Oracle ADF Enterprise Application Development – Made Simple

Second Edition

Successfully plan, develop, test, and deploy enterprise applications with Oracle ADF

Sten E. Vesterli

[PACKT] PUBLISHING   enterprise
professional expertise distilled

BIRMINGHAM - MUMBAI

Oracle ADF Enterprise Application Development – Made Simple

Second Edition

Copyright © 2014 Packt Publishing

All rights reserved. No part of this book may be reproduced, stored in a retrieval system, or transmitted in any form or by any means, without the prior written permission of the publisher, except in the case of brief quotations embedded in critical articles or reviews.

Every effort has been made in the preparation of this book to ensure the accuracy of the information presented. However, the information contained in this book is sold without warranty, either express or implied. Neither the author, nor Packt Publishing, and its dealers and distributors will be held liable for any damages caused or alleged to be caused directly or indirectly by this book.

Packt Publishing has endeavored to provide trademark information about all of the companies and products mentioned in this book by the appropriate use of capitals. However, Packt Publishing cannot guarantee the accuracy of this information.

First published: June 2011

Second Edition: February 2014

Production Reference: 1120214

Published by Packt Publishing Ltd.
Livery Place
35 Livery Street
Birmingham B3 2PB, UK.

ISBN 978-1-78217-680-0

www.packtpub.com

Cover Image by Artie (artherng@yahoo.com.au)

Credits

Author
Sten E. Vesterli

Reviewers
Maroof Ahmad
Vinod Krishnan
Sanjeeb Mahakul
Frank Nimphius
Dimitrios Stasinopoulos

Acquisition Editors
Dhwani Devater
Rashmi Phadnis
Rubal Kaur

Content Development Editor
Arvind Koul

Technical Editors
Manan Badani
Shashank Desai
Shali Sasidharan

Copy Editors
Sarang Chari
Karuna Narayanan

Project Coordinator
Kranti Berde

Proofreaders
Lauren Harkins
Amy Johnson

Indexer
Rekha Nair

Graphics
Yuvraj Mannari
Abhinash Sahu

Production Coordinator
Arvindkumar Gupta

Cover Work
Arvindkumar Gupta

About the Author

Sten E. Vesterli picked up Oracle development as his first job after graduating from the Technical University of Denmark and hasn't looked back since. He has worked with almost every development tool and server Oracle has produced in the last two decades, including Oracle ADF, JDeveloper, WebLogic, SQL Developer, Oracle Portal, BPEL, Collaboration Suite, Designer, Forms, Reports, and even Oracle Power Objects.

He started sharing his knowledge with a conference presentation in 1997 and has given more than 100 conference presentations at Oracle OpenWorld and at ODTUG, IOUG, UKOUG, DOAG, DOUG, and other user group conferences around the world since. His presentations are highly rated by the participants, and in 2010 he received the ODTUG Best Speaker award.

He has also written numerous articles, participated in podcasts, and written *Oracle Web Applications 101*, *Oracle ADF Enterprise Application Development – Made Simple*, and *Developing Web Applications with Oracle ADF Essentials*. You can find his blog at www.vesterli.com and follow him on Twitter as @stenvesterli.

Oracle has recognized Sten's skills as an expert communicator on Oracle technology by awarding him the prestigious title, Oracle ACE Director, carried by less than 100 people in the world. He is also an Oracle Fusion User Experience Advocate and sits on the Oracle Usability Advisory Board and participates in the Oracle WebLogic Partner Council.

Based in Denmark, Sten is a partner in the Oracle consulting company Scott/Tiger, where he works as a senior principal consultant. When not writing books or presenting, he is helping customers choose the appropriate technology for their needs, teaching, mentoring, and leading development projects. In his spare time, Sten enjoys triathlon and completed his first Ironman in 2012.

Acknowledgment

First and foremost, I'd like to thank the members of the ADF Enterprise Methodology Group (ADF EMG). This group meets online, and occasionally in person, to discuss ADF architecture, methodology, and best practice. The discussions I've had in this group have widened my perspective and challenged me to formulate my own methodology clearly. I'd like to extend a special thanks to the group moderator, John Flack, who works tirelessly to keep the signal-to-noise ratio on the discussion forum extremely high. If you are a software developer working with ADF and you are serious about your software craftsmanship, you need to join this group: `https://sites.google.com/site/oracleemg/adf`.

Many people at Oracle have also been contributing with clarifications, comments, and insights that have made this book better. I especially appreciate the efforts of ADF EMG founder Chris Muir, now at Oracle, for responding to my many queries on ADF and JDeveloper 12*c* on the ADF EMG Jira issue tracker.

I would also like to thank the people at Packt Publishing who have been working on this project as well as my reviewers who have improved the book with their excellent questions and suggestions.

Finally, I'd like to thank my wonderful wife for her love and support and for accepting yet another batch of weekends marked with "Book deadline" in our calendar.

About the Reviewers

Maroof Ahmad is an Engineering Graduate (B.Tech) from Integral University, Lucknow. He has majored in Computer Science and Engineering. He has worked on multiple projects with a very large team, where he found freshers who were learning ADF. He also writes a blog on Oracle Fusion Middleware Lab (http://www.ofmlab.blogspot.com/) for providing real challenging solutions and building ADF applications using ADF components and advantages. For more updated details about Maroof, please visit http://maroofgm.blogspot.com/.

He has a rich work experience in ADF and middleware technologies, and he is currently working with Bader Al Mulla and Brothers Company W.L.L. in Kuwait as an Oracle Middleware consultant. He has also worked in CMC Limited (A TATA Enterprise) and HMK INDIA Technologies as a software engineer.

First, I want to thank my Mommy for her encouragement and compromise. After that, it's only possible because of Priyanka; she always stood by me, offering moral and positive support during the time of the review, so a big thanks to Priyanka. I also want to mention a key person and colleague, Ahmad Salman; he always provided comfort when I was working late, leaving the office early, and much more. So, thank you Ahmad Salman for this wonderful journey. I would also like to mention Mohammed Jabarullah and Joby Josheph, who have always supported me in every situation.

Vinod Krishnan has over nine years of experience in the Information Technology industry. This exposed him to a wide range of technologies that include Java, J2EE, WebLogic, Fusion Middleware, SOA, and WebCenter. He has been working with Oracle ADF Technologies since 2005 and enhanced his affinity towards ADF after he joined Oracle India. For the last five years, he has been actively involved in large implementations of next-generation enterprise applications utilizing Oracle's JDeveloper and Application Development Framework (ADF) technologies. He holds a B.Tech. degree in Information Technology from Anna University, Chennai, India. He is currently responsible for building and deploying applications using the Oracle Fusion Middleware technology stack as a project lead in Oracle America. He is an Oracle-certified specialist, and the technologies he has worked on include Oracle ADF, SOA, WebCenter, and Identity Management. His contribution towards JDeveloper and ADF discussion forums is immense. With his experience, he has learned many tips and techniques that will help a new user to learn this technology without any hassles. He writes his own blog (http://vtkrishn.com) that discusses the tips and tricks with using Oracle technologies. He has had a multifaceted career; he has worked in positions such as senior consultant, senior applications engineer, software engineer, and solution architect for MNCs such as Oracle, Capgemini, and Keane. He is the author of the book *Oracle ADF 11gR2 Development Beginner's Guide* — ISBN 978-1-84968-900-7.

Sanjeeb Mahakul is a technical architect who has dedicated his career to specializing in Oracle Fusion products. With over eight years of experience in Oracle Fusion products, such as Oracle ADF, WebCenter Portal, WebCenter Spaces, and WebCenter Content, he has seen the evolution in enterprise application and portals. He leads enterprise architecture and integration and delivers industry-applied solutions for various customers. He is also an Oracle-certified ADF implementation specialist. He is passionate about researching and learning upcoming technologies, architecture, and the industry's best practices. He is also dedicated to helping out and posting in the OTN community and various forums.

I would like to thank all my family and friends who supported me with time and every other way. I would especially like to thank one of my best friends, Mona, who was a constant source of inspiration and a driving force for reviewing this book.

Frank Nimphius is a senior principal product manager in the Oracle Application Development Tools group at Oracle Corporation, specializing in Oracle JDeveloper and the Oracle Application Development Framework (ADF) as well as in mobile application development. Frank runs the ADF Code Corner website, the OTN Forum Harvest blog, and is the co-author of the *Oracle Fusion Developer Guide* book published in 2009 by *McGraw Hill* and the ADF Architecture Square website.

Dimitrios Stasinopoulos is a certified Application Development Framework implementation specialist with more than seven years of experience in Oracle Fusion Middleware and, more specifically, in ADF BC 11*g*. He currently works as an Oracle Fusion Middleware consultant, mainly focusing on Oracle ADF. He has worked in several Oracle ADF projects in various positions, from developer to architect, and enjoys teaching and talking about Fusion Middleware.

In his spare time, he helps the ADF community by answering technical questions in the Oracle ADF and JDeveloper forums and maintains a blog, where he posts his findings and ideas: `dstas.blogspot.com`.

He holds a B.Sc degree in Computer Science from the Technological Educational Institution of Larissa, Greece.

www.PacktPub.com

Support files, eBooks, discount offers, and more

You might want to visit www.PacktPub.com for support files and downloads related to your book.

Did you know that Packt offers eBook versions of every book published, with PDF and ePub files available? You can upgrade to the eBook version at www.PacktPub.com and as a print book customer, you are entitled to a discount on the eBook copy. Get in touch with us at service@packtpub.com for more details.

At www.PacktPub.com, you can also read a collection of free technical articles, sign up for a range of free newsletters and receive exclusive discounts and offers on Packt books and eBooks.

http://PacktLib.PacktPub.com

Do you need instant solutions to your IT questions? PacktLib is Packt's online digital book library. Here, you can access, read and search across Packt's entire library of books.

Why subscribe?

- Fully searchable across every book published by Packt
- Copy and paste, print and bookmark content
- On demand and accessible via web browser

Free Access for Packt account holders

If you have an account with Packt at www.PacktPub.com, you can use this to access PacktLib today and view nine entirely free books. Simply use your login credentials for immediate access.

Instant updates on new Packt books

Get notified! Find out when new books are published by following @PacktEnterprise on Twitter, or the *Packt Enterprise* Facebook page.

Table of Contents

Preface

Welcome to your first real-life enterprise ADF application!

The book you're holding in your hands is about building serious applications with the Oracle Application Development Framework (ADF). You know that actual development work is only one part of a successful project and that you also need structure, processes, and tools.

That's why *Oracle ADF Enterprise Application Development – Made Simple, Second Edition*, will take an enterprise focus, following a complete project from inception to final delivery. Along the way, you will be building a Proof of Concept application, but you will also be setting up and using all of the professional support tools you need for a real-life project.

This book will take you through the entire process of building an enterprise ADF application, from the initial idea through the Proof of Concept, tool choice, preparation, coding the support classes, building the application, testing it, customizing it, securing it, and finally, deploying it.

What is an enterprise application?

Enterprise applications are the strategic applications in the enterprise. They will handle critical business functions and tend to be big and complex. In the past, it was acceptable that users had to take training classes before they were able to use the application, but today, enterprise applications are also required to be user friendly and intuitive. As they are deployed throughout the organization, they will need sophisticated security features. Enterprise applications will remain in use for a long time because of the cost of developing and implementing them.

Application size

An enterprise application is big—containing lots and lots of code modules, interacting in complex ways among themselves and with external systems.

Typically, this means that an enterprise application also has a lot of different screens where the user will interact with the system. However, it is also possible that the complexity of the enterprise application is hidden from the user; a good enterprise application might seem deceptively simple to the average user.

Development team

The complexity of an enterprise application means that it will have to be built by a larger team. It will use several technologies, so you need people skilled in all of the relevant areas. You will need to have people working in parallel on different parts of the application in order to develop it within a useful timeframe because of its sheer size.

An enterprise application cannot simply be partitioned out among developers because of the interdependencies among the different parts of the application. Instead, development work must be carefully planned so that the foundation is laid down before the rest of the house is built while, at the same time, allowing for the inevitable changes as the project progresses.

Development tools

Naturally, you need an Integrated Development Environment (IDE) to build the actual application. This book assumes that the entire team will be using Oracle's free JDeveloper tool for all work. The choice of IDE can be the subject of almost religious fervor, and some projects allow each developer to choose his or her favorite IDE. However, in an enterprise project, the benefits of having everyone use the same tool clearly outweighs any minor benefit achieved by using other IDEs with marginally better support for one or the other task.

In addition to the IDE, you will also need source control—a server holding all of the different versions of the development artifacts and a client on each development workstation. This book uses both Subversion and Git as examples of how to use source control in an enterprise project with JDeveloper.

Another important tool is an issue-tracking tool. This can be used to track defects in code as well as ideas, development tasks, and many other things. In this book, the well-known Jira tool is used, and it is explained how this tool fits the Oracle Team Productivity Center (TPC).

Finally, you need a scripting tool. In a small project, it might be sufficient to build applications directly off of the IDE, but in an enterprise application, you need a tool to ensure that you can build your project in a consistent manner. This book uses Ant as an example of a scripting tool for the ADF projects.

Lifetime of an enterprise application

Enterprise applications are not casually thrown away and rebuilt because of the effort and cost involved in building them. Indeed, many organizations are still running enterprise applications built more than a decade ago.

The longevity of enterprise applications makes it extremely important that they are well built and well documented. Most developers will be familiar with the pain of having to maintain a poorly documented application and understand the need for a good documentation.

However, while documentation is important, it is just as important that the application is built in a recognizable, standard way. That is why this book advocates using the ADF framework in its intended way so that the future generations of developers can look at the code and immediately understand how the application is built.

What this book covers

Before your organization embarks on building an enterprise application using the Oracle Application Development Framework, you need to prove that ADF will indeed be able to meet the application requirements.

Chapter 1, The ADF Proof of Concept, will take you through building a Proof of Concept application using the normal ADF components: ADF Business Components for the middle tier, ADF Faces, and ADF Task Flows for the user interface. The application will access data stored in relational tables and use both the standard ADF components and an ADF Data Visualization component (a Gantt chart). This chapter contains step-by-step instructions and can be used as a hands-on exercise in basic ADF development.

Once you have proved that ADF is capable of delivering the necessary functionality, you need to figure out which components will be part of your application and estimate the total effort necessary to build it.

Chapter 2, Estimating the Effort, will provide checklists of tasks that you must remember in your estimate as well as some guidelines and estimation techniques that you can use to calculate how much time it will take to build the application.

The next step after having decided to proceed with an ADF enterprise project is to organize the development team.

Chapter 3, Getting Organized, explains the skills you need to build an enterprise application and how to organize your team. It also explains which tools you need in your enterprise project and how you should structure your code using separate workspaces connected through the powerful ADF Library functionality for maximum efficiency.

For the team to work efficiently toward the project goal, each developer needs a development workstation with complete integration of all the necessary tools.

Chapter 4, Productive Teamwork, describes how to set up and use the Oracle Team Productivity Center, which serves as an integration hub, connecting your issue tracking system (for example, Jira) and other tools to JDeveloper. It also explains how to work effectively with Subversion and JDeveloper together for version control.

With your workstation all set up and ready to go, you need one more thing before starting development in earnest: templates and framework extension classes. For a small application it might be OK to just start coding and work out the details as you go along. However, in an enterprise application, the rework cost of such an informal approach can be prohibitive.

Chapter 5, Preparing to Build, explains the task flow and page templates you need to build a uniform user interface in an efficient way. It explains why you need your own ADF framework extension classes and how to build them.

Now that all of the infrastructure and templates are in place and the development workstation has been configured with all necessary connections, it is time to prove the entire development flow.

Chapter 6, Building the Enterprise Application, walks you through creating the same Proof of Concept application as in *Chapter 1, The ADF Proof of Concept*, but this time, using all of the enterprise support tools configured and prepared in *Chapter 4, Productive Teamwork* and *Chapter 5, Preparing to Build*. The application is built in a module manner in separate subsystems and integrated together in a master application to illustrate how a large enterprise application should be structured.

By the end of this chapter, you would have proved that the entire enterprise toolset is functional, and you would have rebuilt the Proof of Concept application using the correct enterprise methodology.

All applications need to be tested, but enterprise applications need testing much more than smaller applications, for the following two reasons:

- The size and complexity of an enterprise application means that there are more interfaces where things can go wrong
- The long life expectancy of an enterprise application makes it almost certain that other developers will be maintaining it in years to come

For both of these reasons, it is important that the application comes with test cases that prove correct functionality. It will not be sufficient to have a collection of test scripts that must be manually executed—these will not be consistently executed and will surely become out of date over the lifetime of the application. Your tests must, therefore, be automated so that they can be executed as part of the build process.

Chapter 7, Testing Your Application, explains how to write code tests in the form of JUnit test cases and how to use Selenium to record and playback user interface tests. It also explains how JMeter can be used to load test your ADF application.

Your organization will, of course, have graphical standards that the application must adhere to. In an ADF application, the look of the application can easily be modified in a process known as skinning. By developing several skins, you can even deploy the same application multiple times with very different visual identities—an invaluable feature for independent software vendors.

Chapter 8, Changing the Appearance, explains how to use the powerful skin editor available in JDeveloper 11*g* Release 2 and later versions to create Cascading Style Sheets (CSS) to create a new skin, which corresponds to your enterprise visual identity, for your application.

Looking at the requirements for your application, you might identify a number of pages or screens that are almost, but not quite, identical. In many cases, you don't have to develop each of these individually—you might be able to develop one master page and use functional customization to provide different groups of users with different versions of the page.

The ability to easily customize an application's functionality is one of the truly outstanding features of the Oracle ADF framework. Here, you benefit from the fact that Oracle has developed ADF for real life, large enterprise applications like Oracle Fusion Applications. If you are an independent software vendor, producing software for sale, you can use this feature to easily customize a base application for individual customers.

Chapter 9, Customizing Functionality, explains how to set up an application for customization using ADF Meta Data Services, and how to use the special JDeveloper customization role to perform the actual customization.

Your enterprise application needs a robust, role-based security model.

Chapter 10, Securing Your ADF Application, explains how to secure both user interface (task flows and pages) and data access (Entity Objects) using ADF security features, and how ADF security ties in with WebLogic security features.

Once the individual parts of the application have been built and tested, it is time to build a complete deployment package.

Chapter 11, Packaging and Delivery, describes how an enterprise application deployment package is built and how the development team can set up their own standalone WebLogic server to ensure that the deployment package will work when handed over to the operations team.

An enterprise application might have to be made available in several languages.

Appendix, Internationalization, explains how internationalization works in ADF and how to produce a localized application.

How to read this book

This book follows an enterprise application from inception to final delivery, and you can read the chapters in sequence to learn a proven method for successfully building an enterprise application that meets the business requirements on time and on budget.

However, many chapters can also be read on their own if you just need information on a specific topic. For example:

- *Chapter 1, The ADF Proof of Concept*, can serve as a quick introduction to ADF, thus allowing an experienced developer to get started with ADF
- *Chapter 8, Changing the Appearance*, can be used as a tutorial in ADF skinning
- *Chapter 9, Customizing Functionality*, explains how to harness the power of ADF customization

Are you ready to build a real-life enterprise application? Let's get started!

What you need for this book

To build enterprise ADF applications, you need Oracle JDeveloper and a database, which are as follows:

- Oracle JDeveloper is free and can be downloaded from the Oracle Technology Network (http://otn.oracle.com). The examples in this book use Version 12.1.2, but you should use Version 12.1.3 or a later version if such a version is available by the time you read this book. The examples will also work in JDeveloper 11*g*.

- You can use the free Oracle Database Express Edition 11*g* Release 2, which is also available from the Oracle Technology Network.

Additionally, you need the following:

- Version control software: This book uses Subversion and Git as examples, but there are many other fine version control systems available
- Issue tracking software: This book discusses Jira from Atlassian, but many other options are available
- A scripting tool: This book uses and recommends Apache Ant

Who this book is for

Whether you are a J2EE developer looking for a more productive way to build a modern web application or you are an experienced Oracle developer who wants to start using Oracle's next-generation tools, this book will guide you to a successful enterprise application. With basic knowledge of Java, JDeveloper, and databases, you can easily follow this book.

Conventions

In this book, you will find a number of styles of text that distinguish between different kinds of information. Here are some examples of these styles, and an explanation of their meaning.

Code words in text, database table names, folder names, filenames, file extensions, pathnames, dummy URLs, user input, and Twitter handles are shown as follows:

For example, the `AllTasksVO` view object becomes the view object instance, `AllTasksVO1`.

A block of code is set as follows:

```
(:pResponsible is null or PERS_ID = :pResponsible)
and (:pProgramme is null or PROG_ID = :pProgramme)
and (:pText is null or upper(TEXT) like '%'
   || upper(:pText) || '%')
```

New terms and **important words** are shown in bold. Words that you see on the screen, in menus or dialog boxes for example, appear in the text like this:

When you are done entering the WHERE clause, click on the **Test and Explain** button to verify that your SQL is valid.

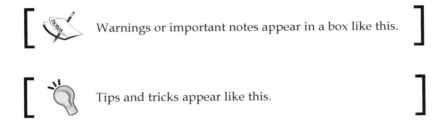

Warnings or important notes appear in a box like this.

Tips and tricks appear like this.

Reader feedback

Feedback from our readers is always welcome. Let us know what you think about this book—what you liked or may have disliked. Reader feedback is important for us to develop titles that you really get the most out of.

To send us general feedback, simply send an e-mail to feedback@packtpub.com, and mention the book title via the subject of your message.

If there is a topic that you have expertise in and you are interested in either writing or contributing to a book, see our author guide at www.packtpub.com/authors.

Customer support

Now that you are the proud owner of a Packt book, we have a number of things to help you to get the most from your purchase.

Errata

Although we have taken every care to ensure the accuracy of our content, mistakes do happen. If you find a mistake in one of our books—maybe a mistake in the text or the code—we would be grateful if you would report this to us. By doing so, you can save other readers from frustration and help us improve subsequent versions of this book. If you find any errata, please report them by visiting http://www.packtpub.com/submit-errata, selecting your book, clicking on the **errata submission form** link, and entering the details of your errata. Once your errata are verified, your submission will be accepted and the errata will be uploaded on our website, or added to any list of existing errata, under the Errata section of that title. Any existing errata can be viewed by selecting your title from http://www.packtpub.com/support.

Piracy

Piracy of copyrighted material on the Internet is an ongoing problem across all media. At Packt, we take the protection of our copyright and licenses very seriously. If you come across any illegal copies of our works, in any form, on the Internet, please provide us with the location address or website name immediately so that we can pursue a remedy.

Please contact us at copyright@packtpub.com with a link to the suspected pirated material.

We appreciate your help in protecting our authors, and our ability to bring you valuable content.

Questions

You can contact us at questions@packtpub.com if you are having a problem with any aspect of the book, and we will do our best to address it.

The ADF Proof of Concept 1

Your organization has decided that the Oracle **Application Development Framework (ADF)** might be the right tool to build your next enterprise application—now you need to set up an experiment to prove that your assumption is correct.

You can compare the situation at the start of a project to standing in front of a mountain with the task to excavate a tunnel. The mountainsides are almost vertical, and there is no way for you to climb the mountain to figure out how wide it is. You can take either of the two approaches:

- You can start blasting and drilling in the full width of the tunnel you need
- You can start drilling a very small pilot tunnel all through the mountain and then expand it to full width later

It's probably more efficient to build in the full width of the tunnel straight from the beginning; however, this approach has some serious disadvantages, as well. You don't know how wide the mountain is, so you can't tell how long it will take to build the tunnel. In addition, you don't know what kind of surprises might lurk in the mountain—porous rocks, aquifers, or any number of other obstacles to your tunnel building.

That's why you should build the pilot tunnel first—so you know the size of the task and have an idea of the obstacles you might meet on the way.

The **Proof of Concept** is that pilot tunnel.

Understanding the architecture of ADF

Since you have decided to evaluate ADF for your enterprise application, you probably already have a pretty good idea of its architecture and capabilities. Therefore, this section will only give you a very brief overview of ADF—there are many whitepapers, tutorials, and demonstrations available at the **Oracle Technology Network (OTN)** website. Your starting point for ADF information is `http://www.oracle.com/technetwork/developer-tools/adf/overview/index.html`.

Enterprise architecture

A modern enterprise application typically consists of a frontend user-facing part and a backend business service part.

The frontend part

The frontend part is constructed from several layers. In a web-based application, these are normally arranged in the common **model-view-controller** (**MVC**) pattern, as illustrated in the following figure:

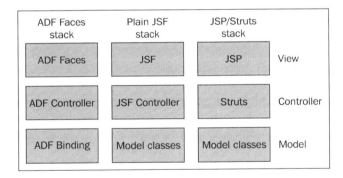

The **view** layer is interacting with the user, thus displaying data as well as receiving updates and user actions. The **controller** layer is in charge of interpreting user actions and deciding which screens are presented to the user in which order. The **model** layer is representing the backend business services to the view and controller layers, thus hiding the complexity of storing and retrieving data.

This architecture implements a clean separation of duties—the page doesn't have to worry about where to go next because that is the task of the controller. The controller doesn't have to worry about how to store data in the data service because that is the task of the model.

Other frontends

An enterprise application could also have a mobile application frontend or even use existing desktop applications, such as Microsoft Excel, to interact with data. In the ADF technology stack, all of these alternative frontends interact with the same model, making it easy to develop multiple frontend applications against the same data services.

The backend part

The backend part consists of a **business service** layer that implements the business logic and provides some way of accessing the underlying data services. Business services can be implemented as API code written in Java, PL/SQL, or other languages, using web services or a business service framework such as **ADF Business Components**.

Under the business services layer, there will be a **data service** layer actually storing persistent data. Typically, this is based on relational tables, but it could also be XML files in a filesystem or data in other systems accessed through an interface.

The ADF architecture

There are many different ways of building applications with Oracle Application Development Framework, but Oracle has chosen a modern SOA-based architecture for Oracle Fusion Applications. This brand new product has been built from the ground up as the successor to Oracle E-Business Suite, Siebel, PeopleSoft, J.D. Edwards, and many other applications Oracle has acquired over the last couple of years.

If it's good enough for Oracle Fusion Applications, arguably the biggest enterprise application development effort ever undertaken by mankind, it's probably good enough for you, too.

Oracle Fusion Applications are using the following parts of the ADF framework:

- **ADF Faces Rich Client** (ADFv): This is a very rich set of user interface components implementing advanced functionality in a web application.

- **ADF Controller** (ADFc): This implements the features of a normal JSF controller, but is extended with the possibility to define modular, reusable page flows. ADFc also allows you to declare transaction boundaries, so one database transaction can span across many pages.

- **ADF binding layer** (ADFm): This implements a common backend model that different user interface layers can communicate with.

- **ADF Business Components** (ADF-BC): This is a highly productive, declarative way of defining business services based on relational tables.

You can see all of these in the following figure:

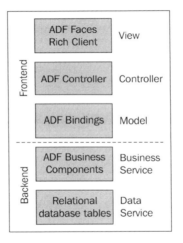

 There are many ways of getting from A to B — this book is about traveling the straight and well-paved road Oracle has built for Fusion Applications. However, other routes might be appropriate in some situations; in the frontend part, you could use ADF Mobile for smartphones and tablets or ADF Desktop Integration to access your data directly from within Microsoft Excel, and in the backend, you could use business services based on Web Services, EJBs, or many other technologies and still use the ADF binding layer to connect the back and frontend parts together.

Entity objects and associations

Entity objects (EOs) take care of object-relational mapping, making your relational tables available to the application as Java objects. Entity objects form the base that view objects are normally built on, and all data modifications go through the entity object. You will normally have one entity object for every database table or database view that your application uses, and this object is responsible for producing the correct SQL statements to insert, update, or delete data in the underlying relational tables.

The entity objects help you build scalable and well-performing applications by intelligently caching database records on the application server in order to minimize the load that the application places on the database.

Like entity objects are the middle-tier representation of database tables and database views, **associations** are the representation of foreign key relationships between tables. An association implements a connection between two entity objects and allows ADF to connect data in one entity object with data in another. JDeveloper is normally able to create associations automatically by simply inspecting the database, but in case your database does not contain foreign keys, you can build associations manually to let ADF know about the relationships in your data.

View objects and view links

While you don't really need to make any major decisions when building the entity objects for the Proof of Concept, you do need to consider the consumers of your business services when you start building **view objects** — for example, what information you would display on a screen.

View objects are typically based on entity objects, and you'll mainly be using them for two purposes:

- To provide data for your screens
- To provide data for lists of values (LOVs)

The data handling view objects are normally specific to each screen or business service. One screen can use multiple view objects. If you have master-detail data, for example, departments containing employees, you create one view object for each master-detail level you wish to display on your screen (for example, one department and one employee view object).

One view object can pull together data from several entity objects. If you need to look up a reference value from another table, you don't need to create a separate view object for this. For example, an employee entity object might contain only the department number. If you want your view object to display the department name, you need to include the department entity object in the view object in order to retrieve it.

The LOV view objects are used for drop-down lists and other selections in your user interface. They are typically defined as read-only, and because they can be reused, you can define them once and re-use them everywhere you need a drop-down list on a specific data set.

View links are used to define the master-detail relationships between the view objects and are typically based on associations (again, they are often based on foreign keys in the database).

The following figure shows an example of two ways to display data from the familiar EMP and DEPT tables found in the SCOTT schema:

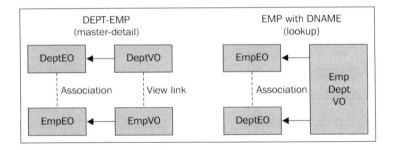

The left-hand side illustration shows a situation in which you wish to display a department with all of its employees in a master-detail screen. In this case, you create two view objects connected by a view link. The right-hand side illustration shows a situation in which you wish to display all employees together with the name of the department they work in. In this case, you only need one view object pulling together data from both the EMP and DEPT tables through the entity objects.

Application modules

Application modules encapsulate the view object instances and business service methods necessary to perform a unit of work. Each application module has its own transactional context and holds its own database connection. This means that all of the work a user performs using view objects from one application module is part of one database transaction.

Application modules can have different granularity, but typically, you will have one application module for each major subsystem in your application. However, there is no limit to the amount of functionality you can put into one application module — indeed, it is possible to build a small application using just one application module.

Application modules for Oracle Forms

If you come from an Oracle Forms background and are developing a replacement for an Oracle Forms application, your application will often have a relatively small number of complex, major forms and a larger number of simple data maintenance forms. You will often create one application module per major form and a few application modules, each of which provides data, for a number of simple forms.

If you wish, you can combine multiple application modules inside one **root application module**. This is called **nesting** and allows several application modules to participate in the transaction of the root application module. This also saves database connections because only the root application module needs a connection.

The ADF user interface

The preferred way of building the user interface in an ADF enterprise application is with **JavaServer Faces (JSF)**. JSF is a component-based framework for building web-based user interfaces that overcome many of the limitations of earlier technologies such as **JavaServer Pages (JSP)**.

In a JSF application, the user interface does not contain any code but is built from the configurable components of a component library instead. For your application, you'll want to use the sophisticated ADF 12*c* JSF component library known as the **ADF Faces Rich Client**.

There are other JSF component libraries; for example, an earlier version of the ADF Faces components (Version 10*g*) has been released by Oracle as Open Source and is now part of the Apache MyFaces Trinidad project. However, for a modern enterprise application, use ADF Faces Rich Client.

ADF Task Flows

One of the great improvements that ADF 11*g* and 12*c* offer over the earlier ways of building web applications is the concept of **ADF Task Flows**.

It had long been clear to web developers that in a web application, you cannot just let each page decide where to go next—you need the controller from the MVC architecture. Various frameworks and technologies have implemented controllers (both the popular Struts framework and JSF have this), but the controller in ADF Task Flows was the first one capable of handling large enterprise applications.

An ADF web application has one **unbounded task flow** where you place all of the publicly accessible pages and define the navigation between them. This corresponds to other controller architectures such as **Apache Struts**. The user can enter an unbounded task flow on any page. However, ADF also has **bounded task flows**, which are complete, reusable mini applications that can be called from an unbounded task flow or from another bounded task flow.

A bounded task flow has a well-defined entry point, accepts input parameters, and can return an outcome back to the caller. For example, you might build a customer management task flow to handle customer data. In this way, your application can be built in a modular fashion—the developers in charge of implementing each use case can define their own bounded task flow with a well-defined interface for others to call. The team building the customer management task flow is thus free to add new pages or change the navigation flow without affecting the rest of the application.

The concepts behind ADF Task Flows have influenced the JSF 2.2 standard, where this approach is known as **Faces Flows**. However, ADF Task Flows have more features and a different technical implementation.

ADF pages and fragments

In bounded task flows, you can define either **pages** or **page fragments**. Pages are complete web pages that can be run on their own, while page fragments are reusable components that you can place inside **regions** on pages.

You can choose to build your ADF application as either a traditional web application or a **Rich Internet Application** (RIA). A traditional web application consists of pages—when the user interacts with the application, the whole browser window will redraw, thus showing the next page of the application. In a Rich Internet Application, on the other hand, you will have a small number of pages (possibly only one) and a larger number of page fragments. These page fragments will dynamically replace each other inside a region on an application page, so the user sees only a part of the page change. If you choose this technique, your application will seem more like a desktop application than a traditional web application.

On your pages or page fragments, you can add content using **layout components**, **data components**, and **control components**:

- **Layout components**: These are containers for other components and control the screen layout. Often, multiple layout components are nested inside each other to achieve the desired layout.
- **Data components**: These are the components that the user interacts with to create and modify data. Data components range from fairly simple components, such as an input field or a checkbox, to very sophisticated components, such as an ADF table.
- **Control components**: These are the buttons and links used to perform actions in an ADF application.

The Proof of Concept

The Proof of Concept serves two purposes:

- To make sure that you can make the technology do what you want it to do
- To gather some metrics about your development speed

If we return to the tunnel analogy, we need to demonstrate that we can drill all the way through the mountain and measure our drilling speed.

Content of a Proof of Concept

The most important part of the Proof of Concept is that it goes all the way through the mountain, or in application development terms, all the way from the user interface to the backend data service and back.

If your data service is data in relational tables and you will be using the ADF technology stack (ADF Business Components and ADF Faces), the part of your Proof of Concept that demonstrates the technology is fairly straightforward.

However, if for some reason, you decide to not use ADF Business Components or you want to base your business components on something other than relational tables, things get more complicated. It might be that your data service is based on Web Services or API code in C++, Java, or PL/SQL. In this case, you will need to demonstrate that you can retrieve data from your data service, display it on the screen, modify it, and successfully store the changes in the backend data service.

You might also have user interface requirements that require more advanced components such as trees, graphs, or even drag-and-drop functionality for the end user. If that's the case, your Proof of Concept user interface needs to demonstrate the use of these special components.

There might also be other significant requirements you need to consider. Your application might have to use a legacy authentication mechanism such as a database login. Another possibility is it might have to integrate with legacy systems for authorization or customization, or you might need to support accessibility standards allowing your application to be used by people with disabilities. If you have these kinds of requirements, you have to evaluate the impact on your project if you can't meet them. If they are critical to your project's success; you need to validate them in a Proof of Concept.

Making the technology work

The ADF technology obviously works. Hundreds of organizations have already followed Oracle's lead and built big enterprise applications using Oracle ADF. It is very straightforward to use the ADF framework with relational tables; the framework handles all of the boring object-relational mapping, allowing you to concentrate on building the actual application logic.

You are likely to inherit at least some of the data models from a pre-existing system, but in rare cases, you will be building a data model from scratch for a brand new application. JDeveloper does allow you to build data models, but Oracle also has other tools (for example, **SQL Developer Data Modeler**) that are specialized for the task of data modeling. Either way, the ADF framework does not place any specific restrictions on your data model—any good data model will work great with ADF.

But your requirements are special, of course. Nobody has ever built an application like the one you are about to build—that's the essence of a project: to do something non-trivial that has not been done before. After all, if you didn't need anything special, you could just pick up a standard product off the shelf. So, you need to consider all of your specific requirements to see if ADF can do it.

ADF can still do it. The ADF framework is immensely powerful as it is, but it also allows you to modify the functionality of ADF applications in myriad ways to meet any conceivable requirement. For instance, if you have to work through a data access API, you can override the doDML() method in entity objects, allowing you to say, "Instead of issuing an UPDATE SQL statement, call this API instead." If you need to work with existing web services for modifying data, you can create data sources from web services.

However, you shouldn't just take my word (or anybody else's word) for it. Building an enterprise application is a major undertaking for your organization, and you want to *prove* that your application can meet the requirements.

Determining the development speed

The development speed of a task mainly depends on three factors: the size of the task, the complexity of the task, and the speed of development.

The size and complexity of the task is given by your requirements. It would be a rare project where all of the requirements are exactly known at the beginning of the project, but if you have a set of detailed requirements, you can make a good estimate of the project's size and complexity.

The speed of development will be the greatest unknown factor if ADF is new to you and your team. Using your previous development tool (for example, Oracle Forms), you were probably able to convert your knowledge of project size and complexity into development effort, but you don't yet know what your development speed with ADF will be.

Your relationship with your development tool will go through a number of phases — not unlike a romantic relationship. Using the terminology of some of the countless relationship coaches on the Internet, we can identify three phases of a relationship:

- Infatuation
- Power struggle
- Co-creativity

During the **infatuation** stage, your development speed is fairly high. You will be building the types of functionalities illustrated in the tool tutorials — fairly simple stuff that the tool supports really well.

After this stage comes **power struggle**. You want to implement some specific functionality and the tool simply refuses to cooperate. During this stage, your development speed drops (and your frustration rises…).

Assuming that the relationship between you and your tool survives this phase, you can move on to the **co-creativity** stage. This is where you understand the tool: you know its strengths and how to overcome its weaknesses. During this stage, your productivity recovers to the initial level and continues to grow to a higher and higher level.

Graphically, it will look as shown in the following figure:

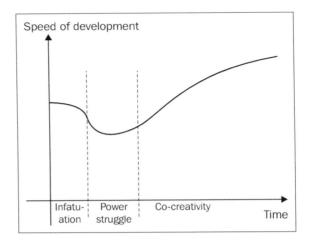

If you have to provide an estimate of development speed very early in the project, you can use your initial development speed as an approximation of the productive development speed you will eventually reach. However, if you do this, you must be aware of the period of lower productivity before you start climbing up with your full productive development speed.

Getting help

Many developers working on their own find that after a few weeks of infatuation, the power struggle phase can take up to 3-6 months before productivity starts to climb again. If you want to move forward faster, you need to break out of your isolation and get some help.

In my experience, typical classroom training is not enough to move through the struggle phase. Try to find an experienced ADF developer who can both teach and offer mentoring and support you on your way to mastering ADF. Also, use the Oracle Technology Network forums (available at otn.oracle.com/ forums), where you'll find a community of experts willing to help.

The Proof of Concept deliverables

The outcome of the Proof of Concept is not an architecture in the form of boxes and arrows on a PowerPoint slide. David Clark from the Internet Engineering Task Force said, We believe in running code—and that's what the Proof of Concept should deliver in order to be credible to developers, users, and management: running code.

If you want to convince your project review board that ADF is a viable technology, you need to bring your development laptop before your project review board and perform a live demonstration.

Additionally, it is a good idea to record the running Proof of Concept application with a screen-recording tool and distribute the resulting video file. This kind of demo tends to be watched at many places in the organization and gives your project visibility and momentum.

The Proof of Concept case study

You are a developer with DMC Solutions, an IT company selling a system for Destination Management Companies (DMC). A DMC is a specialized travel agency, sometimes called an "incoming" agency, and works with clients in the country where it is based.

Running DMC

On an average packaged tour, you will probably not enjoy the services of a DMC. But if you manage to qualify for a company-paid trip to some exotic location, your company is likely to engage the services of a DMC at the destination. If you have ever participated in a technology conference, a DMC will normally be taking care of transfers, dinners, receptions, and so on.

The system that DMC Solutions is selling today is based on Oracle Forms, and the sales force is saying that our competitors are offering systems with a more modern look and a more user-friendly interface. Your mission, should you choose to accept it, would be to prove that ADF is a valid choice for a modern enterprise application, and if so, set up a project to build the next generation of destination management software (the **XDM** project).

The rest of this chapter shows you how to build the Proof of Concept application implementing two use cases. You can simply read through it to get a feel of the tasks involved in creating an ADF application, or you can use it as an ADF hands-on exercise and perform each step in JDeveloper on your own.

Use cases

Your manager has dusted off the specification binder for the existing system and has asked you to implement "Use Case 008 Task Overview and Edit". Additionally, he wants you to implement the newly specified "Use Case 104 Person Task Timeline".

These two use cases represent the application's basic functionality (the ability to search and edit data), as well as a graphical representation of time data, something new that wasn't possible in Oracle Forms.

UC008 Task Overview and Edit

The UC008 Task Overview and Edit screen allows the user to search for tasks by the responsible person, program, or a free-text search, as shown in the following screenshot. Data can be updated and saved back to the database.

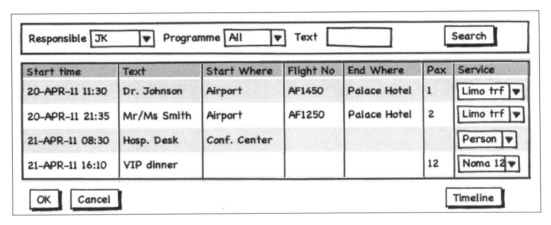

DMC Solutions is a British company, so they use the British English term "programme". This term is used because British English makes a distinction between "programme" (a set of structured activities) and a "program" (something that runs on a computer). The screen is not a dialog box, but uses **OK** to accept changes and save data, and **Cancel** to cancel any changes and revert to the saved data. For simplicity, we will not implement the application menu, but just have a button labeled **Timeline** that invokes UC104 instead.

UC104 Person Task Timeline

Your manager would like something like the Gantt charts he uses to track projects, showing the tasks assigned to each person on a timeline, such as the one shown in the following screenshot:

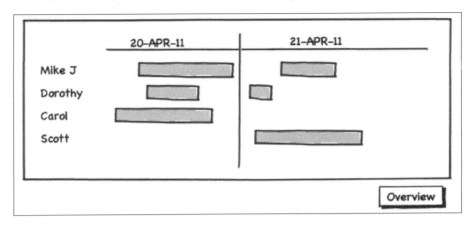

Again, we will not have a menu, just a button called **Overview** for returning to UC008.

Data model

The destination management system starts with events, such as "Oracle OpenWorld 2014". Within each event, there will be a number of programmes (for example, "VIP Pharma Customers"). One person is responsible for each programme. Within a programme, there will be a number of tasks that point to standard elements from the element catalog. Examples of elements could be a limo transfer, a dinner, an excursion, and so on. Each task will be assigned to exactly one person.

The following figure shows just the parts of the (much larger) existing data model that we need for the Proof of Concept:

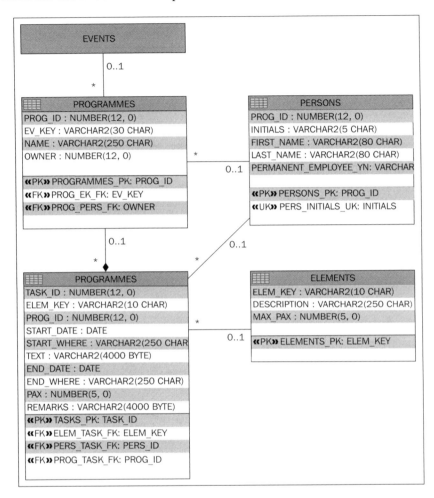

If you want to follow along with the Proof of Concept, building it in JDeveloper on your own workstation, you can download SQL scripts for creating the relevant part of the data model from the book companion website at www.enterpriseadf.com. This script also contains some anonymous data.

Getting started with JDeveloper

Oracle JDeveloper is Oracle's strategic development tool and the only tool with full support for all aspects of ADF development. While Oracle offers a lot of functionalities for Eclipse (with Oracle Enterprise Pack for Eclipse), they have also clearly stated that JDeveloper is the preferred tool for building Oracle ADF applications.

JDeveloper is freely available for download and use from the Oracle Technology Network (otn.oracle.com) — look under **Downloads** and then **Developer Tools**. If you don't already have a free Oracle account, you will have to create one.

The illustrations in this book use JDeveloper 12*c*, Version 12.1.2.0.0. If a later version of JDeveloper is out by the time you read this book, use that instead. The basics of ADF development have not changed over the last couple of years, so you should be able to immediately find the dialogs and options you are looking for. In addition, since Oracle has built a very large application based on JDeveloper, you can be sure that there will be a simple migration path moving forward.

The following steps describe how to create a workspace for an ADF enterprise application — if you want to use this chapter as a hands-on exercise, use the suggested values in each step:

1. Start JDeveloper.
2. Navigate to **File | New | Application**. Choose **ADF Fusion Web Application**. JDeveloper offers you many other types of applications, including **ADF Java Desktop Application**, but you want an **ADF Fusion Web Application**. Click on **OK**.
3. Give your application the name, XdmPoC, choose where to put it in the filesystem (you can leave the default — just note where your projects are stored), and provide an **Application Package Prefix**. Use your organization Java prefix followed by your project abbreviation (for the Proof of Concept, use com.dmcsol.xdmpoc).

Java package prefix

Traditionally, package names start with your organization's Internet domain with the elements reversed. So, if your company domain is mycompany.com, your package names would all start with com.mycompany. However, some organizations (such as Oracle) feel that their names are sufficiently unique, and they don't need to include the first com.

If your organization has ever used Java earlier, your Java package prefix has probably already been chosen and documented somewhere. Ask around.

4. You can simply click on **Next** through the rest of the wizard.

5. This will create a new application containing the two projects, **Model** and **ViewController**. In the main window, JDeveloper will show you the application checklist, as shown in the following screenshot:

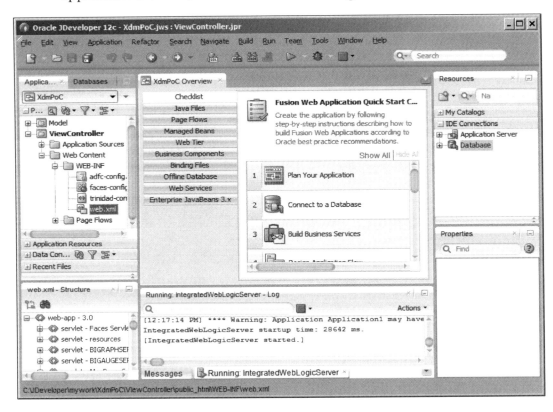

The application checklist actually gives a great overview of the steps involved in building an ADF application, and if you click on the little triangles to expand each step, you'll see links to the relevant JDeveloper functionality for that step, together with links to the relevant places in the documentation. It even has checkboxes that you can check as you complete the different phases in developing your ADF application.

The JDeveloper window and panels

JDeveloper contains a lot of different windows and panels for different purposes. The preceding screenshot shows the most commonly used panels, but you can toggle each of the many panels on and off using the **Window** menu.

If you have not worked with JDeveloper earlier, please take a moment to familiarize yourself with the typical panels shown in the preceding screenshot:

- In the middle is the main window where you will be configuring business components, designing pages, and writing code.

- Below the main window is the **Log** window showing system messages, compiled results, deployment messages, and many other types of information.

- In the top-left corner is the **Applications** window where you can see all of the components in your workspace in a hierarchical structure.

- In the bottom-left corner is the **Structure** window. This important window shows the detailed structure of the component you are working on. For example, when you are working on a page in the main window, the **Structure** window will show a tree with all of the components on the page.

- In the top-right corner is the **Resources** window showing connections to the application servers, databases, and so on. The **Components** window will also appear as a separate tab in this location when editing a page, allowing you to select components to add to the page.

- In the bottom-right corner is the **Properties** window where you can inspect and set properties on the currently selected item.

You can rearrange these panels to your liking by grabbing the tab at the top of each panel and dragging it to a new location, or even dragging it out of JDeveloper to make it a floating window. This can be useful if you have multiple monitors. If you accidentally change the layout to something you don't like, you can always navigate to **Window | Reset Windows To Factory Settings**.

Setting JDeveloper preferences

Before you start working with JDeveloper, you should set the preferences (under **Tools | Preferences**). There are literally hundreds of preferences to set, most of which will not mean anything to you yet. The defaults are mostly fine, but feel free to change the settings. The **Help** section explains the various options well.

One setting that you should change is the business package naming. Open the **ADF Business Components** node and choose **Packages**. Set values for **Entity**, **Association**, **View Object**, **View Link**, and **Application Module**, as shown in the following screenshot:

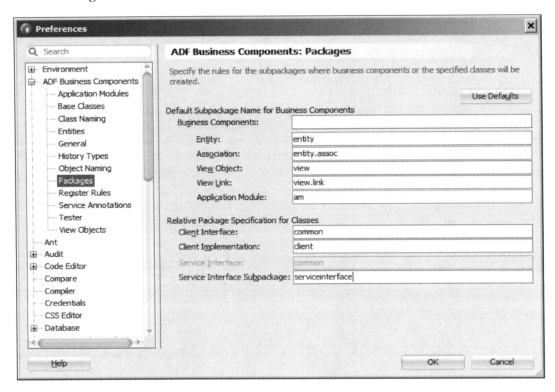

These settings tell JDeveloper to place different types of business components in separate Java subpackages for an easier overview when you have many components. These are just defaults to create a good starting point. As you build your application, you might decide to move your business components and classes to other packages, and JDeveloper makes this safe and easy.

You should also set **Encoding** on the **Environment** node to UTF-8 to have all of your files created in UTF-8 for maximum cross-platform portability. (If you're using Microsoft Windows, this value is probably set to a default Windows character encoding.)

The Proof of Concept ADF Business Components

Once the data model is in place, the next step is to build the ADF Business Components. The description in this book is fairly brief and assumes that you have worked a little bit with ADF earlier, for example, by going through a basic ADF tutorial on the Oracle Technology Network website (`otn.oracle.com`). You can find links to some relevant tutorials on the book companion website (`www.enterpriseadf.com`).

For the Proof of Concept, we will leave all business components in the default location: the **Model** project in the Proof of Concept application workspace. However, when building a real-life enterprise ADF application, you will be splitting up your application into multiple application workspaces and using ADF Libraries to compile these into the master application. Working with smaller workspaces enforces modularity in the code, makes it faster for the developer to find what he's looking for, allows faster checkouts from source control, and JDeveloper also runs faster and better when it is not handling thousands of objects at the same time.

We'll return to the proper structuring of workspaces in *Chapter 3, Getting Organized.*

Creating a connection

As you might have noticed from the application checklist, the first step after **Plan your Application** is to create a connection to the database schema where your application tables reside. Press *Ctrl + N* (or *command + N* on Mac) to bring up the **New Gallery** dialog, choose **Connections** (under **General**), and then choose **Database Connection**.

Each application workspace has its own connections, but you can also create general connections in JDeveloper that you can later copy into your applications. To create general connections, set the value of **Create Connection in** to **IDE Connections**.

In the **Create Database Connection** dialog, give your connection a name (`xdmpoc`) and provide a username, password, and connection information. If you are working locally with the small, free version of the Oracle Database (Oracle Express Edition 11*g*), you choose the "thin" driver, `localhost` as **Host Name**, leave **JDBC Port** at the default value of `1521`, and enter `xe` in the **SID** field. A default local installation of other database editions (version 11*g* and earlier) would use the same values for **Host Name** and **JDBC Port**, but the value of **SID** would be `orcl`.

If you are running against a local Oracle 12*c* database and have decided to implement the multitenant architecture, your data should live in a **pluggable database** (**PDB**), not in the **container database** (**CDB**). If you perform a default Oracle 12*c* database installation and call your database `orcl`, you get a pluggable database called `pdborcl`. To connect to this PDB, set the **Service Name** to `pdborcl.lan`. Just using SID `orcl` will connect to the CDB.

If you are running against a remote database, ask your database administrator for connection information. Click on **Test Connection** to check that you have entered everything correctly and then click on **OK**, as shown in the following screenshot:

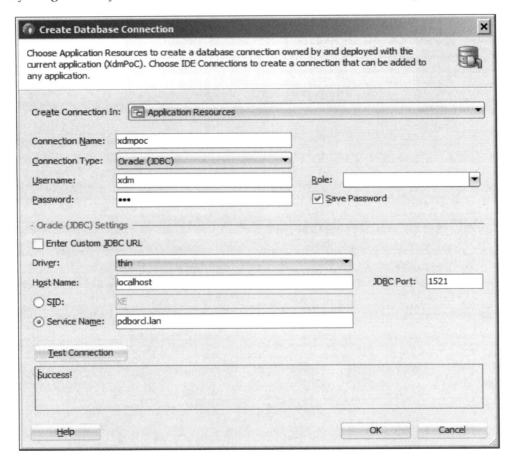

Entity objects for the Proof of Concept

For the Proof of Concept, we will only be building entity objects for the tables for which we need to meet the requirements of the two use cases. To start building, right-click on the **Model** project, choose **New** from the context menu, and then click on **Entity Object**.

Make sure that you select the **Model** project before you start creating business components. A default ADF Fusion Web Application workspace comes with two projects: a **Model** project for the business components and a **ViewController** project for the user interface.

The **Initialize Business Components Project** dialog appears the first time you create a business object. In this dialog, leave the database selection to **Online Database**, select your database connection, and set **SQL Platform** to **Oracle** and **Data Type Map** to **Java Extended for Oracle**. Then click on **OK**.

This book assumes that you use an Oracle database, and the above selections are recommended for this. If you are not using an Oracle database, you can choose **SQL92** as **SQL Platform** and **Java** as **Data Type Map**. Click on the **Help** button in the dialog for more information on these choices.

In the **Create Entity Object** dialog, name the entity object `Person` and enter `XDM_PERSONS` in the **Schema Object** field. You can also click on **Browse** to query the database. Then click on **Next**.

Naming standards

When you start your enterprise application development project in earnest, you need naming standards for everyone to follow. We'll return to naming standards in *Chapter 3, Getting Organized*.

In step 2 of the wizard, just click on **Next** to create entity object attributes for every column in the database. In ADF, there is no overhead at run time for having attributes for unused columns—when the ADF framework issues a `SELECT` statement to the database, it retrieves only those attributes that are actually needed by the view object.

In step 3 of the wizard, you can define the entity attributes in detail. One thing that often needs to be changed here is the type for primary key columns. If the table has a numeric ID column and a database trigger that sets this value when the record is created in the database, you need to set the **Type** to **DBSequence**. Do this for the PersId attribute, as shown in the following screenshot:

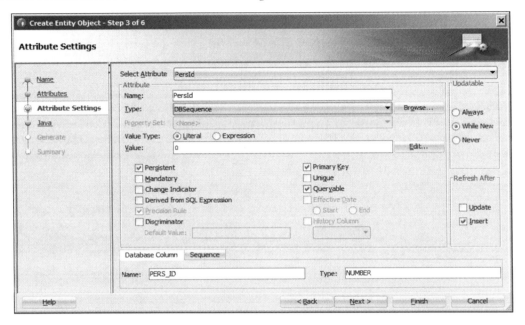

Notice that the ADF framework has now changed the values in the right-hand side of the dialog box: **Updatable** is now set to **While New**, and in the **Refresh After** box, the checkbox for **Insert** is now checked. This means that the entity object will automatically retrieve the primary key value created by your trigger. If you are using an Oracle database, ADF will use the RETURNING feature in Oracle SQL to get the ID back as part of the INSERT command (without having to make a second round-trip to the database).

You don't have to make any changes in steps 4 through 6, so you can simply click on **Finish** here to close the wizard and create your entity object.

For the Proof of Concept, repeat the procedure discussed earlier and create the following entity objects:

- Programme from XDM_PROGRAMMES (choose **DBSequence** for the attribute ProgId)

- Task from XDM_TASKS (choose **DBSequence** for the TaskId attribute)

- Element from XDM_ELEMENTS (doesn't need **DBSequence** for any attribute)

When you are done, the **Model** project in the application navigator should look as shown in the following screenshot:

Building associations for the Proof of Concept

When you have created the entity objects, you will normally find that JDeveloper has automatically discovered the relationships between them based on the foreign keys defined in the database.

If you have configured JDeveloper **Preferences** as recommended in the introduction, all of the associations can be found in the application navigator under `model >` `entity > assoc`, as shown in the preceding screenshot.

The missing link

The ADF framework needs to know about the relationship between entities. In case you have to build an ADF application on an existing database where relations between data records are *not* implemented as foreign keys in the database, you can define the associations in JDeveloper.

Building view objects and view links for the Proof of Concept

To determine which view objects to build, you must look at the screens you need. This allows you to determine both the data you need to present and the value lists you'll need.

Looking at the Task Overview screen (UC008), we see that all data is at the same level (no master-detail level), so we will just need one Tasks view object to display the data.

Additionally, we'll need three value lists:

- Programmes (for the **Programme** drop-down list for search)
- Persons (for the **Responsible** drop-down list for search)
- Services (for the **Service** drop-down list in the data table)

Looking at the Person Task Timeline screen (UC104), there are clearly no value lists. As data is presented graphically, it's not immediately obvious whether the data contains any master-detail relationship. To determine if that is the case, consider how you would display the same information in ordinary fields and tables. Such a screen might show:

- One person
- A number of tasks assigned to that person

This shows us that there is actually a master-detail relationship hidden here, so we need one view object for **Persons**, one view object for their **Tasks**, and a view link connecting the two.

Creating view objects for value lists

To create view objects for persons, right-click on the **Model** project and navigate to **New | View Object**. It's a good idea to give your view object a name that indicates its intended usage as a list of values. For the list of persons, use the name `PersonLOV`. Leave the data source at **Entity Object**.

Always use entity objects

In ADF 10*g* and earlier versions, the recommendation was to use **SQL Query** when you did not need to change the data. Since ADF 11*g*, the benefit of caching those entity objects outweighs the slight performance benefit from executing SQL directly. The recommendation is, therefore, to access data through entity objects always.

In step 2 of the wizard, choose the `Person` entity object and move it to the box to the right. You can remove the checkmark in the **Updatable** box since we will only be using this view object for the drop-down list, as shown in the following screenshot:

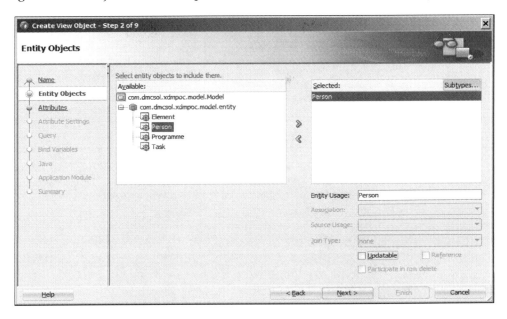

In step 3 of the wizard, move the fields you want to the right-hand side—in this case, we just need `Initials`. Note that the primary key attribute will always be included, as shown in the following screenshot:

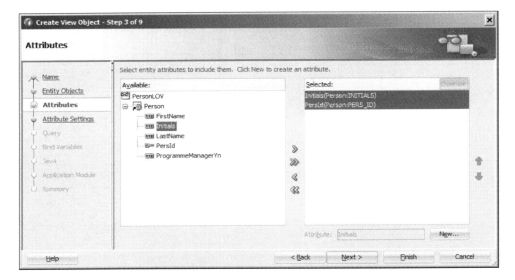

In step 5 (Query), you define the ordering of records by entering Initials in the **Order By** field. Then, click on **Finish** to create the view object.

Repeat this procedure to create the other two value list view objects, which are as follows:

- ProgrammeLOV (based on the Programme entity object, not updatable; select the attribute called Name, order by name)

- ServiceLOV (based on the Element entity object, not updatable; select the attribute called Description, order by description)

Creating a view object for tasks

To create a view object for tasks, look at the Task Overview, Edit page (UC008), and data model. You'll notice that we need fields for date and time, text, start where, flight number, end where, number of passengers, and service. All of this data comes from the XDM_TASKS table through the Task entity object.

Create a new view object (AllTasksVO), leaving the data source at **Entity Object**. In step 2 of the wizard, choose the Task entity object and move it to the right-hand side. As we will actually be updating data through the AllTasksVO view object, we leave the check mark in the **Updatable** checkbox.

In step 3, shuttle the following fields to the right-hand side:

- StartDate
- Text
- StartWhere
- FlightNo
- EndWhere
- Pax
- ElemKey

Note that in the **Available** box on the left-hand side, all attributes are shown in alphabetical order, not in the order you placed them in the entity objects or the order they have in the database table.

Click on **Next** twice and choose to order by start_date. Then click on **Next** to get to **Bind Variables** (step 6).

Bind variables

Bind variables are placeholders in your SQL that you fill with values at run time. The ADF framework enforces the good practice of always using bind variables when you need to change the WHERE condition of a query. You should never simply concatenate values into an SQL statement; if you do, the database can't tell that it already knows the SQL statement and will waste time parsing it again, and a malicious user could potentially insert extra statements into your SQL.

Looking at the search box at the top of the screen sketch, you can see that we need to limit the tasks displayed by responsible person, programme, and text. Use the **New** button to create three bind variables called pResponsible, pProgramme, and pText (all of them of type String). You can leave the other settings in this step of the wizard at their default values.

When you're done, click on the **Back** button to return to step 5 of the wizard and add a WHERE clause that uses the bind variables. It should look similar to the following code:

```
(:pResponsible is null or PERS_ID = :pResponsible)
and (:pProgramme is null or PROG_ID = :pProgramme)
and (:pText is null or upper(TEXT) like '%' || upper(:pText) ||
'%')
```

When you are done entering the WHERE clause, click on the **Test and Explain** button to verify that your SQL is valid. If you do not get the **Query executed successfully** message, fix your SQL.

In this case, we allow null values for the bind variables, so the SQL statement has to contain an OR branch handling this case. We are converting both the database TEXT column and the pText bind variable to upper case to achieve case-insensitive matching. We are also concatenating a wildcard character before and after the parameter value to search for occurrences of the search text anywhere in the database value.

Point-and-click Where clauses

You can also define **Named View Criteria** on your view objects (on the **Query** subtab). These allow you to build a WHERE clause by pointing and clicking. Read about named view criteria and the associated af:query component in the online Help section.

When you click on **Finish**, the AllTasksVO view object is created and appears in the application navigator.

However, we are not quite done with the view object—we still need to define which data elements use lists of values. You might remember from the page layout illustration that **Service** was rendered as a drop-down listbox. Double-click on the AllTasksVO view object to edit it and choose the **Attributes** subtab on the left-hand side. Choose the ElemKey attribute and then select the **List of Values** tab at the bottom of the view object window. Click on the green plus sign to bring up the **Create List of Values** dialog, as shown in the following screenshot:

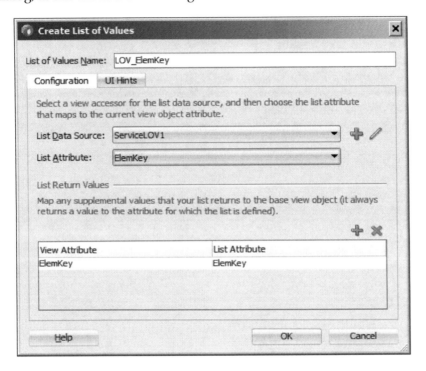

In this dialog, click on the green plus sign to add the **List Data Source**. Choose the ServiceLOV view object and then ElemKey as **List Attribute**.

Since we don't want to display the actual key value (ElemKey) to the user, choose the **UI Hints** tab and move the Description attribute to the right-hand side box. Uncheck the **Include "No Selection" Item** checkbox and then click on **OK**.

The **Attributes** tab also allows you to define some hints to the user interface components about rendering the component. Click on the StartDate attribute and choose the **UI Hints** tab at the bottom of the view object window. Set the label to Start time, set **Format Type** to **Simple Date**, and in the **Format** field, enter the format mask, dd-MMM-yy HH:mm.

The date format string used here is Java `SimpleDateFormat`, not the SQL data format strings you might be familiar with from the database.

Click on the remaining elements and set the label text, referring to the user interface sketch for UC008 (**Format** is only used for date and number objects).

Taking a hint

The control hints defined here are just hints. When building the user interface, these will be the default, but you can still decide to use another label text or format when you use the view object on a page. For simplicity, we are hardwiring labels into the application—in a real-life application, texts should go into separate resource bundles. Refer to *Appendix, Internationalization,* for more information.

Building an application module for tasks

To create an application module for tasks, right-click on the **Model** project and navigate to **New | Application Module**. Name the application module as `EditTaskService`. In step 2 of the wizard, expand the tree in the left-hand side and shuttle the `AllTasksVO` view object to the right, together with the `PersonLOV` and `ProgrammeLOV` that we need to create the search criteria value lists. This is all you need to do, so you can simply click on **Finish** to close the wizard.

Note that the view object instances on the right-hand side get the name of the view object with a number appended to them by default. For example, the `AllTasksVO` view object becomes the **view object instance**, `AllTasksVO1`. The instance name is part of the contract between the business service and the user interface—if you want to change it, do so before anybody starts building the user interface. The reason for this default is that it is possible to have several view object instances based on the same view object in an application module.

Now, you can verify that your application module works the way you expected it to. In the **Applications** window, right-click on the **EditTaskService** application module node (the icon that looks like a little suitcase) and choose **Run** from the context menu. This will start the Oracle ADF Model Tester where you can work with all of the view objects that are part of your application module.

Always test your business components using the Oracle ADF Model Tester before you start using them in pages. Whenever your page doesn't run the way you expected, always use the ADF Model Tester to determine if the error is in the frontend or the backend part of the application.

Double-click on the `AllTasksVO1` view object instance. A pop-up dialog appears, allowing you to assign values to all the bind variables defined in the view objects. To begin, just click on **OK** to leave all bind variables at the `NULL` value. You should see the data in the `AllTasksVO` view object, as shown in the following screenshot:

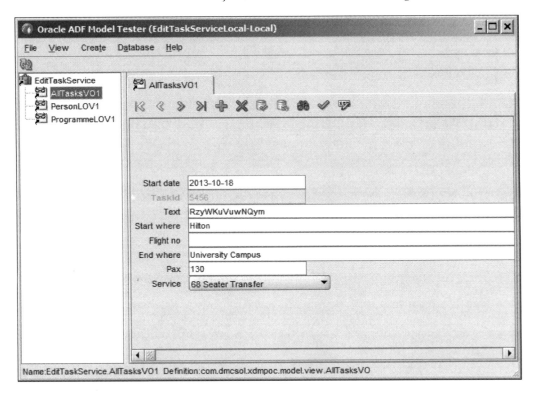

Here, you can page through the existing data, as well as insert and delete rows, using the green plus and red cross symbols. Click on the **Edit Bind Variables** button (to the right of the toolbar, with the little pencil icon) to change bind variable values and notice how the data is filtered.

Creating view objects for scheduling

For the scheduling screen, we need two view objects: one for persons and one for the tasks assigned to persons.

We already have a view object showing persons, but this view object only contains the initials (because it was intended for the Persons drop-down list in UC008). We could create a new Persons view object for UC104; however, we'll change the existing view object instead.

First, you need to change the name of the view object from PersonLOV to PersonsVO to reflect that it's no longer just used for a list of values. Changing the name or package for existing objects is called **refactoring**, and JDeveloper makes this easy. Simply right-click on the PersonLOV view object and choose **Refactor | Rename** from the context menu. JDeveloper will change the name of the object and automatically update all of the references to it, as shown in the following screenshot:

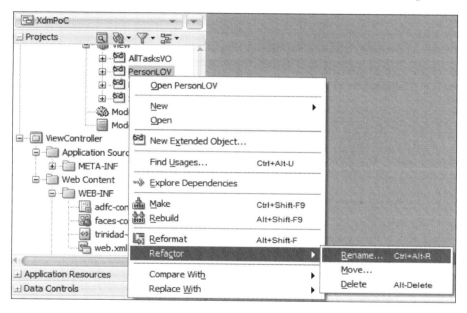

Next, the view object needs some more attributes. To add these, open the view object by double-clicking on it and choose the **Attributes** subtab. Click on the little triangle next to the green plus sign above the attributes and choose **Add Attribute from Entity**, as shown in the following screenshot. Don't just click on the plus sign—you need to select the little triangle to get access to the **Add Attribute from Entity** menu item.

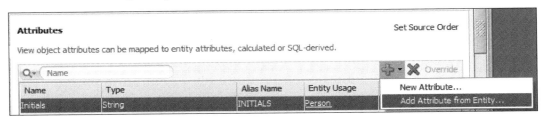

In the **Attributes** dialog, add the `FirstName` and `LastName` attributes to the **Selected** list and click on **OK**. Then, select the new `FirstName` attribute, select the **UI Hints** tab at the bottom of the view object window, and set a **Label**. Repeat this procedure for the `LastName` attribute.

Next, create another view object, giving it the name `ScheduledTasksVO`. In step 2 of the wizard, move the `Task` entity object to the right-hand side. As we won't be updating tasks either, you can remove the checkbox in the **Updatable** field here. In step 3 of the wizard, you only need to select the `StartDate` and `EndDate` attributes—note that the `TaskId` primary key attribute is automatically added.

In step 5 of the wizard, we need to add a `WHERE` clause so that the view object will only show tasks with both, a start and an end date. Enter the following `WHERE` clause:

```
start_date is not null and end_date is not null
```

Then, click on **Finish**.

Since there is a master-detail relationship between persons and tasks, we also need to create a view link. Right-click on the **Model** project and choose **New | View Link**. Name your view link `PersonsTasksLink`.

In step 2 of the wizard, we need to define the relationship between the two view objects. These are connected by the foreign key, `XDM_PERS_TASK_FK`, that defines the connection between a person and the tasks assigned to that person. Leave the **Cardinality** selection at **0..1 to *** (this means that one person may have one or more tasks), expand the `PersonsVO` node on the left-hand side, and choose `XdmPersTaskFkAssoc` at the left-hand side of the link. On the right-hand side, expand the `ScheduledTasksVO` node and choose `PersTaskFkAssoc` again, this time at the right-hand side of the link. Then, click on **Add**. You can see the source and destination attributes added at the bottom of the dialog box, as shown in the following screenshot:

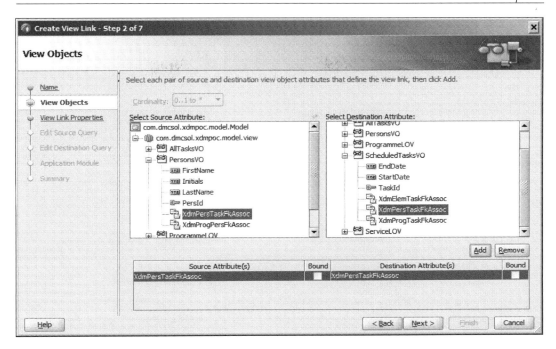

You don't need to change any of the remaining settings in this wizard, so you can simply click on **Next** and then **Finish** to close the dialog box.

Building an application module for scheduling

Create another application module for the UC104 Person Task Timeline screen, giving it the name `ScheduledTaskService`.

One lump or two?

You want to modularize your application so that each piece of functionality is completely developed and delivered by one team. This means that each subsystem gets its own application module. When you put together the final application, you can choose whether you want each subsystem (and each application module) to have its own transaction and database connection or whether they should share the transaction context. We'll return to the discussion of the proper number of application modules in *Chapter 3, Getting Organized*.

In step 2 of the wizard, first move the `PersonsVO` view object to the right-hand side. Then, select the `PersonsVO1` view object instance on the right-hand side and the node `ScheduledTasksVO via PersonTasksLink` on the left-hand side, and click on the **>** button to move `ScheduledTasksVO` to the right-hand side box, as shown in the following screenshot:

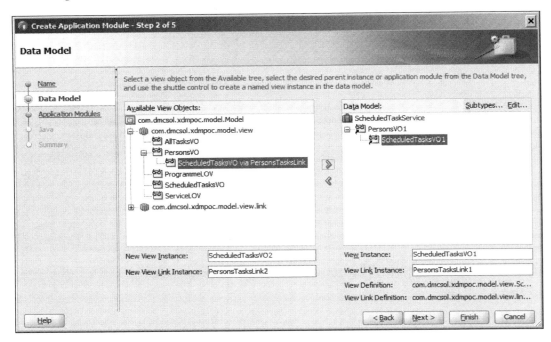

Note the difference between choosing `ScheduledTasksVO` on its own and choosing `ScheduledTasksVO` as a child of `PersonsVO`. If you choose the view object as a child of another view object, the ADF framework will automatically implement the master-detail relationship; the view object will only display the records that are children of the current record in the parent (master) view object. If you choose the view object on its own, it will not have any relationship to the master view object and will simply display all child records.

Then, click on **Finish** to close the wizard.

Run your new application module in the **ADF Model Tester**. In the left-hand side, you'll see the master view object, the view link, and the detail view object. Double-click on the view link to see the master and detail records together. When you use the navigation buttons at the master level, you will see different detail records displayed, as shown in the following screenshot:

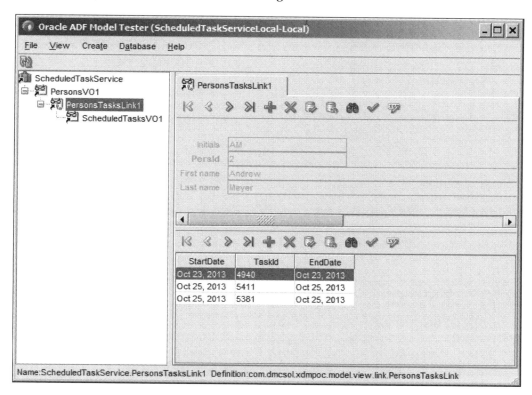

The Proof of Concept ADF user interface

Once you have built all of the business components your application will need, you can start building the user interface. The user interface consists of two parts: **ADF Task Flows** and **ADF Pages**.

Pages or fragments?

As mentioned in the *The ADF architecture* section, an application can use either pages or page fragments. The Proof of Concept uses pages for simplicity, while the professional Proof of Concept we'll be building in *Chapter 6, Building the Enterprise Application*, will use page fragments.

ADF Task Flows

For the Proof of Concept, we will implement one bounded ADF task flow. Right-click on the **ViewController** project and choose **New**. You might notice that the context menu looks different now. That's because the **ViewController** project uses technologies that are different from the **Model** project.

Choose **ADF Task Flow** and name it xdm-poc-flow. Make sure that the **Create as Bounded Task Flow** checkbox is checked and the **Create with Page Fragments** checkbox is *not* checked. Then click on **OK**. You will see a blank task flow diagram in the JDeveloper main window.

> The Proof of Concept is page-based, like a traditional web application. Later in this book, we will see another example where we use page fragments to build a modern Rich Internet Application.

In the component palette in the top-right corner of the JDeveloper window, expand the **Components** heading and drag in a **View** component. Give it the name TaskPage. Drag in another **View** component and name it SchedulePage.

Then, drag in a **Control Flow Case** component (the green arrow) and drop it on the TaskPage. Move the cursor to the SchedulePage and click on it. This establishes a control flow from the TaskPage to the SchedulePage. The cursor will be placed in a box in the middle of the line. Type goSchedule in this box and press *return*. Drop another **Control Flow Case** onto the SchedulePage and drag it to the TaskPage. Name this control flow goTask.

This defines the two pages that we will be using in the Proof of Concept, as well as the possible navigation between them. Your task flow should look like the following screenshot:

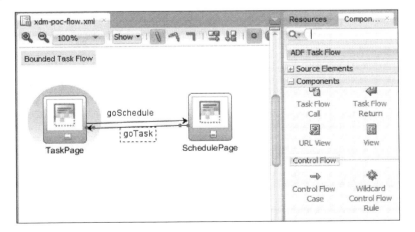

Note the green halo behind the `TaskPage`. It indicates that this page is the default activity — the first thing to happen when the task flow is invoked. You can make another activity (**View**, **Method Call**, and so on) the default by right-clicking on it and choosing **Mark Activity** and then **Default Activity**.

The tasks page

You might notice that the icon in both of the pages in the task flow diagram have a dotted and pixelated lower half. This indicates that the pages don't actually exist yet — they are only defined as placeholders in the task flow.

Creating the tasks page

To create the tasks page, double-click on the `TaskPage` icon in the page flow diagram. The **Create JSF Page** dialog appears. For the Proof of Concept, we start with blank pages (make sure that **Create Blank Page** is selected) — but when actually building the real application, we will, of course, be using the page templates. Set **Document Type** to **Facelets** and click on **OK** to create and open the page.

Facelets is the modern way of rendering a JSF page and is superior to JSP XML. Always choose Facelets for new pages. For more information, refer to the Oracle whitepaper, *JavaServer Faces 2.0 Overview and Adoption Roadmap in Oracle ADF Faces and Oracle JDeveloper 11g*, available at http://www.oracle.com/ technetwork/developer-tools/adf/learnmore/adffaces-jsf20-190927.pdf.

There are two ways of placing ADF components on a JSF page: you can drag them in from the **Components** palette on the right-hand side, or you can drag them in from the **Data Controls** palette in the **Applications** window on the left-hand side, as follows:

- If you drag in a component from the **Components** palette, it is not **bound** to any data control. This means it has no connection to the data in the ADF Business Components. You can create bindings manually, but it is more work.

- If you drag in the data control from the **Data Controls** palette, JDeveloper will automatically present you with a menu of components that you can drop onto the page. If you use this approach, the dropped component is automatically bound to the data control you dragged in.

To add components to the task page, find and open the **Data Controls** panel in the **Applications** window on the left-hand side of the JDeveloper window. You should see two data controls corresponding to the two application modules you have created in the **Model** project: EditTaskServiceDataControl and ScheduledTaskServiceDataControl, as shown in the following screenshot:

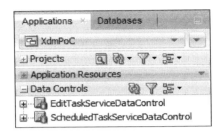

However, before we start dragging in data controls, we need to place a layout component on the page to control where the items are to be placed. If you come from a 4GL background (such as Oracle Forms), you might be used to pixel-precise placement of items. In JSF, on the other hand, the placement of components is controlled by special layout components. This has the advantage that the layout components can arrange, shrink, and expand the components they contain in order to make the best use of the available screen area. The disadvantage of this approach is that it takes a little while to learn to use the right layout components.

For the TaskPage, we start with a **Panel Stretch Layout**. Find this component in the **Component Palette** on the right-hand side of the JDeveloper window (under the **Layout** heading) and drop it on the page, as shown in the following screenshot:

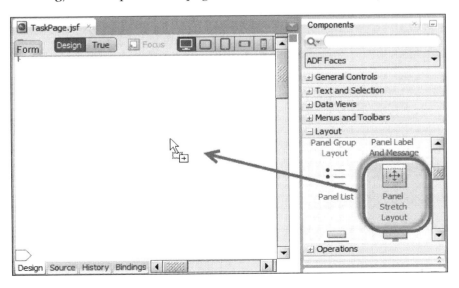

It is a good idea to use a "stretchable" layout component as the outer layer to ensure that your application will utilize the entire browser window.

The structure of your page is represented visually in the work area, but you can also see a hierarchical representation of the components on the page on the **Structure** window (by default, they are placed in the bottom-left corner of the **JDeveloper** screen). If you expand the **Panel Stretch Layout** on the **Structure** window, you will see that it shows a folder-like node called **Panel Stretch Layout Facets** and additional folder-like nodes called **bottom**, **center**, and so on under that, as shown in the following screenshot. Many layout containers contain these containers (called **facets**) that you can place your content in.

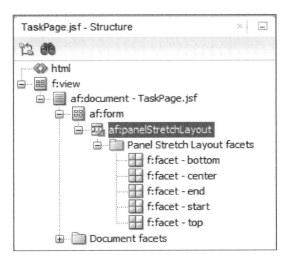

If you refer to the screen design earlier in this chapter, you will see that the **Panel Stretch Layout** matches our requirements: we can place the search criteria on top (in the facet called **top**), the actual data in the middle (in the facet called **center**), and some buttons at the bottom (in the facet called **bottom**). We don't need the **start** and **end** facets, so we don't have to worry about them. Facets without content are not shown at run time.

We will start with the actual data, which we will present using an ADF Table component. Open the **Data Controls** panel on the right-hand side, and then open the EditTaskServiceDataControl node. You will see the AllTasksVO1 view object instance. Grab the entire view object instance (the red and orange icon) and drag it onto the center facet, as shown in the following screenshot:

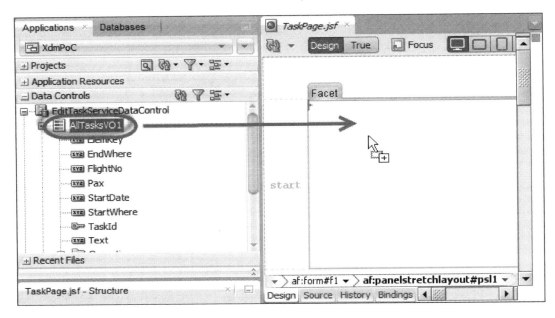

When you drop a data control onto a page, JDeveloper shows a context menu asking you which user interface elements you want to create and bind to the data control. In this case, select **Table/List View** first and then **ADF Table** from the context menu. The **Create Table** dialog appears, as shown in the following screenshot:

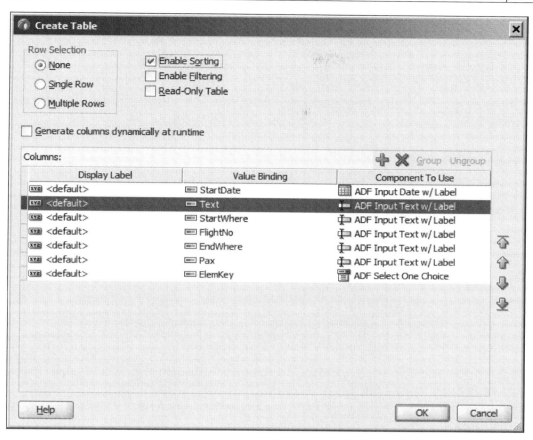

In this dialog box, you can remove the columns that you don't need and re-order the columns if necessary. You will see that JDeveloper has automatically selected an appropriate UI component—**ADF Input Date** for date attributes and **ADF Select One Choice** for attributes where a value list has been defined. For the tasks table, you only need to delete the `TaskId` column. You can also enable data sorting by clicking on the column headers by selecting the **Enable Sorting** checkbox. Then, click on **OK**. You will see a table component in the middle of your page.

Finally, you need to notify ADF which column gets to use any extra space on the screen. Remember that we started with a **Panel Stretch Layout**, which will automatically stretch the components it contains, but a table component doesn't stretch until you specify which column should expand to use any extra space.

First, select the **Text** column and make a note of its **Id** property (look in the **Properties** window in the lower-right corner of the JDeveloper window) — it will be something similar to `c2`. Then, select the entire table (either in the **Design** window in the middle of the JDeveloper window or in the **Structure** window on the bottom-left side). The **Properties** window will now show the properties of the table. Expand the **Appearance** node in the **Properties** window and set the **ColumnStretching** property to the name of the **Text** column (for example, **column:c2**).

Running the initial tasks page

Even though we have not built the search functionality yet, it's about time that we run some code. Simply right-click anywhere on the **TaskPage** and choose **Run** from the pop-up menu.

You will get a warning about running a page that is part of a task flow. This tells you that you cannot navigate to other pages; to do that, you need to run the task flow itself. In this case, we just want to run the page, so we can ignore this error and click on **Yes** to run the page.

In the **Log** window at the bottom of the JDeveloper window, you can see the **WebLogic** server starting up. This will take some time.

Once WebLogic has started, a browser window showing your data will open. Resize the window by checking if the **Text** column expands and contracts. Also, note that you can re-order the columns by dragging the column headers, and you can change the sorting by clicking on the column headers.

You might want to change the initial column size for some of the columns — to do this in JDeveloper, select an **af:column** element in the main window or the structure panel and change the **Width** value (under the **Appearance** heading) in the **Properties** window.

Refining the tasks page

Referring to the drawing of the tasks page, we can see that two groups of items are missing: the search criteria at the top and buttons at the bottom.

JDeveloper makes it very easy to create items that represent bind variables. If you expand the `AllTasksVO1` node, as shown in the following screenshot, you will see all of the attributes in the view object, as well as a node called **Operations**. If you expand the **Operations** node, you will see a number of standard operations that all view objects offer. One of these operations is **ExecuteWithParams**, and if you expand this completely, you will see the bind variables defined in the view object (`pResponsible`, `pProgramme`, and `pText`).

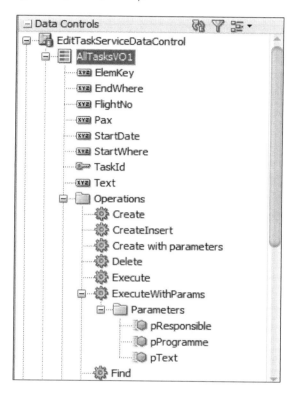

To lay out the search criteria horizontally as required by the user interface sketch, we will use a **Panel Group Layout**. Add this (from the **Layout** section of the **Components** window) to the top facet. In the **Properties** window, set the **Layout** property to **Horizontal** to get the contents (the various search criteria) arranged horizontally.

For tips on the ADF basic layout, refer to the Oracle white paper, *ADF Faces Layout Basics*, available at http://www.oracle. com/technetwork/developer-tools/adf/learnmore/ adffaceslayoutbasics-2046652.pdf.

The first criterion is the person responsible for the programme. To add this criterion to the page, drop the `pResponsible` parameter onto the **Panel Group Layout** in the top facet, as shown in the following screenshot:

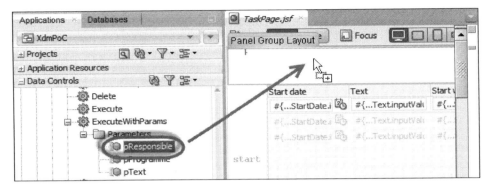

When you release it, a context menu appears. From this menu, select **Single Selection** and then **ADF Select One Choice**. The **Edit List Binding** dialog appears, as shown in the following screenshot:

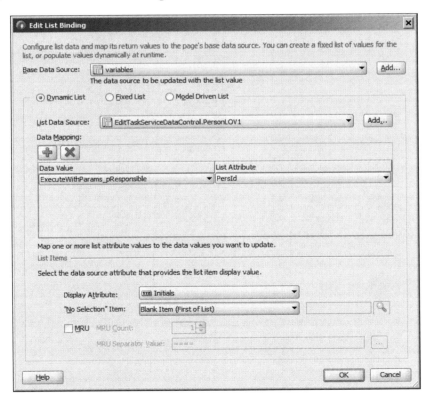

Leave **Base Data Source** as **variables** and click on **Add** to add a new **List Data Source**. Choose the PersonLOV1 view object instance as the source and click on **OK**. In the table in the middle of the dialog, select PersId as **List Attribute** (the value that is bound to the variable). At the bottom of the dialog, choose **Initials** in the **Display Attribute** dropdown and set **"No Selection" Item** to **Blank Item (First of List)**; then click on **OK**.

Set the **Label** property for the **Property Inspector** dropdown in the lower-right corner to Responsible.

> We're taking a shortcut here and hard-wiring a user interface string in. In a real-life application, this should be placed in a **resource bundle** (see *Appendix, Internationalization*).

The second criterion is the name of the programme. To add this, first change the Design view of the TaskPage by clicking on the **Design** tab at the bottom of the window. From the list of parameters (under **ExecuteWithParams**), drag the pProgramme parameter onto the **Panel Group Layout** next to the pResponsible drop-down list and again, drop as **Single Selection, ADF Select One Choice**. Again, leave the **Base Data Source** unchanged and click on the **Add** button next to **List Data Source**. This time, choose the ProgrammeLOV1 view object instance as the data source for this drop-down list and set **List Attribute** to ProgId. Then, set **Display Attribute** to **Name** and again set **"No Selection" Item** to **Blank Item (First of List)**. Then, click on **OK**. In the **Property Inspector**, set the **Label** property to Programme.

If the two drop-down boxes are below each other and not next to each other, it's probably because you have accidentally dropped one of them outside the **af:panelGroupLayout** component. JDeveloper will show you a little red exclamation mark, as shown in the following screenshot:

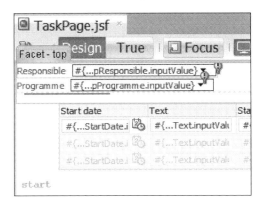

The easiest place to fix this is in the **Structure** window in the bottom-left corner of the JDeveloper window. Grab the **af:selectOneChoice** component that is not indented under the **af:panelGroupLayout** component. Your **Structure** window should look as shown in the following screenshot:

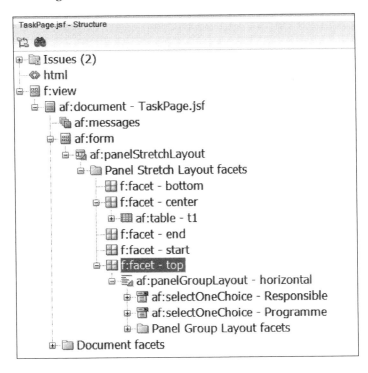

The last criterion is the search text that is matched with the **Text** column. Drop the pName parameter next to the pProgramme parameter, and this time, drop it as **Text** and **ADF Input Text w/ Label**. Set the **Label** property to **Text**.

Finally, you need to create a button that actually executes the search. To achieve this, simply drag the **ExecuteWithParams** operation (the green gearwheel icon) onto the page inside the **Panel Group Layout** next to the three search criteria. As this is not a data element but an operation, your drop choices are different. Choose **Operation** and **ADF Button**. The default text on the button is the name of the operation (ExecuteWithParams). In the **Property Inspector** panel in the bottom-right corner of the JDeveloper window, change the Text property to Search.

 If you don't see all four elements on the same line, one or more of them are outside the **af:panelGroupLayout**. Fix this in the **Structure** window as described earlier.

Fixing the bindings

In the latest version of JDeveloper 12*c* that was available at the time of writing this book (12.1.2.0.0), JDeveloper sets an inappropriate default when you create a list binding for a parameter as we did for pResponsible and pProgramme. It can be argued whether this is a bug or not—hopefully, this default will change in future versions of JDeveloper.

To check and fix this, click on the **Bindings** tab at the bottom of the **TaskPage** window. You will see a graphical representation of the binding layer, as shown in the following screenshot:

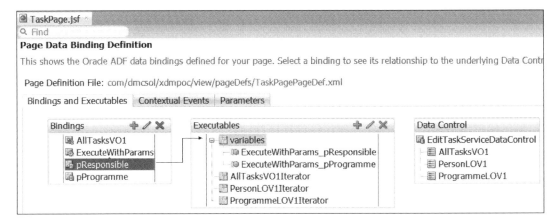

This screenshot shows all of the connections from the user interface to the data model. You don't need to understand everything here as you are starting out with ADF, but you will be returning to the binding view more often as you master ADF and want to implement more sophisticated features.

Right now, you just need to select the pResponsible list binding in the left-hand side **Bindings** box, and in the **Properties** window, open the **Other** node and set **SelectItemValueMode** to **<default> (ListIndex)**, as shown in the following screenshot:

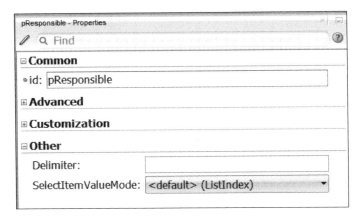

Then, set the same property for the pProgramme list binding.

  If this value is already selected, it just means that you have a newer version of JDeveloper that sets the right value by default.

Running the tasks page with parameters

To make sure we got everything correct, let's run the page again. Right-click anywhere on the **TaskPage** and choose **Run** from the pop-up menu. This redeploys the application to the built-in WebLogic server, but as WebLogic is already running, your page should appear quickly this time.

Play around with the drop-down lists and try different values in the text search field. Each time you click on the search button, the table should update accordingly.

Adding database operations

We can now retrieve data from the database and edit it on the screen. However, we haven't yet created a way to commit these changes to the database. For this, we will choose an operation at the application module level. The **ExecuteWithParams** operation belonged to the `AllTasksVO1` view object. However, if you collapse all of the view objects, you will see that the `EditTaskServiceDataControl` view object also has an **Operations** node with the **Commit** and **Rollback** operations, as shown in the following screenshot:

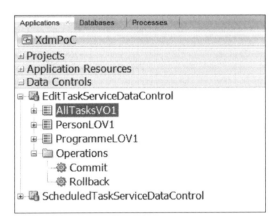

Before you drag these operations onto your page, drop a **Panel Border Layout** in the bottom facet of the page. If you refer to the sketch of the user interface, you'll see that we need some buttons (**OK** to save data and **Cancel** to revert to the previous values) on the left-hand side and the **Timeline** button on the right-hand side. Because a **Panel Border Layout** has a number of facets along the edge, it is a good component to ensure the layout. However, since it does not offer a way to control orientation, we need another component to arrange the **OK** and **Cancel** buttons.

Using the Structure window for arranging layout containers

When you have multiple containers within one another, drop them onto the **Structure** panel in the lower-left corner of the JDeveloper window. This part of the JDeveloper UI will present layout components in a tree structure, making it much easier to control where you drop components.

In the **Structure** window, expand the **af:PanelBorderLayout** component that you just added and drop a **Panel Group Layout** on the **Start** facet. In the **Property Inspector** on the lower-right in the JDeveloper window, set the **Layout** property of this **Panel Group Layout** to **horizontal**.

Start or Left?

You will notice that some elements have both a **Left** and **Start** facets. In Western languages, these will be placed on the same side of the screen. But because ADF actually supports right-to-left languages, there is a difference. Elements placed in the **Start** facet will automatically be shown on the right-hand side if the user runs the application with the language set to a right-to-left language, such as Arabic.

Then, drag the **Commit** and **Rollback** operations from the **Operations** node of `EditTaskServiceDataControl` onto this **Panel Group Layout**, and drop them as ADF buttons. The **Structure** panel should look as shown in the following screenshot. For both of the buttons, use the **Property Inspector** to set the text (to **OK** and **Cancel**) and clear the content of the **Disabled** property (under **Behavior**) to ensure that both buttons are always active.

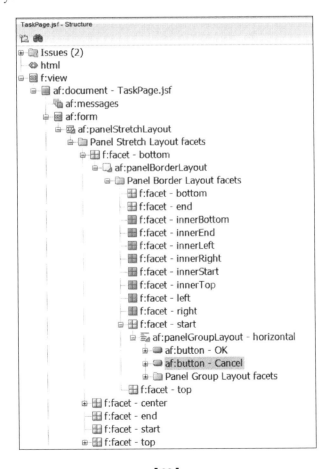

That's all there is to the commit/rollback handling—the ADF application module will automatically handle everything to ensure that your changes are either committed to the database or rolled back.

Running the tasks page with database operations

Run the page again, checking that your buttons are placed where you want them to be. Then, make some changes to the data and click on **OK**. Use a database tool to verify that your changes are committed to the database, or close the browser and run the application again to verify that your changes are actually stored.

We'll get back to the navigation button when we have built the other page.

The scheduled tasks page

To create the scheduled tasks page, go back to the `xdm-poc-flow` page flow. If you have closed the page flow window, you can find it again in the application navigator in the top-left corner in the JDeveloper window under **Web Content | Page Flows**.

Note the difference between the **TaskPage** and the **SchedulePage** icons, as shown in the following screenshot. The **TaskPage** icon now has a solid border and shows a document icon to illustrate that a TaskPage actually exists. The **SchedulePage** icon still has a dashed lower edge and a pixelated lower half to show that the page doesn't exist yet.

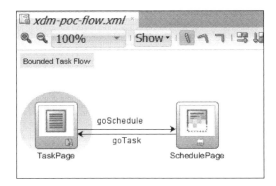

Double-click on the **SchedulePage** icon and then click on **OK** to create the page. JDeveloper remembers the settings you selected the last time you created a page.

Adding the Gantt component

Again, we start by dragging a **Panel Stretch Layout** component onto the page from the **Components** palette.

The component that we need to implement the graphic representation of tasks assigned to persons is a Gantt chart of the type scheduling.

Under **Data Controls**, open the `ScheduledTaskServiceDataControl` node and drag the `PersonsVO1` view object instance onto the center facet and drop it as **Gantt | Scheduling**. The **Create Scheduling Gantt** dialog appears, as shown in the following screenshot:

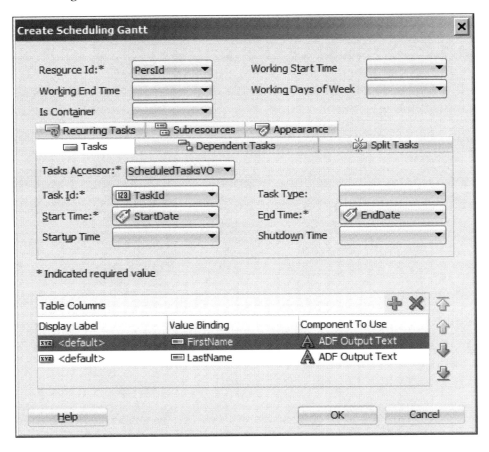

Set the fields in this dialog as follows:

- **Resource Id**: **PersId**
- **Tasks Accessor**: **ScheduledTasksVO**
- **Task Id**: **TaskId**
- **Start Time**: **StartDate**
- **End Time**: **EndDate**

Under **Table Columns**, remove the extra columns, leaving only `FirstName` and `LastName`. Then, click on **OK**. You will see a graphical representation of a scheduling Gantt chart.

> You might see both `ScheduledTasksVO` and `ScheduledTasksVO1` in the **Tasks Accessor** list. Select `ScheduledTasksVO` and *not* `ScheduledTasksVO1`. You can get from one view object to another in two ways: by referring to the view object instance name and by referring to the code method (the **accessor**) that gets built when you define the view link. The Gantt components need the accessor.
>
> Click on the chart and then go to the **Properties** window to set values for the **StartTime** and **EndTime** properties (from `2014-10-15` to `2014-10-31` so that it matches the sample data). The Gantt component does not automatically scale to the dates used, and making it do so involves a bit of code—we have chosen to leave this functionality out of this Proof of Concept.

Right-click anywhere on the page and choose **Run** to see the actual values in the browser and play around with the capabilities of the Gantt chart component. We are using it in default configuration here, but there are many customization options. Refer to the **Help** section (press *F1* with the Gantt component selected) or the documentation for a full description of this powerful component.

Navigation

The last thing that we need to add to the Proof of Concept application is the navigation feature between the pages.

Open the `TaskPage` and look at the **Structure** window. Open the **af:panelStretchLayout**, then the **bottom** facet, and then the **af:panelBorderLayout**. Find the facet called **End** and drag a **Button** component from the **Components** window (in the top-right of the JDeveloper window) across and drop it into this facet. In the **Property Inspector**, set the **Text** property to `Timeline`, and under **Action**, select **goSchedule**.

The **goSchedule** option comes from the page flow—remember that this was the title of the only control flow arrow going away from the TaskPage.

Finally, we need to drop a **Spacer** layout component from the **Components** palette directly onto the **af:panelBorderLayout**. Your **Structure** panel should now look like the one shown in the following screenshot:

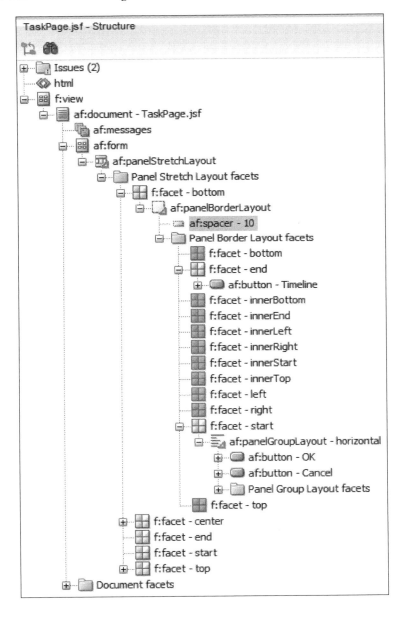

The reason we need the **Spacer** component is that ADF automatically optimizes the page and doesn't show any facets that do not have content. So, if the **Panel Border Layout** doesn't contain anything, the middle part isn't shown and the **Start** and **End** facets are right next to each other. With the spacer in place, the central part will take up all of the available space, pushing the **Start** facet to the left and the **End** facet to the right.

Now, open the `SchedulePage`. Drag a **Panel Group Layout** into the **Bottom** facet and set the **Layout** property to **horizontal** and the **Halign** property to **right**. Then, drop a **Button** onto the **Panel Group Layout**, and set the **Text** to **Overview** and **Action** to **goTask**.

To test the navigation, you can now run the entire task flow. Open the `xdm-poc-flow` task flow, right-click anywhere on the window, and click on **Run**. Your application starts with the default activity (`TaskPage`). Check if you can use the **Timeline** button to go to the `SchedulePage` and the **Overview** button to go back.

 The navigation between pages in the task flow only works if you run the task flow itself — not if you run the individual pages.

Summary

In this chapter, we discussed what a Proof of Concept is and why you need it. You got a very brief introduction to the ADF architecture and saw or built a Proof of Concept application using the entire ADF technology stack, including the advanced Gantt chart component.

You are ready to go to your boss and demonstrate what you can do with ADF. If he or she agrees that ADF is the right tool, your next step will be to produce an overall design and estimate how long it will take to build the next generation of destination management software. This is discussed in *Chapter 2, Estimating the Effort*.

2
Estimating the Effort

You have convinced your boss that the **Application Development Framework (ADF)** has what it takes to build the next generation of destination management software. Now he is asking you how much this new enterprise application will cost, what functionality should go into it, and how long will it take to build.

To be able to answer these questions, you will need to gather the requirements, do a high-level design of the solution, and estimate how long it will take.

Gathering requirements

The first step is to gather the requirements to build the software. This can be done in many different ways depending on your organizational culture and environment, detailed as follows:

- If you are subject to regulatory requirements (for example, in the aerospace or pharmaceutical business), you need a very formal method

- If you are outsourcing development to an external supplier, you need the exact requirements

- If development will be handled by an in-house IT department, you might get by with less formal requirements

At the formal end of the spectrum, you need a complete list of all of the requirements that you can test against. If your organization is used to a more informal approach, you might only produce a fairly complete list of use cases or user stories. For a technology replacement project, where you replace a legacy application developed in, for example, Oracle Forms, the requirements might be simply, "it should work like the old system."

> **Know the requirements**
>
> Aim for as complete an understanding of the requirements as possible. Even if you are doing Agile, iterative development, everybody on the team should still start out with a complete picture of the end result in their minds.

Building it just like the old system

Many ADF projects are technology replacements, often from older Oracle technologies such as Oracle Forms. In this case, the application to be replaced has typically been developed over many years; the documentation is outdated and sparse or non-existent. As neither the business nor the IT department can articulate what the system does, the requirements tend to become "it should work just like the old system."

From an estimation standpoint, you're on very thin ice here—nobody knows exactly what the system does, but the business still wants to know how long it will take to build an equivalent system. If you are in this situation, try to minimize the project risk by setting up a small project scope (redevelop just a few modules of the system).

From a cost-effectiveness standpoint, you're on equally thin ice—you know it is going to take time and effort to redevelop the modules, but if you build the new system just like the old system, you are providing no benefit to the business. Think about stepping back from the existing screens in order to see what the business processes that the system needs to support are. Often, the business processes have changed a lot since the old system was built, and it would be a shame to miss this opportunity to design an application that really matches what the business needs today. In order to maximize the business benefit from the new system, establish written user requirements as described in the following sections—do not simply write a specification that matches the existing system screen by screen.

Use cases

Often, requirements are specified in the form of use cases. Each use case describes how to perform some task, so your complete specification will consist of multiple use cases. A small system might have less than 10 use cases, while several dozens or even hundreds might be used to specify a large system.

A use case describes the interaction between a person (called an "actor" by convention) and the system. It describes what the system does for the user to provide business value to the actor, thus focusing on what is to be done and not on how it is to be done. It should therefore not contain any technical details about the implementation.

Use cases can be written at different levels of detail, as follows:

- **Brief use case**: This will be just a few sentences to use in overviews and diagrams

- **Casual use case**: This explains the use case in more detail, but still takes up less than a page of text

- **Fully dressed use case**: This is a formal specification containing a number of fields such as purpose, summary, actors, normal flow, exception flows, and business rules

If you need a high degree of formality because of regulatory requirements or because the application is being developed by a supplier for a customer, you will need a fully dressed use case. However, if you are an in-house IT department building an application for internal use, you might start out with only brief or casual use cases and flesh out the details as the project progresses.

In the previous chapter, we worked on "Use Case 008 Task Overview and Edit." A more realistic version of the screen for this use case might look like the following screenshot (with a link to a separate screen to edit all of the details):

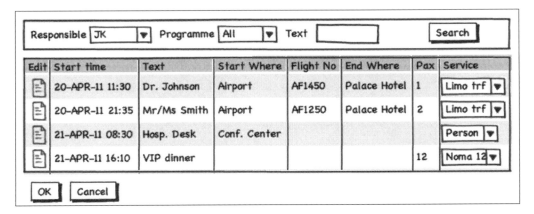

In a formal description, the preceding use case could look as follows:

Item	Description
Name	Find and edit tasks
Number	UC008
Version	1.2
Goal	To update task details if the situation changes
Summary	The programme that is responsible can search for tasks by responsible, programme, or text. The basic task attributes can be changed directly from the overview screen; all of the attributes can be changed in a pop-up detail screen.
Actors	The programme that is responsible
Preconditions	A programme has been defined
Trigger	For example, it becomes necessary to change the task details because the flights or number of passengers change.
Primary flow	• The user selects a responsible person, programme, free text, or combination of these and initiates a search.
	• The system shows only the tasks that meet all of the conditions (free text matched anywhere in the Text field). The attributes shown include Start Time, Text, Start Where, Flight no., End Where, Pax, and Service.
	• The user makes the necessary changes.
	• The user approves or cancels the changes.
Alternative flows	• The user clicks on the Edit button next to the task.
	• The system shows a detail screen with all of the task attributes.
	• The user makes the necessary changes.
	• The user closes the detail window.
	• Rejoin main flow at 4.
Post conditions	All of the tasks remain valid.
Business Rules	BR024 Task start time after programme start time
	BR025 Valid flight number
	BR026 Task pax <= service max pax
Notes	Adding new tasks is out of scope for this use case
Author and date	Sten Vesterli, 2011-03-26

User stories

Agile software development methods tend to find fully dressed use cases too heavy and prefer to work with shorter descriptions, usually called user stories. By tradition, these are supposed to be so short that they can be fit on a single 3 x 5 index card. In principle, there is no difference between a casual use case and a user story.

User stories are only useful as requirements if supplemented with some kind of acceptance test description, thus establishing a common understanding between the business user and developer about what constitutes a successful implementation.

Critical success factor: the user

A requirement for success with Agile development is that the business users are always available to answer questions throughout the project. Unless you have a solid buy-in to this process from your business users, Agile development is unlikely to succeed.

Non-functional requirements

In a software development project, it is normal to focus mainly on the functional aspects—what the system should do. However, there are many other aspects to software quality; for example, ISO-9126 defines the following aspects:

- Functionality
- Reliability
- Usability
- Efficiency
- Maintainability
- Portability

It is important that non-functional requirements are documented in a measurable and testable way, just like the functional requirements. Response time requirements need to be specified in seconds (or fractions of seconds) for a specific function:

Requirement	Description
NFR002	The time from which the user initiates the search until the filtered data is shown on the screen is < 0.5 seconds

Performance/capacity requirements need to specify the exact load the system is expected to handle (for example, 50 concurrent users sending a request every second and receiving a response within 0.5 seconds).

One common non-functional requirement is that the system is user-friendly. This is a very inexact requirement and needs to be detailed into something measurable. For example, an untrained user is able to enter five expense report items and submit the expense report in less than three minutes.

Requirement lists

If you are working with formal requirements, you need to collect all of the requirements in a common list where each requirement is given a unique ID. When you are building your test cases to prove that the application works as specified, you can map the test cases to the requirements. If all of the requirements are covered by a test case and all of the test cases succeed, your application is complete.

Ensuring complete test coverage of the requirements for an enterprise application is a major undertaking typically requiring a test management professional.

Screen design

In many enterprise applications, there are a small number of central screens where most of the day-to-day work is being done. Additionally, there might be screens with specific layout and design criteria, for example, graphic dashboard-style screens. If you have produced a use case list, you should be able to identify these special screens easily. You might even have built some of these as part of your Proof of Concept.

If you are redeveloping an existing Oracle Forms application, you can often identify the central screens simply by looking at the size of the FMB files. A typical enterprise application exhibits a few fairly large and complex modules and a "long tail" of smaller and rarely used modules. The following illustration shows the size of all Oracle Forms FMB files ordered by size in an enterprise application:

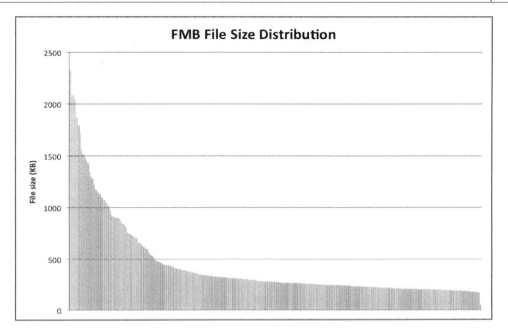

For these large and commonly used screens, it makes sense to specify the screen layout in some detail as part of the requirements process. With more than 150 ADF components available, it is a good idea to create a component catalog and design all of the screens using components from the catalog only. This provides a more uniform user interface and makes it easier for the development team to build it.

Documenting the component catalog

Each component in the catalog should be documented for both developers and end users. Developers need to know where and how to use each component, and end users need to know what behavior to expect from each component (how a drop-down list box reacts to keystrokes, how a shuttle component works, and so on).

As the UI design is actually a rather small part of the overall development time in an ADF application, and as the UI tends to evolve over the lifetime of the project, it is not cost-efficient to produce a detailed layout for every screen. Typical data maintenance screens will be totally acceptable in the default layout achieved when dropping a data control on to a page as, for example, an ADF Form.

You should design these screen layouts (sometimes known as "wireframes") in a tool that makes it easy to make changes. You can use a specialized tool for wireframe screens such as Balsamiq (`http://balsamiq.com`), which deliberately produces a handwritten look to make it clear to users that this is just a sketch and can be freely changed until exactly the right design has been achieved. The sketches in *Chapter 1, The ADF Proof of Concept*, and earlier in this chapter have been produced with the Balsamiq tool.

An alternative is to produce high-fidelity prototypes using a tool like Microsoft Visio—Oracle has made a set of Visio stencils available at `http://www.oracle.com/technetwork/indexes/samplecode/jdeveloper-adf-sample-522118.html` that you can download and use.

Be careful about using these high-fidelity prototypes (or actual JSF pages) as requirements—you might run into several problems, which are detailed as follows:

- It enables the misconception that the application is almost done
- It tends to fixate a very specific image in your users' minds—if an alternative design idea appears during development, it can be hard to deviate from the almost-finished screen the user believes to have seen
- You are more likely to get bogged down in detailed discussions about colors and fonts in a project phase, whereas the focus should be on the functionality

Deciding how to build it

Once you know what you need to build, you need to decide how you want to build it. There are three major decisions that you need to take. They are as follows:

- How much do we build at a time
- How much do we build ourselves
- How do we integrate

Deciding how much to build at a time

If you are building a new system to support a process that has not had IT support earlier, you can build it in one large chunk or in several smaller chunks. The advantage of the large chunk is that you only have to spend resources on one go-live process. On the other hand, if something does not work, you might have developed hundreds of screens with a wrong approach and have to change them.

If you are replacing an existing system (for example, an Oracle Forms-based system), you need to decide if you want to attempt a "big bang" replacement of the entire old system with a new one or if you want a phased approach. As it is much easier to run one system than to run two, some people prefer the "big bang" approach. The problem with this approach, however, is that it carries a much larger risk. If the new system does not perform satisfactorily in the production environment or if unexpected errors pop up, you risk the entire business grinding to a halt while the IT guys work out the kinks in the new system.

Based on my experience, I generally recommend a phased approach, thus building smaller chunks of functionality at a time. If you are building a new system, this approach allows you to find any potential problems early and implement corrections cheaply before you are too far down the road. If you are replacing an existing system, it pays to think carefully about how to run the systems in parallel and accept a bit of extra complexity in order to avoid the risk of business-threatening catastrophic failure.

Deciding how much to build yourself

When you look at the requirements, always ask yourself: "Might someone else have needed this before?"

The complete Oracle palette contains a lot of products, and it might make more sense for you to use Oracle's content management rather than build your own. Similarly, you might want to leverage the advanced layout and customization features of **Oracle WebCenter** rather than build your own portal framework.

If the Oracle license cost places these products out of reach, look to see if you can integrate cheaper or free frameworks instead of building everything yourself.

Deciding how to integrate

Finally, you need to decide how you want the system to integrate with external systems. As an ADF application uses modern three-tier architecture, you have three places to integrate. They are as follows:

- In the browser
- In the application server
- In the database

Frontend integration in the browser requires good knowledge of JavaScript. It is possible for your ADF application to exchange data with other web applications through the use of JavaScript in your ADF application and/or the other web application. However, this type of integration tends to be rather brittle and subject to various problems due to different JavaScript implementations in different browsers.

Integration on the middle tier is the typical way a modern web application interacts with other applications. Most often, this is done by having your application consume the web services offered by other applications or by your application offering web services to other applications. This can be done in an ad hoc fashion via a portal framework such as Oracle WebCenter or via a central integration point in **Service-Oriented Architecture (SOA)**. You can also use various messaging protocols and servers to connect applications.

Integration on the database is often the way you integrate with legacy systems. These systems often do not offer modern web service interfaces but can access a database. If your new ADF application is replacing an existing Oracle Forms application, it is often easier to integrate in the database for the period of time when both applications will be running.

Application architecture

Once you have found out what you need to build and how much you want to build, you now have to choose your application architecture. The architecture determines how many workspaces you have and which components go into which workspace.

The ADF framework is very flexible and allows you to build applications in many different ways, so there is a large number of possible architectures. Three good ones are:

- Simple
- Modular
- Enterprise

In a simple architecture, you build the entire application in one workspace. You saw an example of this approach in the Proof of Concept application in *Chapter 1, The ADF Proof of Concept*. Business components go into a model project in the workspace, and task flows and pages go into a view/controller project. This approach works well for small applications that will be built by one or two developers.

If your application is larger than 5-10 bounded task flows and/or more than two people need to work on it, a modular architecture is a good approach. In this approach, you place common elements (templates, visual identity, entity objects, and view objects for value lists) in a common application workspace and then use the output of that workspace in a number of subsystem workspaces. As described earlier, your subsystems then each contain a specific subset of the total application functionality (view objects, task flows, and page fragments), and all of the subsystems are collected into one master application workspace. This architecture is illustrated in the following figure:

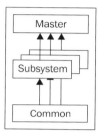

If your organization is going to be building many ADF applications, it makes sense to extend the modular architecture to the enterprise architecture. In this approach, you keep the enterprise common objects (base-level templates, visual identity, possibly entity objects, and view objects for global entities) in an Enterprise Common Workspace and then use the output from this workspace in a number of Application Common Workspaces. These Application Common Workspaces add features that are specific to each application (entity objects and value lists specific to the application). Like in the modular architecture, each application is then built with a number of subsystems that are collected into one or more master application workspaces. This architecture is illustrated in the following figure:

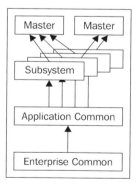

Note that the enterprise architecture allows you to build several master applications and even use the same subsystem in two different applications.

Example Work Breakdown Structure

When you know the requirements and have a screen design for the most important screens, you can start designing the solution. This does not mean that you need to know every piece of code you're going to write, but you do need to be able to break down the work in manageable chunks.

This is typically done in the form of a hierarchical **Work Breakdown Structure (WBS)** that decomposes the entire application-development effort into a number of work packages. The following list contains the work packages you will probably need when building an enterprise ADF application. Many of the items listed here haven't been explained yet but will be covered in the subsequent chapters—they will make sense when you return to this chapter after reading the rest of the book.

Your WBS is likely to include:

- **Technical design**: This is a detailed design document providing any information that the programmer will need that is not already in the requirements.
- **Server setup**: This requires the following aspects:
    - You need both a development and test environment with a WebLogic application server and a database.
    - You need a source control repository (Subversion, Git, and so on) if you don't already have one.
    - You need an issue tracking tool (for example, Jira) if you don't already have one.
    - You need a development Wiki if you don't already have one.
- **Development workstation setup**: This involves getting each development workstation set up with JDeveloper and a local database + connection for source control and issue tracking.

- **Development standards**: These cover the following aspects:
    - ° Everything a new developer needs to know to work on your project—they include how to structure workspaces and projects, how to work with the database, how you intend to do version control, build management, configuration management, and issue management. They also include naming conventions, security strategy, test strategy, UI guidelines, and HOWTOs for any common development tasks (for example, how to display an error, how to create an ADF Library, and how to write localizable strings).
    - ° Place this information in the development Wiki—development standards written in a word processor tend to languish unread on a network drive somewhere.

- **Prototyping**: This means creating standard ways of handling common functionalities to be documented in the HOWTO sections on the development Wiki, possibly multiple work packages for prototyping different things.

- **Framework extension classes**: These are your own base classes that all your ADF Business Components should be based on. If you decide on the enterprise architecture and this project is the first in the organization, remember that you will be building both enterprise framework extension classes and project-specific ones.

- **Data model**: If you don't already have a data model, you need to create tables and other database objects.

- **Entity objects for all tables**: If you are working directly with relational tables, this should be a small task. Include any special data access coding if you are not working directly with relational tables.

- **View objects for common queries (for value lists)**: These are used for including a common application module.

- **Graphical design**: If you are designing a public-facing application, you might have very strict graphical-design guidelines. This is likely to take less effort for internal applications. Output from the graphical design should be example HTML pages.

- **Skinning and templates**: These help in creating page templates and a "skin" for your application, thus defining its visual identity.

- **Usability testing**: A developer can't guess what a user finds easy. Usability testing is a specialty of its own and requires trained professionals.

- One work package per subsystem, subdivided into the following steps:

    1. Task flows (typically one for each use case)

    2. Data model for each screen (view objects and view links)

    3. Screens (JSF page fragments)

    4. Test cases

    5. Technical documentation

How much testing?

How you plan to test your use cases will make a big difference to your estimates. An explorative test where the developer plays around with the screen following a short checklist doesn't take much time, but recording a replayable user interface test does. Decide on this before you estimate. We'll return to testing in a later chapter.

- **Business logic package**: This can be anything from one small work package to a collection of large ones, depending on your requirements.

- **Integration package**: This is typically one work package per interface (web service, file load, and so on) depending on your integration needs.

- **Master application**: This work package will collect all of the bounded task flows from the subsystems into the final application.

- **Automated build procedure**: This is used to set up Ant, Maven, or a similar tool to automatically build your completed application directly from the source in your version control repository. It might possibly include setting up a continuous integration server.

- **System integration testing**: This tests the whole application — testing individual components should happen in the use case work packages. Reserve at least 10 percent of your total development time for integration testing.

- **Coordination and project management**: For example, 5 percent of the total development effort is spent in coordination time — remember that a two-hour project meeting is already 5 percent of a workweek. For project management, use, for example, 20 percent of the total development effort (but typically not more than one full-time resource).

Estimating the solution

With your Work Breakdown Structure in hand, you can start estimating the real work involved in each group of tasks. Estimate the effort needed to perform the task in hours or days (measured in ideal engineering hours, assuming concentrated, uninterrupted work on the task). Don't fall into the trap of estimating in duration— duration estimates will vary wildly depending on how much non-project work the person doing the estimate expects to be doing at the same time.

Use small tasks

If you find that a work package has an estimate of more than 80 hours, revisit the Work Breakdown Structure and split the task into smaller subtasks. An estimate of 80+ hours very often indicates an incomplete understanding of the task and carries a large risk of overrunning the estimate.

The individual subsystem work packages might break the 80-hour limit and are, therefore, divided into subpackages.

Top-down estimate

If you are an experienced project manager, you can probably produce a rough estimate of the total effort involved in the project. For this, you rely on your experience with similar projects and your intuition.

Some project managers don't like the idea of using "intuition" because it does not feel scientific and exact. However, your other-than-conscious mind can process a lot of information and will be able to produce some quality input to your estimation process.

Of course, you don't start a multi-man-year project based solely on intuition—you combine the top-down estimate with a bottom-up estimate.

Bottom-up estimate

In order to produce the bottom-up estimate, you ask people capable of performing each task how much effort (in hours or days) it will take to produce the necessary output. Some projects prefer to let several people do independent estimates, while other project methodologies like Scrum prefer team estimates using collaborative techniques such as planning poker (see http://www.planningpoker.com).

Your work on the Proof of Concept will already have given you an idea of the effort involved in some common ADF development tasks, and the productivity you observed during the "infatuation" stage can provide a rough estimate of the final development speed.

You need to make clear what you include in the estimate—developers typically forget to include things such as technical documentation and repeatable test cases.

> The rest of this section describes an estimation technique often used for formal estimates that go into agreements and contracts—for example, when a system integrator is making an offer to a customer to build an application according to the agreed specifications. If you are an IT department building an application for internal use, Agile methods like Scrum, where development is done in a number of fixed time windows (called "sprints"), might fit your needs better.

Three-point estimates

If you ask someone for just one estimate, it is natural that the estimate will be padded with a bit of buffer time. All sorts of unforeseen complications may emerge, so a developer will try to anticipate these and include them in his or her estimate.

Unfortunately, even if complications do not occur, the task still tends to take the estimated time.

In order to respect the uncertainty of the task without padding every task with buffer time for worst-case scenarios, developers and others producing estimates should produce a three-point estimate for each task, detailed as follows:

- **An optimistic estimate**: This is the best case if things are easier than expected. You stumble upon a framework class that can perform the task, a wizard in JDeveloper generates code for you, and so on.

- **A likely estimate**: This is the time you realistically expect the task to take.

- **A pessimistic estimate**: This is the worst-case scenario if things are harder than expected. The class you thought you could use doesn't do exactly what you want it to, you run into a baffling bug when testing with multiple users, and so on.

  Don't allow the pessimism to take overhand; you do not need the pessimistic estimate to include tornadoes destroying the test server.

Three-point estimates like these will clearly show the project manager which tasks are not clearly specified or carry a greater risk. If the pessimistic estimate is much higher than the likely estimate, the person doing the estimate is unsure about either the task or the means to complete it. This can be addressed by specifying the task in greater detail and possibly performing a short, dedicated Proof of Concept to allay any doubts the developer or other estimator has about the task.

The data set from three-point estimates can also be used to calculate an expected time according to the formula in **Program Evaluation and Review Technique (PERT)**. This technique was developed by very clever people building Polaris nuclear submarines in the 1950s and has been used ever since.

The expected time is calculated as follows:

$$t_{expected} = (t_{optimistic} + 4 \; x \; t_{likely} + t_{pessimistic}) / 6$$

This time takes the uncertainty into account and produces a better number than just using the most likely time. The three points will also be used for some clever math when we get to the end of the chapter, where we'll be adding everything up.

Grouping – simple, normal, and hard

Your Work Breakdown Structure is likely to include many tasks of similar complexity. Naturally, you are not going to estimate each of these individually but rather estimate an average complexity for the whole group and simply multiply this effort with the number of code modules in the group to arrive at a total estimate.

For an ADF application, you might use the following grouping:

Element	Simple	Normal	Hard
Entity objects	Based on relational tables	Based on the API offering insert/ update/delete functions (for example, a PL/SQL API)	Based on the API that doesn't map directly to insert/ update/delete operations
Value list	Based on relational table	Dependent value lists (the content depends on other selections)	
Data model for a screen	Data maintenance, one view object	Average screen, 2-5 view objects	> 5 view objects

Element	Simple	Normal	Hard
Task flow	1-3 pages	4-10 pages with simple flows	> 10 pages or complex flows and custom transaction handling
Screen	Simple data maintenance on one view object	Normal screens based on 2-5 view objects, no special components	Based on > 5 view objects or using complex components (for example, tree, visualization, drag-and-drop)

You can use more groups if your application has a wider variety of tasks, or you might estimate a few hard tasks individually if they are of a higher complexity than your other "hard" tasks.

Estimation: art or science?

Three-point estimates, as described earlier, are a way to add some scientific rigor to the experience-based estimates produced by developers. There are other estimation techniques like Function Point Analysis (http://en.wikipedia.org/wiki/Function_point) that attempt to apply an even more scientific method to the estimating process.

More input, better estimates

Research shows that the average of independent estimates from several people is likely to be closer to the correct value than any one estimate. Many Agile development methods also recommend you to involve developers, architects, testers, and customers in discussions of the estimate.

You can try this in the office: ask your colleagues what the distance between two well-known cities some distance away is. You'll find that the average of just five people will be pretty close to the real distance, even if some of the estimates are way off.

You don't need multiple estimates for all of the items in your Work Breakdown Structure, but for critical tasks or tasks where the worst-case estimate is far from the likely estimate, consider getting a second, third, or fourth opinion.

Just like the old one – the dangers of groupthink

If your requirements are a new system "just like the old one" and you are part of the team that built the old system, this averaging technique is not sufficient to arrive at a reasonable estimate. Developers who are intimately familiar with an application will underestimate the complexity of the solution dramatically. If you only have an estimate by developers of the legacy system you are replacing, experience shows that it is prudent to multiply that estimate by a factor of 2.

The following table shows examples of what estimates could look like for a few of the items from the WBS described earlier in the chapter. All estimates are in ideal engineering hours:

Task	Optimistic	Likely	Pessimistic
Server setup			
• Test server	8	16	24
• Subversion, Jira, and Wiki	4	10	20
Entity objects (55 tables)	11	27	55
Graphical design	20	40	60
Skinning and templates			
• Skin	4	10	40
• Page template incl. menu	8	16	24
Usability testing	40	80	160
UC 008 Task overview and edit			
• Task flow	1	2	3
• View objects	1	3	5
• Overview screen	2	4	8
• Detail screen	3	6	12
• Test cases	2	4	6
• Technical documentation	1	2	3

You'll notice that some tasks have larger variation than others. For example, usability testing is likely to take 80 hours, but might take up to 160 hours. The reason for the high pessimistic estimate is that we might need several iterations before the usability is as good as we want. For other tasks, the optimistic, likely, and pessimistic values are very close together. This indicates well-defined, low-risk tasks that we're pretty sure how to complete.

Adding it all up – the final estimate

When you have gathered all of the detailed task estimates, you need to add up the details to a total estimate for the entire project.

As a starting point, you add up all of the expected task efforts. Remember that these are calculated based on your three-point estimates using the formula earlier in this chapter. This total is the total effort most likely needed to complete the project.

Swings and roundabouts

A fairground owner will say: "What you lose on the swings, you gain on the roundabouts." A developer will recognize this: some things take longer (closer to the pessimistic estimate), and some take shorter (closer to the optimistic estimate). However, it is extremely unlikely that everything takes as long as the pessimistic estimate—just as it is extremely unlikely that everything goes swimmingly according to the optimistic estimate.

A statistician will illustrate this fact with a normal distribution curve showing probability or likelihood on the vertical axis and project effort on the horizontal axis. This bell-shaped curve is high in the middle, indicating that it is most likely that your total project effort will be somewhere near the sum of all of the expected task efforts. It drops off toward the ends, showing how likely or unlikely it is that your project duration will be dramatically different from the middle value.

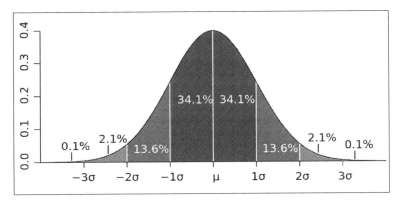

The shape of the curve is defined by what is known as the standard deviation that can be calculated from your three-point estimates. There is some math behind it, but the net result is that it is 95 percent likely that your total project effort falls within the plus/minus two-standard deviations. (If you're interested in the math, there is a good treatment on Wikipedia: http://en.wikipedia.org/wiki/Standard_deviation).

Calculating the standard deviation for a task

You can calculate the standard deviation for each task using your three-point estimates. Simply use a spreadsheet program like Microsoft Excel and the standard deviation function (STDEVP in Excel). The inputs to this function should be six figures (one optimistic, four likely, and one pessimistic), just like we used when calculating the expected time for a task.

This calculation will show a large standard deviation (and greater uncertainty) if your optimistic and pessimistic values are far from the likely value.

Calculating the standard deviation for a project

To get from the standard deviation of the individual tasks to the standard deviation for the whole project involves a bit of math. What you do is calculate the square of the standard deviation (also called the variance) and then add up the variance values for each task. You then take the square root of the sum of the variances to get the standard deviation for the entire project.

Remember from the preceding context that it was 95 percent likely that the actual value is within plus/minus two-standard deviations from the middle value. So, if your most likely total effort is 1450 hours and the calculated standard deviation for the entire project is 150, you can tell the business: "We expect the effort of the project to be 1450 hours with a 95 percent probability of falling in the interval from 1150 to 1750 hours."

The following table illustrates how to calculate a final estimate. As the entire estimate would take up several pages, this calculation example uses just four tasks from the Work Breakdown Structure. The tasks are detailed as follows:.

Task	Optimistic	Likely	Pessimistic	Expected	Std.dev.	Variance
Development Server	8	16	24	16	5	21
Page templates	4	10	20	11	5	22
Graphical design	20	40	60	40	12	133
Usability testing	40	80	160	87	36	1289
Total				153		1466
Proj. std. dev				38		

The values in the expected column are calculated according to the formula earlier in this chapter. In Excel, it would look something like `(B2+4*C2+D2)/6`.

Your spreadsheet software can calculate the values in the standard deviation column. In Excel, this would look like `STDEVP(B2;C2;C2;C2;C2;D2)`. This calculates the standard deviation of one optimistic value, four likely values, and one pessimistic value.

The values in the variance column are simply the square of the standard deviation. In Excel, this could look like `POWER(F2;2)`.

Finally, you calculate the sum of all of the variance values and take the square root of this sum to get the standard deviation for the whole project. A statistician can explain to you why you can't just add up the standard deviations. In Excel, this calculation would look like `SQRT(G6)`.

With a total expected time of 153 hours and a standard deviation of 38 hours, you get the following aspects:

- The expected project effort is 153 hours
- It is 95 percent likely that the project effort will fall between 77 and 230 hours (plus/minus two times the standard deviation).

If this is too wide a span for the business to sign off on, you need to address the major uncertainties. If, for instance, you were to limit usability testing to a maximum of 100 hours, the expected time for this task drops to 77 hours and the project standard deviation to 22. This leads to an expected project effort of 143 hours with a 95 percent confidence interval of 99 to 188 hours.

Again, this estimation methodology is intended for formal estimates where you need to agree on the project effort upfront. If you do not need to commit to a fixed time and cost at the beginning of the project, Agile development methods might fit your needs better.

Sanity check

Once you add up all of your bottom-up estimates, you should arrive at a total close to the project manager's top-down estimate. If the estimates are not fairly close, your project contains some uncertainty that you need to examine.

The project manager might find that the bottom-up estimate is higher because it includes the tasks he or she did not consider in the top-down estimate. That's fine. However, if you have a major discrepancy and cannot find the reason, you need to revisit your estimates. As described earlier, you get better estimates if you let more people do the estimation and then calculate the averages. Do this for both your top-down and bottom-up estimates until the total bottom-up estimate is approximately the same as the top-down estimate.

From effort to calendar time

Remember that we have been discussing effort in this chapter, calculating it in ideal engineering hours. You need to convert this into actual calendar time, taking into account vacation, illness, training, the support of the existing systems, tasks for other projects, company meetings, and many other things.

If you have already implemented detailed time tracking in your organization, you can get a good idea of the development efficiency of each developer from historical data. If you do not have this data, start your project plan assuming 50 percent efficiency for everyone. Then, follow up on how many hours are actually spent on development tasks for each person. This can be very different from person to person because of the varying other tasks each team member will have.

Summary

You gathered all of the requirements, decided how you will build the application, and decided on a modular architecture. You then created a Work Breakdown Structure for the XDM project, and together with the other developers in DMC Solutions, you created three-point estimates for each task in your project. Then, you calculated the total effort needed to build DMC Solutions' next-generation destination management.

Your boss was impressed with your detailed estimate and liked the fact that you had calculated a 95 percent probability worst-case value. He has now gone to the CEO for the funding—if he gets the go-ahead, your next task is to get the project team organized. That's the topic of *Chapter 3, Getting Organized*.

3
Getting Organized

You've proved that ADF is the right tool for your enterprise project. You have estimated how long it will take to build the application, and the business has approved the project.

Time for some programmers to get together and start coding, right?

Wrong. If you are to build a successful enterprise project, you need to think about the skills and people you need before you start. In addition, you will need to set up a few tools and establish some guidelines to ensure that everyone on the team will be working efficiently together to achieve the common goal.

Skills required for an ADF project

For a small application, you might have to do all of the work yourself. If you have ever built a whole application, you might remember that some parts were fun and others were less fun. And, while being functional, your application probably did not win any prizes for design or usability.

If your enterprise application is going to be a success, people should *want* to use it. That means it has to be visually attractive and user friendly—public sites such as Facebook, Flickr, and the various Google applications have set the bar fairly high. Your users *expect* the enterprise application that you are building to live up to the sites they see and use regularly.

These applications are *not* built by one person. They are large (like your application), so they need a sizable team of programmers. But, they are also complete — the visual identity and usability is as much a part of the overall experience as the code. If you are to live up to these high demands, you need a team with many different skills, including:

- ADF framework knowledge
- Object-oriented programming
- Java programming
- Database design and programming
- XML
- Web technologies (HTML, CSS, and JavaScript)
- Regular expressions
- Graphics design
- Usability
- Testing

We'll examine these necessary skills in more detail in the following sections.

ADF framework knowledge

Everybody on the team will need basic knowledge of the ADF framework. This includes project managers, testers, graphic designers, and usability experts, too. Having a common understanding of what the framework can and cannot do will make communication within the team much easier.

The programmers will, of course, need a deeper understanding of the framework — but, not everybody has to be an expert. An experienced programmer should just need a basic training class for one week and about a month of work under experienced supervision in order to be productive with ADF.

Finally, you need at least one person with a deep understanding of how ADF works. This person will define the project standards and provide guidelines on how to use ADF effectively. The same functionality can be implemented in many ways in ADF — it is the task of the ADF expert to ensure that you use the framework as much as possible and do not code things that ADF can handle declaratively.

If you do not have anyone in your organization with these skills, you should seriously consider hiring an experienced consultant to help you get your project off the ground in the right direction. Once you have built up some level of skill with ADF, you might get by with a part-time expert as long as that person is on call by phone or e-mail to prevent you from getting stuck or traveling too far down a wrong path.

Work with the grain

When a carpenter picks up a planer to shave a piece of wood, he will be working with the grain of the wood. This allows him to produce a smooth surface with a minimum amount of effort. If he works against the grain, the plane iron will lift the wood fibers. This makes it harder to push the plane, and the surface will be rough.

Similarly, you need to work with the grain of the ADF framework in order to produce a good-looking, efficient enterprise application with the minimum amount of effort.

Object-oriented programming

You also need someone on the team who understands the principles of object-oriented programming (OOP), but again, not every programmer on your team needs this skill.

The ADF framework takes care of most of the heavy lifting that you need to build a Java application on top of a relational database. But, you will need to build your own layer of framework extension classes that fit into the Java object hierarchy between the standard framework classes supplied by Oracle and the ADF Java objects that you are building in your application. If you are using the Enterprise ADF architecture as described in *Chapter 2, Estimating the Effort*, you might also have classes common to the enterprise that will be extended and specialized in each application. Additionally, you might also occasionally need to develop support classes in Java, and because Java is an object-oriented programming language, some OOP skills are necessary to have on the team.

Java programming

Not everybody who writes needs the skills of Shakespeare, but everybody who writes need to follow spelling and grammar rules in order to make themselves understood.

All serious frameworks provide some way for a programmer to add logic and functionality beyond what the framework offers. In the case of the ADF framework, this is done by writing Java code. Therefore, every programmer on the project needs to know Java as a programming language and be able to write syntactically correct Java code. But, this is a simple skill for anyone familiar with a programming language. You need to know that Java uses { curly brackets } for code blocks instead of BEGIN-END, you need to know the syntax for if-then-else constructs and how to build a loop and work with an array.

But, not everyone who writes Java code needs to be virtuosos with full command of inheritance, interfaces, and inner classes.

Database design and programming

In a modern three-tier application, you have two servers at your disposal: the application server and the database server. You can build your entire application using just the ADF framework and the application server. But if you are running your application on top of an Oracle database, why not make full use of the features the database offers?

Some tasks are better handled in the database—for example, if you need to process many rows according to some rule, without needing any input from the user. It is inefficient to pull all of the data to the application server, process it, and push it back to the database. If your program stored procedures in the database (using PL/SQL in the case of the Oracle database), your application server simply needs to tell the database to start working and can then return to handle the interaction with the user.

It will, therefore, be an advantage to have someone on your team with database programming skills.

Additionally, in case you are building a brand new enterprise application that does not have to work with the existing data and tables, you may need someone on your team who understands database design. The database design is the foundation on which your enterprise application stands—you will have a very hard time building a robust enterprise application if the foundation is not rock solid.

XML knowledge

The ADF framework is metadata driven. This means that most of the application is not actually *programmed* in a programming language such as Java, but is instead *defined* through JDeveloper. These definitions are stored in the form of **Extensible Markup Language (XML)** files. You will notice that, for example, Business Components have a **Source** tab, allowing you to see the raw XML file.

You do not have to write XML files to use ADF, but it will be an advantage to know a little bit about XML so that you can read the files built by JDeveloper.

Powerful and dangerous

JDeveloper also allows you to actually edit the XML files directly by changing to the **Source** tab. This is not necessary during normal development—you can perform almost all changes through the wizards and dialogs in JDeveloper. An experienced ADF developer might sometimes edit the XML directly; this is a powerful, but also dangerous approach that can wreck your application or worse, introduce subtle and very-hard-to-find errors. As a beginning ADF developer, don't edit the XML.

Web technologies

When your ADF application is running, the end user is interacting with a web page in a browser. This means that your application must use the web technologies that the browser understands: HTML, **Cascading Style Sheets** (**CSS**), and JavaScript. The ADF framework takes care of most of the details for you, but it is good to have someone on your team who understands these technologies. That person can both help you understand any limitations that you might encounter and how to work around them.

If you are planning to do any frontend integration (between your web application and other web applications running in the browser), you definitely need someone who understands JavaScript well on your team.

Regular expressions

JDeveloper allows you to use **regular expressions** to define validation rules. Regular expressions are arcane, almost magical constructs that can express complex requirements in a very compact form. For example, the following regular expression can be used to validate an e-mail address:

```
[A-Z0-9._%-]+@[A-Z0-9.-]+\.[A-Z]{2,4}
```

This is clearly much shorter than writing a block of Java code, but unfortunately, it is also impossible to read for someone who does not know regular expression syntax.

If you don't want to learn regular expressions, that's OK. But in an enterprise application, you'll probably be defining so many special validation rules that it will be worth the effort for someone to learn this syntax.

In case you are interested, the preceding regex reads as follows:

Any number of characters from a-z, digits ranging from 0-9, periods, underscores, percents, and dashes, followed by an @, followed by any number of characters from a-z, digits from 0-9, periods, and dashes, followed by a period, followed by 2 to 4 characters from a-z.

Graphics design

Have you checked Facebook today? Or YouTube, LinkedIn, or Pinterest? Have you been on amazon.com or eBay? Do these sites look like the enterprise applications that you use at work?

Probably not, unless you are running Oracle Fusion Applications, as shown in the following screenshot by Oracle:

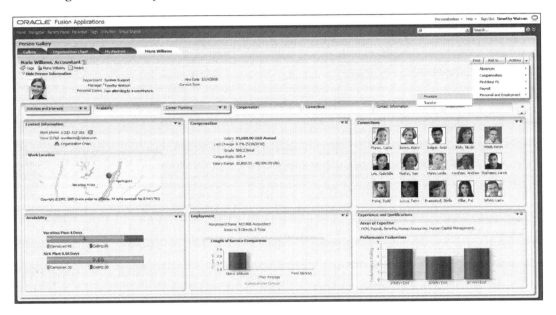

Your users experience modern web applications every day and expect your enterprise application to be as visually attractive and user friendly as those applications. Is the average programmer able to produce such an experience? Left alone, he/she would probably not. That's why you should have someone with graphic design skills on your team.

Usability

Speaking of Facebook, did you take a Facebook class? No, you didn't. Modern web applications are built with such a focus on usability that everyone can use them right away. Your users are expecting the same thing from you. The enterprise application that you build is so user friendly that they can use it without taking training classes.

That's not at all easy. Programmers tend to be people with a specific way of thinking, and without guidance, they build applications for people like themselves. The purpose of usability studies is to ensure that the applications are built for the people who will be actually using them.

Usability experts will use a variety of tools, from low-tech paper prototypes to high-tech eye tracking equipment, to achieve this goal.

Testing

When the original `amazon.com` website went into beta testing, it had of course already been tested thoroughly by the developers. But Jonathan Leblang, one of the beta testers, immediately found that you could order a negative number of books—meaning that Amazon owed you money and would refund it to your credit card.

This anecdote illustrates that developers typically make poor testers. They have full knowledge of all of the things that the application is supposed to do, so they tend to test only a narrow range of variations on the normal case. A professional tester, on the other hand, will test the entire range of possible inputs (including negative numbers).

Organizing the team

A complete enterprise application development project team needs to fill the following roles:

- Project manager
- Software architect
- Lead programmer
- Regular programmer

- Build/configuration manager
- Database and application server administrator
- Graphics designer
- Usability expert
- Quality assurance
- Test manager
- Tester

Additionally, if you are building an application from scratch or are making significant changes to an existing application, you will also need a data modeler.

This does not mean that your team has to have a dozen people—if your enterprise application is not very big, you can get by with fewer people. But, you do need to fill all of these roles—one person can often fill more than one role.

Project manager

Naturally, you need a project manager to run an enterprise project. Project management is a well-documented discipline that we won't be discussing in this book.

Danger! Programming project manager

The programming project manager is the equivalent of the player-coach in sports. It might work in amateur football, but it doesn't work in professional sports. And it doesn't work in enterprise application projects. If the project manager starts writing code as the deadline looms larger, project management deteriorates, and the project ends up late and over budget.

The project manager should not be allowed to write code.

Software architect and lead programmer

The **software architect** and **lead programmer** work together building an enterprise application just as an architect and a builder work together to build a house.

The software architect designs the application, making key decisions about the ADF architecture, and including the use of unbounded and bounded task flows, application module granularity, and security. The lead programmer leads the team that is building the application. In principle, he/she could build the whole application himself, but in most of the real-life enterprise projects, he/she will build only a few key parts and spend most of their time supervising other programmers.

Both the software architect and lead programmer need a good understanding of databases, Internet technologies, and the ADF framework, and must be willing to work with the grain of the tool.

Work with the grain

Since ADF is a very powerful framework that does a lot of work for you, some developers distrust it and build a lot of code themselves. While this might be fun for the developer, it means that the business will be spending more time and money building a more fragile application. The lead developer must ensure that the ADF framework is used effectively and efficiently.

Apart from an enthusiasm for building enterprise applications fast with good tools, the lead programmer, of course, also needs good Java programming skills and some years of experience.

Regular programmers

The regular programmers are the people who do most of the work. They are not necessarily great artisans—simply being a competent craftsman is enough to build great applications with ADF.

The programming tasks in your enterprise development project are likely to include:

- Building Business Components
- Building the user interface
- Skinning
- Templates
- Defining data validation
- Building support classes
- Building database stored procedures

In a typical project, the total functionality will be parceled out among the team members, who will each be building both Business Components and user interface elements for specific subsystems. However, large projects might specialize further, with some people exclusively building Business Components and others building the user interface.

More specialized development tasks will typically be handled by one or two persons on your team.

Building Business Components

While building Business Components, the developer will spend most of their time in JDeveloper using the wizards and dialog boxes that are a part of JDeveloper. During this task, the developer will occasionally need to read the XML files where JDeveloper stores the metadata for a Business Component, and will also occasionally need to write short pieces of Java code when the default functionalities of the Business Components do not meet the requirements.

Developing Business Components typically takes between one-third and half of the total development time.

Building the user interface

Building the user interface is not a trivial task. In the **JavaServer Faces (JSF)** technology used in ADF applications, components are not placed in specific locations but are placed within layout containers. The layout containers determine how and where they are rendered on the screen, automatically resizing the components to make the best possible use of the browser window.

Depending on your previous experience, this can be easy or hard:

- If you are used to tools with pixel-precise placement of components (for example, Oracle Forms), it will take some time to get used to working with layout containers.
- If you have built Java swing applications, you will already be familiar with the concept of layout managers.
- If you have experience building web applications using HTML tables, you will recognize some of the challenges. Fortunately for HTML programmers, the new Panel Grid Layout component (available in 11.1.1.7 and 11.1.2 onward) works much like an HTML table.

Much of this work can be greatly simplified by creating common design patterns and documenting their use on the project Wiki or in a shared document.

The individual developer will normally be building page fragments and should focus on the functionality and arrangement of items—the exact visual appearance is controlled through templates and skinning, as described in the following section.

The user interface also typically takes between one-third and half of the total development time.

Skinning

Skinning is normally understood as the process of removing the skin from an animal to get to the meat, to use the fur, or both. However, the word also means "to cover with skin." It is this second meaning that has been picked up and redefined in IT application development.

In ADF application development, skinning refers to the act of creating a **skin** for an application. The skin is purely visual and does not affect functionality—just like a panther (black leopard), which is the same animal as a spotted leopard.

The person developing the skin needs a good understanding of CSS. If your team includes people who have built web applications, they might already know some CSS. Developing an ADF skin is not a trivial task, but with the ADF Skin Editor that is part of JDeveloper 11*g* R2 and later, the work is much simpler than before. If you want to retrofit a new skin over an application that is maintained in JDeveloper 11*g* R1 (the 11.1.1.x versions), you can download a standalone skin editor from the Oracle Technology website (available at `http://otn.oracle.com` and search for `adf skin editor`).

You do not need to define the visual attributes of every component. You can start from one of the standard skins delivered with JDeveloper and change only those parts you want to look different. Always define a skin for your application when starting the project, even if you don't plan to change anything. Having a skin defined makes it easy to change the visual appearance of the application later.

You just need one person to develop and tweak the skin. This is a small, part-time task after the initial skin definition. You don't want every developer to set detailed styles on the components—have the person doing the skinning to explain the possibilities to the rest of the team to make the maximum use of this powerful ADF feature.

Templates

In ADF, your pages are normally based on templates, and you can also define page flow templates that serve as the basis of your task flows.

These templates will often be built by the lead programmer or another ADF-experienced developer on the team.

From JDeveloper 11*g* R2 onward, templates can be based on other templates, allowing you to create a hierarchy of templates. Don't go overboard with this feature—there is a performance penalty and rarely a good case for using more than two levels of templates.

Defining data validation

An enterprise application is likely to make extensive use of data validation to ensure that only the right data gets into the database. You can define validation in all of the following three layers of the application:

- In the user interface
- In the Business Components
- In the database

Validation in the user interface is handled by the `Validate` operations that you can place on user interface components. This validation happens in the browser without placing any load on the server.

A large number of validations can be defined declaratively in the Business Components; additionally, the ADF framework also allows you to specify validation using regular expressions, Groovy, or Java code. These validation rules are well integrated into the ADF framework and validation errors are easy to present to the user. Of course, Business Component validation places a small load on the application server.

Finally, you can place validation rules in the database itself using the PL/SQL code. These rules have the advantage that they will always be applied, no matter how the data gets into the database (through the application or any other way). A disadvantage is that the validation errors are more difficult to present to the user in the ADF pages.

Much of your validation will be built by the programmers who build the Business Components and user interface; on a larger team, you might want to appoint someone with an experience of regular expressions as a validation specialist.

Building support classes

Before the industrial age, a farmer would produce his own tools using only the village blacksmith for the few tasks that he couldn't do himself. As industrialization took hold, more and more specialized tools came into use—from steam-driven auto threshers to today's GPS-controlled combine harvesters. This has allowed a dramatic increase in output, but it also means that the farmer is no longer able to repair his own tools.

Many developers tend to prefer the pre-industrial model when it comes to programming—they build their own utility classes and tools instead of leaving this task to a specialized tool builder. However, it is much more efficient to appoint someone from the team to build the utility and support classes that you need. This ensures that each tool is only built once, documented, and can be re-used through the whole application.

If your team is more than a handful of people, consider appointing one developer as the tool builder delivering the utility classes needed by other programmers. Because the code written by this person will be widely used in the application, the tool builder should be one of the more experienced team members.

Building database stored procedures

If you need to cut one log into planks, you can call a friend and get out your two-man saw. But if you need to cut a hundred logs, you will ask a sawmill to do it.

If you need to process one data record, you can retrieve it from the database, process it in the application server, and store it back in the database. But if you need to process a hundred, a thousand, or a million records, you will have to ask the database to do it.

If your application calls for this kind of batch processing, your team needs to include database programmers who can build stored procedures in your database. If your application is based on an Oracle database, the language of choice is PL/SQL, but other databases also have stored procedures in other languages.

Additionally, if data gets into your database through means other than the enterprise application, you need to implement validation and business rules at the database level to make sure that your logic is applied to all of the data.

Build/configuration manager

There are two parts to building an application: the thinking and the doing. The thinking is best done by a human, while the doing is best done by a machine. For more on the build machine, refer to the *Automated build system* section later in the chapter.

The human is the build and configuration manager, who oversees the release and distribution of ADF Libraries. When building an enterprise ADF application, your team will be working in different workspaces, and these workspaces will release their content in the form of ADF Libraries. The build and configuration manager has the final word on which versions of libraries are used throughout the project, and is the person who knows that Version 0.3 of your application contains the Common Code Library of Version 0.2.1 and Version 0.4 of the `CreateEmployee` task flow.

This person is also in charge of the source control system, authorizing code branches and overseeing merges of code back into the main development track.

Try to avoid using a developer as a build/configuration manager. A good build/configuration manager is careful, well-organized, and methodical. These are typically traits of a good systems administrator or database administrator, but not necessarily of a developer.

What is a good day?

When you are putting together the team for your enterprise application, ask each prospective participant this question: What does a good day at work look like?

The people who talk about new, exciting tasks should be developers. And the people who talk about all systems running smoothly should be build and configuration managers, database administrators, and system administrators.

Database and application server administrator

If your application was a ship, the database and application servers would be the engine—an indispensable part of the ship but one that's rarely seen by most of the passengers and crew. And just as the crew can use the engine order telegraph to send instructions to the engine room, an ADF developer can use the ADF framework to send data and instructions to the database.

The ADF developer, of course, needs to understand the data model—just as the captain needs to understand the physical capabilities of his ship's engine.

Every captain knows that to keep a ship in operation, you need a trained and experienced professional in charge of the engine department: the chief engineer. An ADF application needs the equivalent, a database and application server administrator. A large organization might split this task into separate database administrator and application server administrator roles.

Apart from keeping the database and application servers humming along, the administrator can also help with performance problems. The ADF framework contains many ways of ensuring optimal performance, but it is still possible to run into a performance problem.

In some cases, this is caused by resource contention—for example, too many users trying to access the same application module at the same time. Your application server administrator can tell you in detail how your application is running and help you to configure most of the ADF tuning settings.

In other cases, this is caused by the application trying to tell the database *how* to answer a specific question instead of just asking the question and letting the database figure out the most efficient way of finding an answer. If you want the sum of all orders and your application is asking for each order separately, then there is something wrong with your application. Just ask the database for the sum, and it will happily and quickly respond. Your database administrator can tell you what your application is really asking the database—if the database is not being asked the question you thought that your application was asking, you need to look at your code.

Graphic designers

You need one or two graphic designers to create the visual identity of your application. Some organizations will already have a detailed style manual, describing colors, fonts, and other visual attributes. In other cases, your designers have a free hand to create the look of the application.

Graphic designers tend to prefer working in very visual tools such as Adobe Photoshop, sometimes leaving the programmers to struggle with the challenge of converting their visual ideas into running code. To avoid wasting time in designing something that cannot be built, ensure that your graphic designers have access to the ADF component catalog. (Oracle is hosting an online demo at `http://jdevadf.oracle.com/adf-richclient-demo`).

If you don't have graphic designers in your organization, this task can be subcontracted. Graphic design is an area that lends itself well to online collaboration—you can send your specifications to a designer in another country, discuss drafts online, and receive the finished design electronically. You can even hold online graphic design content through sites such as `www.99designs.com`.

Usability experts

To verify that your users can actually understand and use the pretty user interface designed by your graphic designers, you need usability experts to perform usability tests with prospective users. This is a must to happen early in the development cycle, where the screens might be little more than drawings on paper or simple wireframe mockups, and it is cheap and easy to change the UI.

If you can afford it, have at least two usability people in your team—two people can bounce ideas off each other and have a much better chance of coming up with creative ideas if you hit areas where your users just don't understand your application.

Because usability is a specialized topic, you can also consider subcontracting the whole usability task to an external supplier. However, this task *cannot* be sent out to someone to perform online—you need the usability people onsite with your users to capture all of their input.

Cross-training
While graphic design is a separate skill from usability, graphic design and usability people must work closely together; often, the same people will fill both roles.

Quality assurance, test manager, and tester

If you are working in an environment with strict regulatory requirements, or if you are a vendor delivering a software product to a customer for a fixed price, you are likely to need a quality assurance manager. This person has the responsibility to ensure that the agreed quality procedures are followed.

Additionally, someone must be in charge of testing the application to prove that all of the requirements are met. For this, you need a test manager to write the test plan, ensuring full test coverage of the agreed functionality. The test manager also supervises the actual testing work and might be responsible for tracking all of the defects discovered by testing. Sometimes, the roles of the QA manager and test manager are combined and done by one person.

Finally, someone will have to write the detailed test scripts, possibly record automated test cases, and perform the test—this is the task of the professional testers.

Data modelers

If you are building your application from scratch, or by adding more than just a few tables to an existing data model, you need someone with an understanding of data modeling. The data model is the foundation of the whole application, and if the foundation is not well built, the whole structure will be wobbly.

The inhabitants of Pisa in Italy might be happy to have the Leaning Tower today, but the duke commissioning the construction was probably not happy in the 12th century when his beautiful *campanile* started leaning.

Users

You are building the application because it will fill the need of a specific group of users. You need user involvement to follow two purposes:

- To answer questions about the subject area
- For usability testing

For the first purpose, you need one expert who can explain the subject area and answer any questions you might have. If you are working with formal, detailed requirements and documents, you might not be asking many questions, but if you are working according to an Agile development methodology, it is imperative that an expert user is always available.

For the second purpose, you need multiple users with different experience levels to make sure you are building an application that is easy to use for casual users and still efficient for the experienced power users. Depending on your ambitions for usability, you can involve anything from a handful of users up to several dozen.

Consider your representative users to be part of your team—send them the project newsletter, and give them access to the project website. A new enterprise application will be a big change for many people; you want the users with whom you work to be your advocates and evangelists spreading enthusiasm for the new application across the organization.

Worst practice: design by committee

Work with one person at a time—sit down with your expert to have your questions on the subject area answered, or present your user interface prototypes to one representative user at a time to gather feedback.

Having a committee of a dozen people or more questioning every aspect of the design and moving buttons and fields around on your screen designs will take months of extra development time without improving the final product.

Gathering the tools

In the past, many people held such strong beliefs that they felt it was completely justified to burn people of a different opinion at the stake. Mysteriously, similar strong passions often emerge among programmers when someone performs the heresy of proposing a different source control or build automation system.

The recommendations in this section are about the types of tools that you need to manage your enterprise ADF project through the entire project development process and into production—commonly called **Application Lifecycle Management (ALM)** tools. Please do not burn this book if the recommendations do not match your particular programming religion—simply use the tool of your choice in each area.

Source control

In the 1930s, builders expected about one fatality per million dollars in construction costs. For the Golden Gate bridge in San Francisco, this meant that 35 people were expected to lose their lives. Actually, only eleven died. Nineteen people were saved by a revolutionary new invention: the safety net.

When building an enterprise application, your source control system is your safety net—the one tool you absolutely and definitely need.

Your source control system provides a centralized location for all of your code on a professionally managed server, securely located in your data center or with a hosting partner. This ensures that your precious source code is backed up and that everyone can get access to all of the code whenever they need to.

It also allows you to go back to an earlier version for whatever reason—the business might change their mind about the requirements (yes, it's been known to happen)—you might need to implement a change that proves to have unforeseen side effects, and a file might become corrupted due to a hardware failure. There is no excuse for not having source control in place before the development starts.

A good example of a traditional, centralized source control system is **Apache Subversion (SVN)**. It is fairly widespread, so your development team is likely to have encountered it before. It integrates directly into JDeveloper, and there are many standalone clients available.

Some developers prefer a distributed system, where every developer has a complete copy of the repository and can commit changes locally without access to a central server. The local changes can then be pushed to a central server and the new code can be pulled from the server. **Git** is an example of this type of system that is rapidly gaining popularity. Later versions of JDeveloper 11*g* R1, as well as JDeveloper 12*c* support Git (but 11*g* R2 versions do not).

So, before you write the first line of code of your real application, talk to your systems management people to find out what source control system is already being used by your organization. If there is no system available for your development project, you can easily set up a source control repository on a development server.

> If it is up to your team to decide on a version control system, take some time to investigate centralized versus distributed systems. They have different advantages and disadvantages and are used in different ways, so one might fit your development approach better than the other.

With the low cost of hard drives today, it is recommended to configure this server with multiple disks in a fail-safe RAID configuration to avoid disrupting development in case of a hard disk failure. Additionally, talk to your system administrator to make sure that the machine with your source code repository is included in the daily backup routine.

Bug/issue tracking

"In the unlikely event" (as they say in the airline industry), that your code does not work perfectly the first time, you need some system to track the issues and defects. Many of these tools are also used to assign tasks to developers.

There is a wide variety of tools available, for example:

- **Jira**: This is a popular, commercial tool. It is full-featured and user friendly. Mobile clients are available (just in case you want to read bug reports on your iPhone)and are free for noncommercial use. This tool is available at www.jira.com.

- **Bugzilla**: This is an open source bug-tracking tool that scales to many thousands of bugs/issues (not that you'd have that many, of course). More focus is on functionality than user interface—it can be fairly intimidating for new users. This tool is available at www.bugzilla.org.

- **FogBugz**: This is another commercial tool for complete project management, including bug and issue tracking. The focus is on the support given to end users, with automated classification of e-mail bug reports and a screenshot tool for testers and end users. This tool is available at www.fogbugz.com.

All of these can either be hosted externally or installed locally—again, talk to your systems management department to see if your organization already has a bug/issue tracking system that you can use. If not, you can install one of these tools on a development server.

If you use a project development server for bug/issue tracking, make sure that it is backed up regularly. For an ADF project, Jira and Bugzilla have the advantage that Oracle has already built adapters integrating them into the **Oracle Team Productivity Center (OTPC)**. However, if you already have a bug/issue tracking system running, there is no need to throw your existing system away. It is perfectly feasible to run your bug/issue tracking system without integrating it with OTPC, or you could build an OTPC adapter yourself.

Collaboration

Even if every member of your team works in the same office, and you have regular project meetings, you still need collaboration tools to facilitate communication in the team. Several types of collaboration tools can be useful:

- Shared documents
- Discussion forums
- Online chat

There are many free, open source collaboration tools available. If you would rather have something prebuilt and pre-integrated, you can subscribe to web-based services or even buy sophisticated (and pricey) tools such as Oracle WebCenter Spaces (part of the Oracle WebCenter Suite).

Shared documents

The most basic collaboration tool is shared documents, and you will definitely need this. This is where you put your development guidelines, and naming and code standards. If you have high security needs, keep your shared documents on your internal network—there is both commercial and open source Wiki software that you can install. It is even quicker to use a cloud-based Wiki or shared online documents such as Google Docs.

The important part about shared documents is to make sure that everyone can edit them. You do *not* want to wait for the project manager to come back from some meeting before you can update a standards document with some great idea or much-needed improvement.

Because everyone can edit the documents, the other feature that you will need is a full version history so that you can easily go back to the previous version and compare the versions.

Discussion forums

Stop sending e-mails to your team. E-mail is so last century… But seriously, e-mail is not really useful for collaboration.

For one thing, everybody's e-mail inbox is already overflowing with meeting invitations, promotional e-mails from all of the companies to whom you gave your business card at the last conference in return for a free t-shirt, funny pictures of cats that your friends think you need to see, Viagra ads, and mails from friendly people who need to borrow your bank account to transfer a couple million dollars. This almost ensures that someone will miss the crucial e-mail that you send about the changes to how the code should be checked into source control.

Secondly, collaboration is not about individual messages but about discussions. And e-mail programs don't really show discussions well. What you need is a real tree view of who said what, and in which order. If someone changes the subject of the e-mail slightly, the e-mail program gets confused and is unable to follow the thread.

So, set up a discussion forum—if you don't have the software, you can use a private group on Google Groups or another online service. One-to-many communication and announcements go into the shared documents, and all other communication goes to the discussion forums.

Online chat

Some people love online chat systems, and other people can't be bothered. This is not a required part of your collaboration toolkit, but if you think it might be useful, try it out.

There seems to be a generational divide in online chat—younger people who have grown up with multiple forms of digital communication tend to like it, and older people tend to find that the constant online chatter impedes their productivity.

The teams that typically achieve the greatest benefit from using an online chat application are geographically dispersed teams in approximately the same time zone. If you are all in the same office, you can get help by walking down the corridor, and if you are in different time zones, the person with the answer might not be online when you need to ask a question.

Oracle Team Productivity Center, which we will talk about in the next chapter, contains a chat client.

Test and requirement management

Your quality assurance manager and test manager can work with spreadsheets and documents, carefully mapping test cases to requirements. However, for an enterprise project, you should look into professional software solutions (such as HP Quality Center and other similar ones) for managing requirements and test cases. Many of these professional tools will also allow you to automate your application testing.

Automated build system

The final tool that you should strongly consider is a build tool. Think about all of the following tasks involved in building your application:

1. Check out the latest version of the code from your source control system (you do have one, don't you?).
2. Compile all of the code.
3. Run all of the unit tests that you have defined.
4. Generate Javadoc and/or other documentation.
5. Audit the code for quality issues.
6. Package the whole application into a deployment package.
7. Deploy it on your test/integration server.
8. Run any automated user interface tests.

Once you have set up your build tool, you can have the tool to perform all of these tasks automatically — saving developer time, reducing bugs due to manual errors, and improving the quality of your code.

Several tools are available for this, for example:

- Apache Ant (http://ant.apache.org)
- Apache Maven (http://maven.apache.org)

In addition to the pure build tools that actually execute the tasks that you define, you can also use **continuous integration** tools that will automatically invoke your build tool based on specific rules. For example, you might compile and run unit tests every time a developer checks something into your source code repository, and run a complete build every night at 2:00 a.m. The tools for continuous integration include:

- Hudson (http://hudson-ci.org)
- CruiseControl (http://cruisecontrol.sourceforge.net)

All of the preceding tools are open source, but there are commercial tools available, as well. If your organization or someone on your team already has experience with one of them, stay with that tool. If you don't have any preferences, have someone spend a day researching tools and choose the one that appeals most to you.

Structuring workspaces, projects, and code

Your ADF application is going to consist of lots of files and development artifacts collected into JDeveloper application workspaces that contain projects. Confusingly, JDeveloper sometimes just calls them "applications", but that's really a misnomer—only a fairly simple application will be contained entirely within one workspace.

To avoid this confusion, the following sections will refer to application workspaces as just workspaces. Each application workspace can contain multiple projects. Depending on the ADF architecture you choose, you'll have various numbers of workspaces.

Using projects

Within an application workspace, you can have one or more projects. If you are using a modular or enterprise ADF architecture, you will have a number of subsystem workspaces that will each contain at least the following two projects:

- Model project
- View/controller project

When you create a new application workspace of the type **Fusion Web Application**, JDeveloper will automatically create a model and a view/controller project for you. You should not use the default project names, as this will cause problems when you combine ADF Libraries from multiple projects in the master workspace.

Instead, name both projects after your subsystem with the suffixes, `Model` and `View`, respectively. For example, if your subsystem is called `TaskHandling`, you should use project names such as `TaskHandlingModel` and `TaskHandlingView`.

Simple architecture

As we discussed in the last chapter, only fairly simple applications should be built in one application workspace—that's the *simple* ADF architecture pattern. Having a large application in one big workspace places a heavy load on JDeveloper that will be noticeable even on a powerful development workstation.

Because you work with version control at the workspace level, having a big workspace also means that your source control operations (updates and commits) will take more time. Additionally, if there is more than one developer working on the workspace, you will run into situations where two developers have both changed the same file, and you'll have to merge the two versions of the file.

Only show me what I need

If you find that JDeveloper is showing you too many objects that are not relevant to your task, you can define **working sets**. These are configurable filters on your application workspace that you can define under **Application | Filter Application**.

In a simple architecture, you'll have a model and a view project, as described previously.

Modular architecture

In a modular architecture, you'll partition your application into several workspaces, as follows:

- Application Common Workspace
- Database workspace (if you are building a new database)
- A number of subsystem workspaces
- One master workspace

The output of each workspace is one or more ADF Libraries. Technically, these are standard .jar files (one from each project in the workspace), but with added metadata that allows JDeveloper to recognize the contents as ADF artifacts.

Workspaces that depend on objects from other workspaces will then import the latest ADF Library released by that workspace. The subsystem workspaces will include the ADF Libraries released by the Application Common Workspace, and the master workspace will include all of the common and subsystem workspaces, as shown in the following figure:

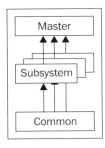

Get it right the first time

Think carefully about how you want to split your system into subsystems. A subsystem should represent a logical grouping of functionality to minimize dependencies between subsystem workspaces and should be implemented by a small team, ideally not more than two or three developers.

Unfortunately, it is not easy to move objects and code between workspaces once you have started building the application. Only change the division of code in subsystems if you find major issues.

As part of your configuration management, you need to keep track of the versions of the ADF Libraries are used in other workspaces.

Application Common Workspace

The Application Common Workspace is where you place all of the foundation code that will be used by the subsystems of your application. You can decide to keep the items in this workspace in one project (and therefore, in one ADF Library), or you can use multiple projects if you have several developers working in the Application Common Workspace.

If you decide to use multiple projects, a good structure is to have the following three projects:

- Application Common Code
- Application Common User Interface (UI)
- Application Common Model

Application Common Code project

The Application Common Code project contains your framework extension classes (we'll return to these in *Chapter 5, Preparing to Build*) and any utility classes that you develop.

The people who work here will be the hardcore Java and ADF coders—the lead programmer or the most senior programmers in the team. These classes should be well-written and extend the existing classes in the right way. The work done in this project will affect the entire application, so it is important to get this code right.

Once the first version of the application Common Code ADF Library has been released, new releases should be relatively rare due to the impact this Library has across the entire application. Each new release of the Common Code Library should trigger comprehensive regression testing across the entire application.

Application Common Model project

In the Common Model project, you keep all of your entity objects for the whole application. Since there will be only one entity object for each relational table, it makes sense to gather these together in one project and create an ADF Library that can be shared with all of the subsystem workspaces.

This project will also contain the view objects built for use in value lists across the application, and the application module will contain these view objects. Additionally, this project needs default view objects for each entity object so that you can test the EOs.

Once the initial components in this project have been built, only the validation programmer is likely to be working much in the project, with occasional visits from a business component developer, if the need for a new value list pops up.

Expect one initial release containing all of the entity objects, and then a number of releases can be expected with small changes involving validation rules as the project progresses. Unless you make major changes involving the removal of entity objects, you do not need much regression testing when releasing a new version of the ADF Library from the Application Common Model project.

Application Common User Interface project

The Application Common UI project is where you keep all of the common elements that define the visual identity of your application. This includes the application skin, page templates, and page flow templates.

Both the skin developer and the page and page flow template developers work in this project. Unless you have a large team, these two roles are likely to be filled by the same person.

A skin defines the look of an application. Even if you don't anticipate customizing the look of the application, you should create your own skin at the beginning of the project. It doesn't take much effort to create a skin (you can base it on one of the skins delivered with JDeveloper), and it gives you a place to change the visual identity of the application, if you later decide you need this. We'll return to skinning in *Chapter 8, Changing the Appearance*.

You can expect many minor changes to happen in the Application Common UI project, mainly to the skin or visual identity of the application. The changes that only affect the skin can be rolled out without affecting the functionality of the application. The changes that affect the page and page flow templates need a bit of regression testing to ensure that the pages still work as you expect them to.

Database workspace

If you keep your data model in JDeveloper, you should have a separate workspace for the offline tables and other data elements, as well as any database diagrams that you use.

You do not need to keep your database definition in JDeveloper. While it might be easier to use the same tool for everything, there is no real integration benefit from having your data model in the same tool as your business objects. If you prefer to use the Oracle SQL Developer Data Modeler or another tool with which you are already familiar, feel free to do so.

Subsystem workspaces

You'll generally be implementing one task flow for each use case or user story. This means that your application can have anything from a handful to hundreds of task flows.

You should group these task flows together in subsystem workspaces, each developed by a small team. That team will be creating the specific view objects that are necessary for the task flows in the model project of the workspace, and the task flow and pages in the view/controller project of the workspace.

A subsystem workspace will import the output of the common workspace through the latest ADF Libraries released by each of the projects in this workspace.

Master workspace

The master workspace is where the build and configuration manager puts everything together. This workspace depends on all of the other workspaces and contains almost no code of its own—it simply serves as a container for all of the task flows that make up your application. The final application deployment package (the .ear file) is built from this workspace.

Enterprise architecture

An enterprise architecture is similar to a modular architecture, but adds an additional Enterprise Common Workspace and opens up the possibility of building several separate applications from your subsystems. As you saw in *Chapter 2, Estimating the Effort*, the enterprise architecture looks as shown in the following figure:

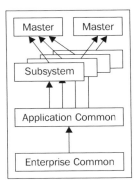

Enterprise Common Workspace

The Enterprise Common Workspace is similar to the Application Common, but it is used to place foundation code that will apply across all of the ADF applications that the organization builds. As in the Application Common Workspace, you can decide to split the contents of the workspace up into multiple projects and ADF Libraries or leave everything together.

Having this extra workspace provides an additional level that can be used to ensure consistency across multiple applications. For example, an organization will often develop one skin to be used for all of the ADF applications. This would go into the Enterprise Common Workspace, and the ADF Library from this workspace is then used in the Application Common Workspace. Inside the Application Common Workspace, the skin might be tweaked slightly if specific modifications are required for a particular application.

Master application workspaces

In an enterprise architecture, you might have multiple master workspaces to produce multiple ADF applications (as `.ear` files). Often, each master application workspace will only use subsystems specifically developed for that application, but the flexibility of the architecture pattern allows you to re-use subsystems. This might be useful if, for example, you develop a customer-handling subsystem that multiple applications might use to create customers.

Naming conventions

The better your standards—and the better they are adhered to—the easier your code will be to develop and maintain. You can use some or all of the following standards and add your own code. Whenever JDeveloper automatically generates names for things, consider if these are good enough—write a naming standard that deviates from the standard JDeveloper's way only if you feel that the rule has significant benefit.

Your standards should be easily available to everyone on the project in a Wiki or shared document.

This section lays out a proposal for naming the various elements of your ADF application. Oracle has also produced an official naming guidelines document that you can find at `http://www.oracle.com/technetwork/developer-tools/adf/learnmore/adf-naming-layout-guidelines-v2-00-1904828.pdf`.

General

You need to decide on an application name: an abbreviated project name or an acronym that can be used in package names. You will be writing this over and over, so make it as short as possible—preferably of just three or four characters, (for example, `xdm` for the project `neXt generation Destination Management`).

Java packages

All of your Business Components and Java code will be placed in packages and displayed in the package hierarchy in the **Applications** window in JDeveloper. To make it easy for all of the team members to find everything, determine your Java package naming hierarchy from the beginning.

Project code

As you remember from *Chapter 1*, *The ADF Proof of Concept*, the base of all of your Java package names is, by tradition, the Internet domain name of your organization with the elements in reverse order. This is called your **organization base package**—for DMC Solutions, it would be `com.dmcsol`. Under the organization base package, all code belonging to the project should be placed under your project name for the XDM project; this would be `com.dmcsol.xdm`. This is called the **project base package**. All of your project code should be placed in subpackages under the project base package.

Your package naming could look as shown in the following table (where <pbp> is short for the project base package):

Package	Usage
<pbp>	Project base package; no code directly used here
<pbp>.common	Common utility classes for this application
<pbp>.framework	Framework extension classes for this application
<pbp>.model.entity	Entity objects (always common to the whole application)
<pbp>.model.entity.assoc	Associations between entity objects. It is also common to whole application
<pbp>.model.view	Common view objects (for example, lists of values used across the whole application)
<pbp>.model.resources	Resource bundles for the Common Model
<pbp>.<subsystem>.model	Java classes common to the backend (model) part of this subsystem
<pbp>.<subsystem>.model.view	All view objects built specifically for <subsystem>
<pbp>.<subsystem>.model.view.link	View links for <subsystem>
<pbp>.<subsystem>.model.am	Application module(s) for <subsystem>
<pbp>.<subsystem>.model.resources	Resource bundles for the <subsystem> view objects
<pbp>.<subsystem>.view	Java classes common to the frontend part of the subsystem (for example, managed beans for the task flows of the subsystem)
<pbp>.<subsystem>.view.backing	Backing beans for individual pages
<pbp>.<subsystem>.view.resources	Resource bundles for the frontend part of the application (page flows, pages, and page fragments)

Enterprise Common Code

If you are using the enterprise ADF architecture pattern, you will also have Enterprise Common packages outside any specific project (the classes found in your Enterprise Common Workspace). These should be placed in a separate .adf subpackage under your organization base package. For DMC Solutions, this ADF enterprise base package would be com.dmcsol.adf.

Your package naming for Enterprise Common Code could be as shown in the following table (where `<aebp>` is short for the **ADF enterprise base package**):

Package	Usage
`<aebp>`	Base package; no code directly used here
`<aebp>.framework`	Framework extension classes
`<aebp>.common`	Enterprise Common utility classes

Database objects

If you are working with an existing database, you should use the existing naming conventions. If these are not documented, look at the existing objects and use similar naming—do not change the naming if you inherit an existing database even if the naming conventions are not to your liking.

If you are building a new database, you need to set naming standards for at least the following database objects:

- Tables
- Columns
- Views
- Primary key constraints
- Foreign key constraints
- Sequences
- PL/SQL packages
- Triggers

Table names should be prefixed with the abbreviation of the application even if they reside in a database schema only used for the application. During the lifetime of your enterprise application, people are likely to use the data in your tables together with other data for those purposes which nobody has thought of from the beginning. Prefixing your table names clearly identifies them as part of a specific application. Each table name should be the plural of the record that it contains, for example, XDM_TASKS.

Primary key **columns** should be named with the table abbreviation (three to eight characters) and the _ID suffix, if they contain a system-generated number. Use the suffix _KEY, if the value is an alphanumeric key. For example, PROG_ID or ELEM_KEY.

Normal **views** should have the suffix _V. If you are using updatable views with the INSTEAD-OF triggers, use the suffix _UV.

Primary key constraints should have the name of the table with the suffix _PK, for example, PERSONS_PK.

Foreign key constraints should be named with the abbreviation of the table where the constraint is defined, followed by the abbreviation of the table referred to, with the suffix _FK. For example, TASK_ELEM_FK.

Sequences should have the suffix _SEQ.

Triggers should have the name of the table, with a three-part suffix indicating their usage:

- The first part should be B or A, indicating BEFORE or AFTER.
- The second part should be a combination of the letters I, U, and D, indicating INSERT, UPDATE, or DELETE.
- The third part should be R or S, indicating ROW or STATEMENT level.

An example of a trigger name could be TASKS_BIR, which means Before insert at the row level.

ADF elements

You should set naming standards for at least the following ADF elements:

- Entity objects
- Associations
- View objects
- View links
- Application modules
- Task flows
- Pages

Entity objects should have the same name as the table on which they are based, but singular and without the project prefix. The entity object for the XDM_TASKS table should thus be called Task.

By default, **associations** get the name of the foreign key on which they are based, with the suffix Assoc. There is no need to change this (even if the associations do inherit a superfluous Fk prefix).

View objects should be named for functionality or the data they include — there is no need to force an artificial correspondence to the entity object names. Use a VO suffix for the main view objects, for example, EmploymentHistoryVO. Use a LOV suffix for simple view objects that are only used for value lists, for example, ServiceLOV.

View links should be named with the detail view objects (without the VO suffix), followed by the master view object (without the VO suffix), and the suffix Link. For example, TaskPersonLink.

Application modules should be named according to the service they provide (typically, the name can be derived from the subsystem that uses the application module). Use the suffix, Service. Inside application modules, JDeveloper by default gives the individual view objects that use the name of the view object a numeric suffix (for example, TasksVO1). In most cases, the numeric suffix is unnecessary and can be removed when adding a view object instance to an application module.

Task flows have both a **Task Flow ID** (which is also the name of the XML file) and a **Display Name** field that is shown in the Application Navigator in JDeveloper. The ID should be brief and might refer to the use case number or user story that it implements. Use the suffix, -flow, for example, for timeline-flow. Use the **Display Name** if you feel you need a more detailed title to identify the task flow.

File locations

Each project has a base directory in the filesystem that is defined when the project is created. Under the base directory, an src subdirectory is created, and all of your Java code and ADF Business Component XMLs will be placed in subdirectories under src matching your package names.

Your ADF view/controller project also contains a subdirectory called public_html. The content of this directory is shown in JDeveloper under the **Web Content** node in the Application Navigator. Everything in this directory is accessible from a browser when the application is running, except for the content of the WEB-INF subdirectory.

Pages should be left in their default location (**Web Content** in JDeveloper, corresponding to public_html in the filesystem).

Page fragments should be placed in the /WEB-INF/fragments subdirectory because there is no need to access them outside the context of the bounded task flow they are part of. When creating page fragments by double-clicking on a view object from a task flow, you can simply add this directory name to the end of the content of the **Directory** field, as shown in the following screenshot (this causes JDeveloper to create the subdirectory):

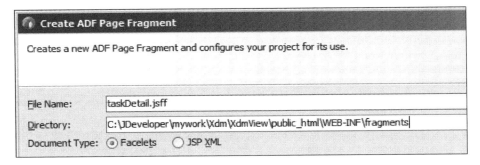

Your page flows and page templates also do not need to be directly accessible, so you should place these under the WEB-INF directory. This prevents a malicious user from snooping around in the application's internal files.

Test code

If you are using the Maven tool, you should follow the Maven conventions for the placement of test code. If not, you can create a separate test project in each workspace and place your unit tests in this project.

Having the tests separate from the code makes it easier to deploy the final application without including test code unnecessarily at runtime.

Summary

You have learned which skills you need in order to build an enterprise ADF application. Talking to your colleagues in the development department of DMC Solutions, you found that most of the skills were available, but you also had to find external resources to fill a few of the roles in the development team for the XDM project.

Talking to the system administrators in DMC Solutions, you found that there was already a Git repository available that you could use for your project, but you also had to install a couple of additional tools for issue tracking and collaboration on your development server.

On the project Wiki, you have described how your team should use application workspaces to build the application in a modular fashion, and you have documented the naming conventions that should be used by everyone on the project.

The next task is to get the development team together for the official kickoff and tell everybody how to use the tools so that you can build the XDM solution in the most efficient way. That's the topic of the next chapter.

4
Productive Teamwork

You have put together your team so that all the necessary skills are available and you have set up your development servers (versioning, issue tracking, and collaboration). You have already documented the XDM project standards in the project Wiki—now you need to get everybody together for the kick-off and the first official project session telling everybody how to set up their development workstations to work productively with the tools.

The secret of productivity

In order to be as productive as possible with JDeveloper, you need the following:

- A large screen area
- To work effectively with Version Control
- To use a task/issue tracking system
- To focus on one task at a time
- To integrate other support tools into your workflow

More pixels give better productivity

When you start working with JDeveloper, you are likely to find that your screen is too small. If you are wasting time minimizing and resizing panels, you need a bigger screen. Get at least a 1600 x 1200 resolution, preferably bigger (or even better, get two). With the current monitor prices, the payback time for extra screen area can be calculated in weeks.

Research from the University of Utah compared an 18-inch monitor, a 24-inch monitor, and two 20-inch monitors. They found that users with a 24-inch monitor completed tasks 52 percent faster, and people using two 20-inch monitors were 44 percent faster than the people with the 18-inch monitor.

Version control

As we discussed in *Chapter 3, Getting Organized*, you absolutely need to use some kind of version-control system in an enterprise development effort. You should even use it if you are the only developer in your team!

Oracle JDeveloper comes with extensions for many different source control systems that you can download and install using the **Check for Updates** functionality by navigating to **Help**. The supported systems include Subversion (SVN), Git, CVS, Perforce, ClearCase, and many more.

This chapter describes in detail how to work with Subversion and Git. If you have already decided for one or the other, you can of course skip the section on the other tool.

Avoiding spreadsheets

One of the tools you need for efficient enterprise development is a bug/task/issue tracker. Valuable time of the developer and project manager should not be spent keeping lists of issues in spreadsheets.

Jira from Atlassian is a popular, user-friendly tool that integrates well with Oracle Team Productivity Center, but there are many others (Wikipedia lists over 50 issue-tracking systems).

Split your project into tasks

When starting a project, the project manager should convert the project plan into a list of tasks for each developer and register these as work items in your bug/issue/task tracking system. This allows each developer to write comments and register progress on tasks, split tasks into more manageable subtasks, and even reassign tasks to the other team members.

Focus

Don't you just hate it when you're in the middle of something and your boss comes up to you with an urgent request that you just must start on right away? You need to put away what you're doing, get into the new task, finish it, and then get back into what you were doing before.

Productivity experts call this a context switch. It's much more expensive in terms of lost productivity than most people realize. Estimates of lost time vary but typically range from ten minutes to an hour of lost productivity. To be more productive, you need fewer context switches.

This book can't really offer advice on how to minimize the boss-induced context switches—but it can offer some guidelines for minimizing the context switches you can influence yourself.

Integrate your tools

An experienced computer user can switch applications in a fraction of a second—but the context switch takes much longer than the time it takes to press *Alt + Tab* or *cmd + Tab*.

First, you are likely to have more than two applications that you can switch between. This means that every once in a while you will have to actually look at your screen to determine just how many *Alt + Tab* presses you need. Second, once the desired application is on the screen, you need to reorient yourself every time. Your brain has to determine the location of the window, find the mouse pointer, and then instruct your hand to scroll or move. Third, you'll occasionally have to actually use information from the second window in the first one. You can either resize both windows to a smaller size or cut and paste the information you need, both of which take time.

That's why you don't want to switch between applications—you want as much as possible integrated into your development environment. Earlier, Oracle's solution to this need for integration would have been to connect JDeveloper to some of their own software, such as the Oracle Projects module of the E-Business Suite. Fortunately, Oracle has moved on from the monolithic "buy-everything-from-us" approach, and with **Oracle Team Productivity Center** (**OTPC**), it offers a modern, loosely-coupled integration solution.

Later in this chapter, we will see how to set up and use Oracle Team Productivity Center.

Version control with Subversion

Subversion is very popular among JDeveloper users, for several reasons, which are detailed as follows:

- It's well integrated into JDeveloper
- It has been supported in JDeveloper for a long time
- It's widely used—lots of other people are using it, and many other tools can read your Subversion repository

- It's free—always a good point
- It's atomic—either your whole commit goes into the repository or nothing does. Since ADF projects consist of many interdependent files, this is very much desirable

To use Subversion, you need a Subversion server and client. The Subversion server is available for all platforms—if your version control server is based on Microsoft Windows, you can use the VisualSVN (`http://www.visualsvn.com/server`), which comes as a standard Windows MSI install file.

JDeveloper comes with a Subversion client for working with code, but if you keep other files in Subversion as well, you probably want a standalone client to update and commit to the repository. A very popular (and free) client is TortoiseSVN (`http://tortoisesvn.tigris.org`), which integrates directly into the Windows Explorer context menu when you right-click on it.

Effective Subversion

If you have never used Subversion before, you need to familiarize yourself with the tool. There are many excellent resources available on the Internet—a good place to start is the free e-book on Subversion (`http://svnbook.red-bean.com`).

There are many ways to use a tool such as Subversion, but for an enterprise ADF project you should do the following:

- Use the standard structure of trunk, branches, and tags
  - **Trunk**: This is where you keep your main development code.
  - **Branches**: These are where you store variations of the code. Each branch is a copy of the code as it looked when you created the branch.
  - **Tags**: These are where you store copies of your code corresponding to a specific tag. You typically create a tag for each released version of your code.

Efficient storage

Even if it looks like Subversion, it keeps many copies of your code; the branches and tags copies do not take up any significant space—they are only pointers or virtual copies.

- In your trunk, create folders for each application workspace with the same name as your application workspace

- Use Copy-Modify-Merge (in general, don't lock the files)
- Check out and commit at the application workspace level (use **Commit Working Copy**, not just **Commit** for a single file)

Handling new files

You might not always notice additional files that JDeveloper sometimes create for you—for example, the data binding that is created the first time you drop an item from the **Data Control** panel onto to a page.

To make sure that everything is added to Subversion, you should set a JDeveloper preference. Under **Tools | Preferences | Versioning | Subversion | General**, check the checkbox **Automatically Add New Files on Committing Working Copy**. If you want to manually control when new files are added to Subversion, you can leave this checkbox unchecked and then explicitly add them from the **Pending Changes** window on the **Candidates** tab. Clicking on the green plus sign on this tab will change the file status from **Not Versioned** to **Scheduled for Addition**, as shown in the following screenshot. This means that they will be imported into Subversion the next time you commit your working copy.

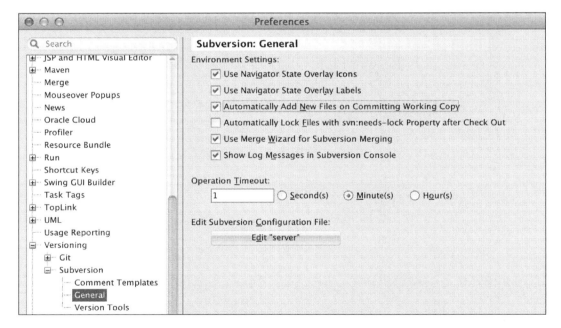

Starting with Subversion

As soon as you have created the application workspace and the first few functioning objects, add your application to the Subversion repository (in Subversion terminology, this is called importing).

To import your application workspace, select a project in the workspace and navigate to **Team | Version Application**. If you have more than one connection to a versioning system, JDeveloper prompts you to select one of them.

The first time you import an application workspace into Subversion, you will be prompted to create a connection, as shown in the following screenshot:

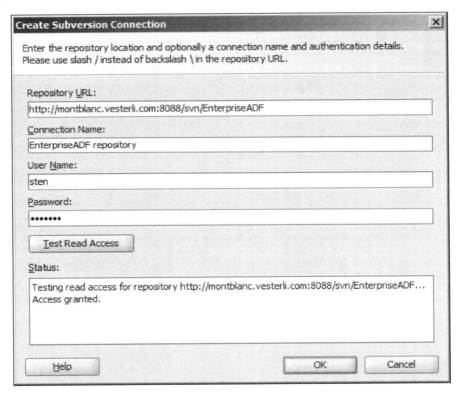

The **Import to Subversion** wizard starts and guides you through the initial import as follows:.

1. In the **Destination** step, choose **trunk** and then click on the little add folder icon above the path box to the right. In the **Create Remote Directory** dialog, enter the name of your application workspace as directory name and provide a comment.

2. In the **Source** step, check that the **Source** directory is your application workspace directory. Provide a comment such as `Initial import` and click on **Next**.

3. You don't need to change anything in the **Filters** step.

4. In the **Options** step, leave **Perform Checkout** checked to immediately check out of your application to continue working.

5. In the **Summary** step, review the options and click on **Finish**.

You can see your import running in the **SVN Console Log** window.

Once the import is complete, you'll notice the following changes in the **Application Navigator**:

- The projects now show the repository server where the files are stored.

- Each file now has an indicator showing its state. Right now, all of them have the status **Unmodified**, but you will see this change as you and your team members work on the project.

- Each file now shows a version number. Don't worry about the numbering—they will seem to increase in uneven jumps. In fact, the Subversion version number increases every time anybody on the project commits anything. Refer to a Subversion book (for example, the free e-book at `http://svnbook.red-bean.com`) for a more detailed explanation.

Working with Subversion

If you have structured your application as described in *Chapter 3*, *Getting Organized*, and have chosen the modular or enterprise architecture, you will have a number of different application workspaces. For some workspaces, you might be the only developer, but most of the time there will be a small team of developers working on the code at the same time. As you work with your project, you will notice different icons on your files and directories. They can be seen in the following screenshot:

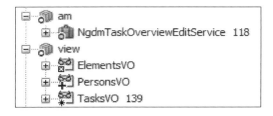

The little circle with the yellow center indicates a versioned object that has not been changed since the last commit, and the object marked with an asterisk (TasksVO) is an object that has been changed since the last commit. The file with a little white X in a box (ElementsVO) is a new, unversioned file, and the file with the plus sign (PersonsVO) is a new file that is scheduled for addition on the next commit.

You can also navigate to **Versioning | Pending Changes** to call up the **Pending Changes** window showing the files changed locally (outgoing), new files (candidates to be placed under version control), and files changed by other users on the server but not yet applied to your working copy (incoming).

Every time you have made a significant change (and tested it, of course), you check your changes into the central repository by navigating to **Team | Subversion | Commit Working Copy** from the menu bar.

If you are only using Subversion (and not Oracle Team Productivity Center), the **Commit Working Copy** only prompts you for a commit comment. If you are using Oracle Team Productivity Center together with Subversion, the dialog changes slightly to allow you to associate the commit with one or more work items. This allows Oracle Team Productivity Center to register the association, so you can find commits related to a specific work area later.

Comment templates

If you like, you can configure a number of standard comments as Comment Templates under **Tools | Preferences | Versioning | Subversion | Comment Templates**.

When you click on **OK**, you see the Subversion commands issued to commit your changes in the **SVN Console Log** window. The icons in the **Application Navigator** also change, and the **Pending Changes** window should now be empty.

Getting a new copy

When another team member needs to start working with an application workspace already imported into Subversion, that person simply navigates to **Team | Subversion | Check Out**. He then defines a Subversion connection using his Subversion credentials and navigates to the application workspace folder under the trunk of the version tree. JDeveloper will now get the latest version to the local machine as that person's working copy.

Getting other people's changes

When a colleague commits new files to the application workspace you are working on, these files will show up in the **Pending Changes** window as incoming. To get these files, you navigate to **Team | Subversion | Update Working Copy**. This will make your working copy up to date with the changes committed by other team members.

Automatic merge

Occasionally, you and another team member have both made changes to the same file. Of course, Subversion doesn't just allow the second developer to overwrite the changes made by the first. Instead, if your colleague committed his or her change first, you will get a message from Subversion when you try to submit your file. The message will be something similar to the following screenshot:

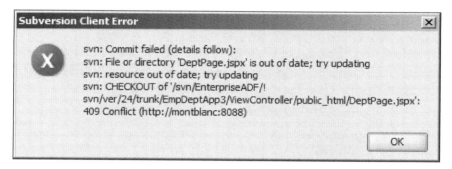

This message tells you that the file has changed in the repository since you originally retrieved it. If you look at the **Pending Changes** window, you will also see that the same file is listed both as *Outgoing* (with your change in it) and as *Incoming* (with the other developer's change in it).

If you now perform an **Update Working Copy**, Subversion is clever enough to automatically merge your change and the incoming change to a new file containing both your updates. You can see the changes by right-clicking on the conflicting file and selecting **Compare With**—this allows you to compare all versions of the file.

Handling conflicts

However, what happens if your colleague has changed some code, and you then change *the exact same lines of code* in your working copy? Initially, you will get the **...try updating** message. When you try updating, you'll discover that several things are happening. They are detailed as follows:

- You suddenly have four versions of the file in question in the **Application Navigator**—one of them with an exclamation mark indicating a conflict, as shown in the following screenshot:

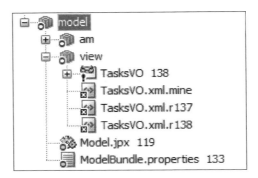

- The SVN Console Log will show a conflict
- The **Pending Changes** window will show your outgoing file with the status, Conflicts

Since Subversion doesn't pass judgment on which change is better, you and your colleague will have to decide how to handle the conflict. Fortunately, JDeveloper has a very nice graphical interface to help you implement your decided conflict resolution. Simply right-click on the conflicted file and choose **Resolve Conflicts**. This brings up the file in the merge mode, showing your version on the left-hand side (the .mine file), the other person's code on the right-hand side, and an editable, final version in the middle. You can use the > and < buttons to move code from either side to the middle, or you can simply edit the central file if the result of your merge contains parts from both sides, as shown in the following screenshot:.

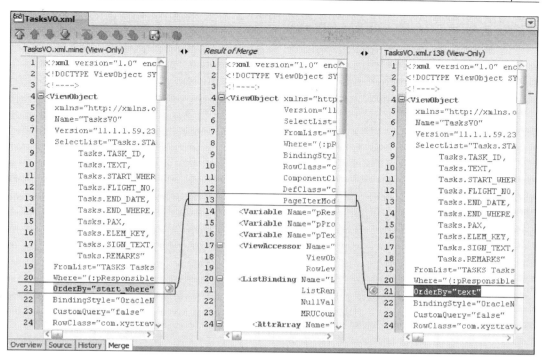

When you're done merging, click on the **Save** and **Complete Merge** buttons in the toolbar above the files (a little diskette icon with two colored circles). This completes the merge, and you can now commit your working copy to the repository.

After committing your working copy, you can click on the little refresh button (two blue arrows in a circle). You'll see that the extra versions of the file (the two .rXXX files and the .mine file) are now gone, thus indicating a successful conflict resolution.

Version control with Git

Git is another version control system that is rapidly gaining popularity. It is architecturally different from Subversion, in that it is an example of a **distributed version control system** (**DVCS**). It is popular in open source projects for several reasons, which are as follows:

- It is fast
- It supports large development teams
- It allows developers to work without a connection to a central repository
- It's widely used in the open source community
- It's free
- It's atomic (like Subversion) — either your whole commit goes into the repository or nothing does. Since ADF projects consist of many interdependent files, this is very much desirable

To use Git, you need the Git software. Since the system is distributed and every user has a complete copy of the entire repository, the concept of a server and a client does not really apply to Git — there is just the Git software.

If you plan on using only Git for your JDeveloper code, you do not have to install Git — JDeveloper comes with a Git extension that contains everything you need. However, if you want to version other files in your Git repository as well, you probably want a separate Git software installation to work with your repositories.

Git is available for all platforms — you can download it from `http://git-scm.com/downloads`.

A convenient way of working with Git in a Windows environment is the free TortoiseGit software (`http://code.google.com/p/tortoisegit/`) that integrates directly into the Windows Explorer context (right-click) menu. TortoiseGit is just a convenient frontend and requires you to install the "regular" Git first.

Effective Git

If you are new to Git, you should take a moment to learn how to use Git; this is especially important if you are switching to Git from a centralized version control system. Start with the official Git documentation page (`http://git-scm.com/documentation`) where you can find both a book and a number of video tutorials. This page also contains a link to a page pointing to a number of other resources to learn Git.

Because of the distributed nature of Git, you can arrange your repositories in many different ways. If you are new to Git, use a simple centralized workflow as shown in the following figure:

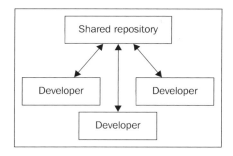

In this workflow, each developer will work in the following way:

1. Every morning, pull the latest version of the code from the shared repository.
2. When starting on a task, create a new branch for that task and check out that branch.
3. Perform your work.
4. Commit often while you work (commit a working copy, not just a single file).
5. When you have completed the task, check out the master branch.
6. Merge your task branch into the master branch.
7. When done for the day, push your code to the shared repository.

There are other workflows for more complicated project organizations—see the Git manual (`http://git-scm.com/book/en/Distributed-Git-Distributed-Workflows`) for some other examples.

Staging and committing

Git works with the concept of **staging** files. A file can be new or modified, but unless you **stage** it, it will not be included in the next commit. Unless you really know what you are doing and want very fine-grained control over your files, you will not need to worry about staging.

To ask JDeveloper to handle all of this for you, there is a JDeveloper preference you should set for Git. Under **Tools | Preferences | Versioning | Git | General**, check the **Automatically Add New Files on Committing Working Tree** checkbox. This simply changes the default setting for the **Commit non-staged files** checkbox in the **Commit All** dialog to be checked by default, thus adding all new files when committing.

If you want to manually control the staging, you can leave the **Commit non-staged files** checkbox unchecked. This means that you take responsibility for choosing which files to add. You do this from the **Pending Changes (GIT)** window. This window appears at the bottom of your JDeveloper window and has two tabs: **Outgoing** and **Candidates**. All your changes will appear on the **Candidates** tab, and all your new files will appear on the **Outgoing** tab. However, none of these will be included in a commit unless you explicitly add them by clicking on the green plus sign. The status changed depending on the current status as follows:

- When you add a new file (from the **Candidates** tab), the file changes status from **Unversioned** to **Scheduled for Addition Staged** and moves to the **Outgoing** tab
- When you add a modified file from the **Outgoing** tab, the files changes status from **Changes Pending Not Staged** to **Changes Pending Staged**

Only files with a **...Staged** status are committed to your repository unless you check the **Commit non-staged files** checkbox.

Preparing your local repository

Remember that Git is a distributed version control system. This means that there will be a local repository on your development workstation and other repositories elsewhere. There are many possible Git architectures for very large organizations as well (the entire Linux kernel is kept in a Git repository), but for the purposes of this book, we will assume an architecture with local repositories and a single shared repository on a server somewhere.

Free Git hosting

If you want to play around with a remote Git repository for your personal use and don't want to set up a server, you can sign up for a free plan at GitHub. This plan only offers publicly available repositories—if you want private repositories or want to use GitHub in a commercial organization, you need to sign up for one of their paid plans. See https://github.com/plans for details. There are also other providers who offer hosted Git.

You need to initialize your central repository first and then clone your remote repository to your local machine. To do this, start by creating a directory to hold all your Git repositories, for example, `C:\gitrepos`.

Then, in JDeveloper, navigate to **Team | Git | Clone**. This starts the **Clone from Git** wizard. In step 2 of this wizard, you provide the URL for your remote repository. Your Git administrator can tell you what this URL is. If you are using GitHub, you find the clone URL in the bottom-right corner of your repository screen, as shown in the following screenshot:

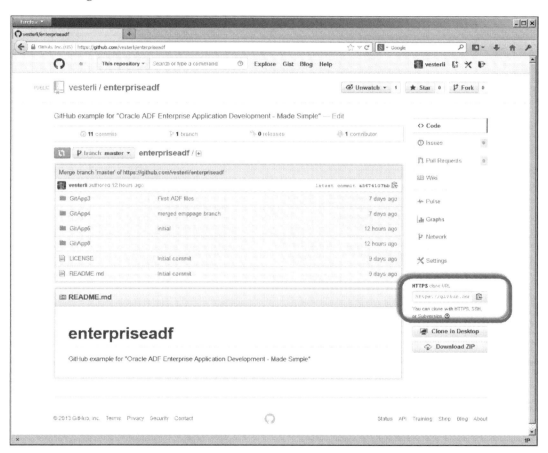

You can click on the **Copy to Clipboard** button next to the field to copy the URL. A GitHub URL has the form `https://github.com/<username>/<repositoryname>.git`, for example, `https://github.com/vesterli/enterpriseadf.git`.

Once you have the URL, fill in your name and password for the **Remote Repository** as shown in the following screenshot:

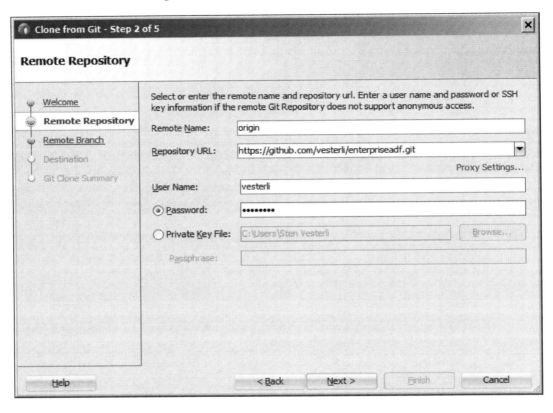

In step 3, include all the branches (there will often only be one branch called `master`).

In step 4, point to the directory where you want to keep all your repositories, let the clone name be the same as the name of your remote repository, and check out the branch master, as shown in the following screenshot:

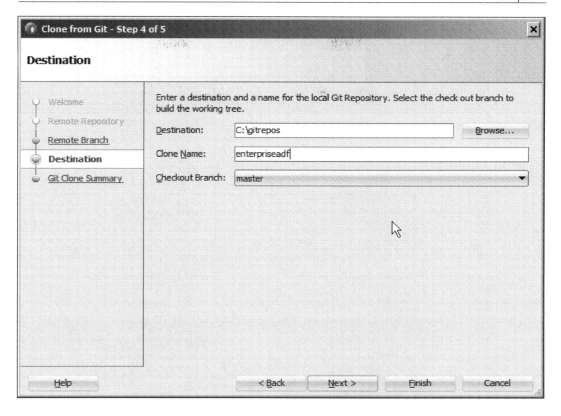

When you finish the wizard, your remote repository is cloned to the local location you specified, and you will see any remote content in a directory with the clone name under the destination directory you specified.

> It is also possible to connect an already existing local repository to a remote repository. However, this requires some Git command-line incantations. Make it simple for yourself, and clone an existing remote repository instead.

Initial load of a workspace

When you have cloned your remote repository, you can add your application workspace to the local repository.

To do this, select any project in the workspace in the **Applications** window and navigate to **Team | Version Application**. If you have the extension for more than one versioning system installed, JDeveloper prompts you to select one of them. Select **Git**.

The **Import to Git** wizard starts and guides you through the initial import, as follows:

1. In the **Source and Destination** step, you can leave the **Source Directory** value unchanged, but change the **Destination Directory** to a subdirectory in your local repository matching your application workspace name. If you created the C:\gitrepos directory for your repositories and cloned it into enterpriseadf, the destination for the XdmCommon workspace should be C:\gitrepos\enterpriseadf\XdmCommon, as shown in the following screenshot:

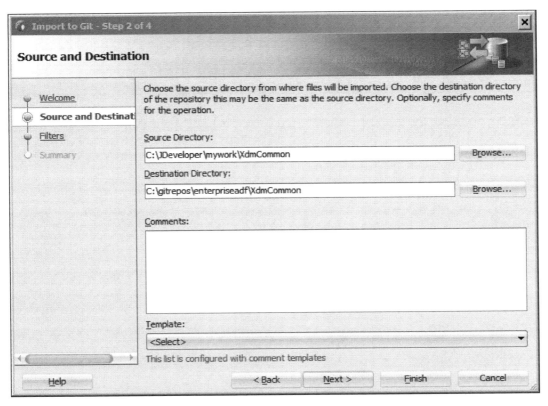

2. You don't need to change anything in the **Filters** step.

3. In the **Summary** step, review the selections and click on **Finish** to import your code to the local repository.

Your import runs quickly—you can see what happened in detail in the **Messages** window.

Once the import is complete, you'll notice the following changes in the **Application Navigator**:

- The projects now show the branch they are on (initially, the master branch).

- Each file now has a little indicator icon in the bottom-left corner of the main icon showing its state. Right now, all of them have the **Git: No Change** status, but you will see this change as you and your team members work on the project.

Working with Git

As mentioned earlier, a good way of working with Git is shown in the following workflow:

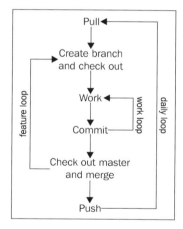

If you are used to a centralized versioning system such as Subversion, you will notice two differences:

- Lots of branches
- Lots of commits

As you work against a local repository, all of your operations are very fast. This allows you to quickly create branches for everything and quickly merge them back into your master branch. This also allows you to create a throw-away branch if you are trying out various approaches. You can also commit freely (even if your code is not complete) because your commits are only to your local repository.

Starting the day

At the start of each day, you navigate to **Team | Git | Pull**. This gets all the changes from the central repository to your local repository. If there are many branches in the central repository, you can select them to pull only the **master** branch.

If you get a message about a conflict while doing this, see the section on Merge Conflicts later in this chapter.

Starting work on a task

When you start working on a specific feature or bug, you create a new local branch by navigating to **Team | Git | Create Branch**. Give your branch the name of your task or bug—this will often be an issue number from your issue-tracking system.

Then navigate to **Team | Git | Checkout** and click on the **Select Branch** button in the **Checkout Revision** dialog. Open the **Local** node in the branch tree and select the branch you just created, as shown in the following screenshot:

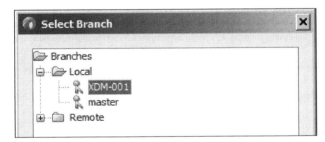

In the **Applications** window, you will now see your project names followed by the branch name.

Committing often to a task

Every time you are done with some part of the task, commit to your local repository by navigating to **Team | Git | Commit All**. Since you are only committing locally, you are not messing up anybody else's work, so you can commit as often as you want. This allows you to commit, try something out, and revert back one version if your approach didn't work.

Remember to provide a reasonable commit comment, so you can identify each commit in case you have to revert to an earlier version.

 Sometimes, your project gets messed up in some mysterious way and refuses to work. You might have unknowingly introduced an error in a file, or maybe JDeveloper crashed. Committing often gives you many different points in time to revert back to.

Completing a task

When you are done with your task, you switch to your local master branch and merge your development branch into it. To do this, navigate to **Team | Git | Checkout**, click on **Select Branch**, and choose your local `master` branch.

Then, navigate to **Team | Git | Merge**, click **on Select Branch**, and choose your local feature branch to merge in. When you click on **OK**, the changes in your feature branch are merged into your local master branch.

 You should not have merge conflicts at this time because you have not changed your local master branch since you pulled the latest changes from the shared repository in the morning.

Now, continue with the next task as described earlier, keeping each feature on its own branch.

Ending the day

At the end of each working day, push the changes from your local repository onto the shared repository by navigating to **Team | Git | Push**. In the **Push to Git** wizard, you normally select to push only your `master` branch, as shown in the following screenshot:

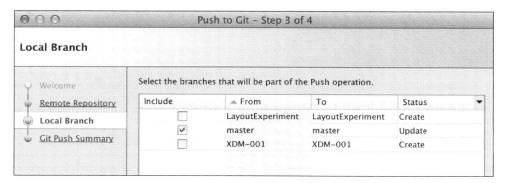

You might want to push one of your local branches to the central server if you explicitly want to share a specific feature branch with another developer (for example, to have someone else help troubleshoot an issue you're having).

If you have a conflict, see the following section.

Handling conflicts

If a file has been modified by several developers in separate local repositories, you might get a merge conflict when pushing or pulling the files. Sometimes, Git can work out how to merge the file, but at other times it has to ask a human for help.

A merge conflict shows up the **Messages** window with the **Following files contain unresolved conflicts** text, and the file or files with conflict are shown in the **Applications** window with an exclamation mark on its icon, as shown in the following screenshot:

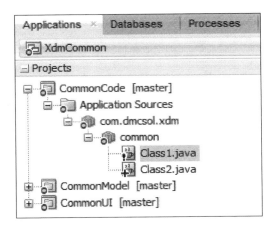

The file also appears in the **Pending Changes (Git)** window with the **Merge Conflicts** status.

If you open the file, you will see that JDeveloper is showing both versions of the file with a slightly cryptic syntax, as follows:

```
package com.dmcsol.xdm.common;

public class Class1 {
    public String myMethod(String v) {
<<<<<< HEAD
        return "Greetings, " + v;
```

```
      }

=======
        return "Hello " + v;
      }
>>>>>>> branch 'master' of https://github.com/vesterli/enterpriseadf.
git
}
```

Fortunately, you do not need to understand this syntax or edit the file manually.
Instead, you can navigate to **Team | Git | Resolve Conflict** to bring up the visual
conflict resolution tool built into JDeveloper, as shown in the following screenshot:

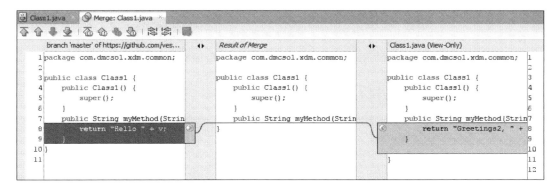

Here, you can use the green angled brackets to move the code from either side into
the merge result column in the middle, or you can simply edit the central column
manually. When you are done, you can click on **Save** and then on the **Complete
Merge** button (the right-most button on the button bar in the merge window) to
save the merged file and indicate that the conflict is resolved.

The file changes to the **Changes Pending Staged** status and can now be committed.
After committing, you can now complete your push or pull operation.

Avoiding conflicts

It takes time to resolve conflicts, so you should make an effort to avoid them. There are
both soft and hard methods that you can use for this. The soft methods are procedural
(ways in which you agree to work in your team), and the hard methods are technical;
they are implemented using the capabilities of your version control tool.

The first soft method is to take the approach recommended in the previous chapter and split your application into a number of separate workspaces connected via ADF Libraries. If you do this, you have already reduced the risk of version conflicts significantly.

The second soft method you can use is to assign owners to the files that are often the source of version conflicts. If you decide that only Bob, the lead programmer, is allowed to commit changes to the two files that the whole team keeps fighting over, he can keep the purpose and entire structure clear in his mind. If anybody else needs to make a change, they can tell Bob and let him make the change.

Unfortunately, some of the files that you might want to assign an owner to are the files that are updated by many different ADF wizards. In this case, a developer might not even realize that he is making a change to a contested file. To avoid this, some tools (such as Subversion) offer a hard method: explicitly locking files. If you are using Subversion, you can right-click on a file and navigate to **Versioning | Lock** from the context menu. This will prevent anybody else from checking on a change to the locked file. Use this method with caution—you can seriously disrupt the work of other developers if you lock important ADF files.

Unmergeable files

Some files cannot be merged; you will have to either assign an owner to these files or lock them to avoid wasted work. Examples of unmergeable files are JDeveloper diagrams, word processing files, spreadsheets, and images.

Focusing for maximum productivity

In order to reach maximum productivity, you need to focus on the task at hand. However, you cannot stay fully focused for an entire 8 hour (or longer) working day. I suggest you to split your working day into three different kinds of time, detailed as follows:

- **Work mode**: In this, you work on small tasks that do not require deep concentration. This might be fixing a misaligned user interface, simple refactoring, moving accidentally hardwired strings into a resource bundle, and similar tasks. Handling e-mails can also be done in Work mode.

Never check e-mails in the morning

Always start the day in Focus mode. In most projects and workplaces, there is absolutely no need to check e-mails other than at mid-morning and mid-afternoon.

- **Focus mode**: In this, you work on complicated stuff that requires your full concentration. This might be programming a Java method or debugging a difficult issue.

- **Recharge mode**: In this, you do something else to revitalize your body and mind. You might read a few postings on a forum or website you follow, but preferably, get away from the computer. Go down the hall for a cup of coffee or outside for a breath of fresh air. You should not be in the Recharge mode for more than 5-10 minutes at a time—after that, you are losing more time at the water cooler than you are making up for in increased productivity later.

You are already using all of these modes, but the productivity trick is to make a conscious decision about which mode you will be in. If you have decided to be in the Focus mode, disable all the notifications on your computer, such as new mails, Twitter messages, chat, and so on. Set a timer for a specific interval, for example, 30 minutes. Few people can stay in Focus mode for longer than that; on the other hand, committing to 30 minutes before checking e-mail or Twitter will increase your productivity.

Go with the flow

Sometimes, you reach the happy state called **Flow**, where everything just comes together effortlessly as if by magic. If you get into Flow, feel free to stay there for as long as you like.

Between periods of Focus, place Work, and Recharge phases as necessary. There is no need to set a strict regimen—different phases of your project will have a different balance between Focus and Work time.

If your team uses a chat program, you can allow that to be open during Work mode in order to be able to help out your team members as needed.

Read *Be Excellent at Anything* by Tony Schwarz for more details on how to use your focus for maximum efficiency.

The Integrated Solution – Oracle Team Productivity Center

As we saw at the beginning of this chapter, we want to avoid context switching as much as possible in order to achieve maximum productivity, and Oracle's solution for this is the **Oracle Team Productivity Center (OTPC)**. This free product from Oracle connects to different repositories of information and presents data directly in JDeveloper. OTPC consists of three parts, as follows:

- JDeveloper TPC Client.
- Team Productivity Center Server.
- Team Productivity Center Connectors.

The architecture of OTPC looks as follows:

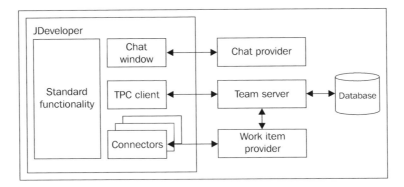

The Oracle Team Productivity Center client is built into JDeveloper. However, the connectors to various repositories are not initially installed—you need to use the automatic update feature (**Help | Check for Updates**) to install the ones you need.

The Team Productivity Center Server is a Java application offering a number of services that the client uses. It contains a password vault storing credentials for third-party repositories, so the user can seamlessly connect to different products as well as a simple task database in case you do not have any third-party repositories you want to use.

The Team Productivity Center Connectors expose third-party repositories of information to the client. Using a standards-based interface, a connector allows create/update/delete operations on the underlying repository, so the developer can do all the work without leaving JDeveloper. Team Productivity Center comes with prebuilt connectors for Jira, Bugzilla, Rally, and Microsoft Project Server, as well as the built-in simple task repository.

If you want to integrate a tool for which Oracle does not yet offer a connector, you can develop your own connector. This is explained in this chapter under Developing Applications with Oracle Team Productivity Center at `http://docs.oracle.com/ middleware/1212/jdev/TPCUG/creating_connectors.htm`.

In order to use OTPC, you need to install the OTPC server software on a server machine and connect each individual development workstation to the server.

Installing the server

If you decide you want to work with Oracle Team Productivity Center, you need to install the OTPC server component on a server in your environment. If you don't want to allocate a dedicated server for this (and you don't have to), you can install the OTPC server components on your test/integration server.

The server software needs a database with a schema where it can store its items and a Java application server to run the server-side code. The database can be any database that allows a JDBC connection, for example, MySQL, the free Oracle XE database, or one of the commercial Oracle database versions. If you decide to install the Oracle Team Productivity Center server components on your test/integration server, you can use the database already in place—simply create a separate schema for the OTPC components. The application server can also be any JEE application server—if you install it on your test/integration server, you can use the same WebLogic server that you use for your test. If you install on a separate server, a free, open source product like Tomcat will be sufficient.

You can find the installer on the Oracle Team Productivity Center web page on the Oracle Technology Network website (`otn.oracle.com`)—at the time of writing this book, it could be found at `http://otn.oracle.com/developer-tools/ tpc/downloads`. If you can't find it, use the site-search feature to search for `Team Productivity Center`. On this page, you can also download the server-side connectors for the repositories you want to connect to.

There is a short installation guide that you need to follow to install the Oracle Team Productivity Center server. During this process, you can also download and install the relevant connectors as well as plugins to connect to continuous integration servers, as shown in the following screenshot:.

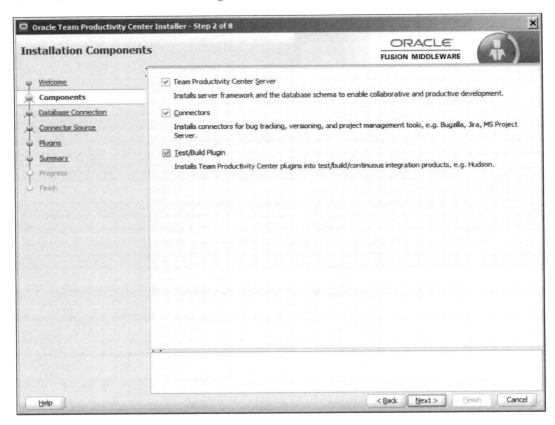

Connecting JDeveloper to repositories

In order for to Oracle Team Productivity Center to connect to a remote repository, the necessary connector must be installed into JDeveloper. You do this using the automatic update feature (**Help | Check for Updates**), as shown in the following screenshot:

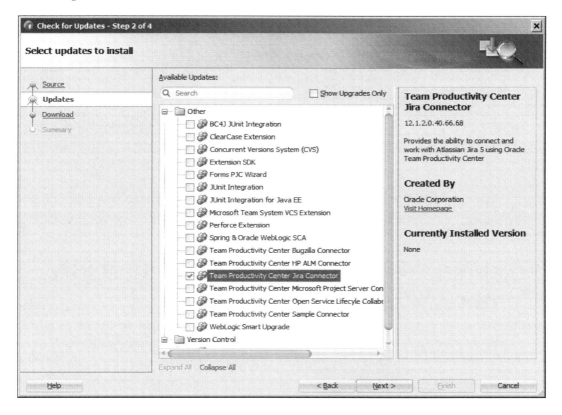

Administration tasks

Before you start using OTPC, you need to appoint an OTPC administrator. That person needs to do the following:

- Connect various repositories to the OTPC

- Assign repositories to teams

- Create and manage users and groups, which includes assigning them to teams

- Manage roles to ensure that each team member has only the necessary access

To perform team administration, first connect to the team server with the admin user you created during the installation of Oracle Team Productivity Center (**Team | Connect to Team Server**). Then, navigate to **Team | Team Administration** to bring up the **Team Administration** dialog. Here, you can define users, roles, and teams as well as set up connections to work on item repositories and version control systems.

The Developing Applications with Oracle Team Productivity Center manual (`http://docs.oracle.com/middleware/1212/jdev/TPCUG/tpc_admin.htm`) describes how to perform the necessary administration tasks.

Working with Oracle Team Productivity Center

In order to work with Oracle Team Productivity Center, you need to connect to the server by navigating to **Team | Connect to Team Server**.

You will be prompted for the server and port where the OTPC server is running as well as your OTPC user credentials. Your OTPC administrator can give you this information.

Once you have connected, the **Teams** window opens (by default, to the left of your JDeveloper window as a new tab next to **Applications**). If you are a member of several teams, select the team you want to work on behalf of from the dropdown at the top of the window. This window has three headings. They are as follows:

- **Team Members**: In this, you find all members of your team. If you have connected to a chat server, as described later in the chapter, you also see the status of each member (available, away, and busy).

- **Work Items**: In this, you see the **Active Work Item** at the top followed by all the repositories you have connected to (Jira, Rally, Bugzilla, and so on). Under each repository, lists of work items from that repository are shown. Oracle Team Productivity Center does not store the work items itself—you define queries either at the team level or just for yourself, and these queries show a number of work items.

- **Versioning**: In this, you find connections to the versioning system you use on the project. The functionality here is the same as in the **Versions** window; the advantage of defining versioning as part of Oracle Team Productivity Center is that the team administrator can specify the repository URL for the team.

Working with work items

The items in the repositories that OTPC is connected to are called work items, irrespective of what the underlying product calls them (task, bug, issue, and so on).

Your project manager has probably already created some tasks for you based on the project plan. Depending on the level of detail you want, you might have a complete use case as a task (UC 008 Task Overview and Edit), or you might have a detailed breakdown with multiple tasks (UC 008 Task flow, UC 008 View objects, and so on).

Finding work items

To find your assigned work items, you open the work item repository and perform a query. You can define your own queries based on various criteria, or use a team query defined for you by your team administrator. Note that you can also use tags as part of your search criteria.

Setting the active work item

When you have queried an item, you can right-click on it and choose **Make Active** to make this work item your active item. When you have an item on screen, you can click on the **Make Active** button at the top to set that item as your current or active item. The active work item is shown at the top of the **Work Items** list in the following screenshot:

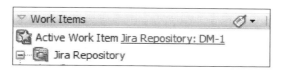

Whenever you commit your changes to your version control system, Team Productivity Center will by default associate your commit with the active work item.

 As described in an earlier section, always keep an active work item selected. This serves as a subtle hint to your brain to stay at the task at hand and increases your productivity.

Linking work items

It is possible to link work items to each other; for example, a bug in Bugzilla could be linked to a task in Microsoft Project Server.

To create and view these links, you use the **Relationships** subtab to the left of the item itself.

Here, you can see the relationships the work item is part of and add new ones. If you activate this subtab, you have the option to link the active work item to another open work item or an item you have tagged.

Tagging work items

You can select a number of work items by tagging them. You are free to define your own tags with whatever meaning you want—this could be today's work, stuff for next release, items to discuss with Michael, or anything else.

You can add a tag to an item when you first create it or anytime later you have the item open. Simply click on the **Tags** subtab to the left of the work item tab to add and remove tags.

Saving and restoring context

Remember the discussion from the beginning of the chapter about the cost of context switching? Oracle Team Productivity Center contains a very nice feature to minimize the cost of context switching: the ability to save and restore context.

To use this feature, open a work item and click on the **Save Context** button in the button list at the top of the work item. This will save your current context, including information about all open files in the main window, the currently active workspace, and the state of the **Application Navigator**. When your boss walks up to you with an urgent task that requires you to drop everything, you can simply perform the following steps:

1. Save your JDeveloper context.

2. Peform the urgent task and return to JDeveloper.

3. Click on **Restore Context** (the button to the left of **Save Context**).

JDeveloper will open all the files that were open when you saved context and will open the application workspace you were working on, exactly as you left it.

The Boss Key

Many years ago, before multi-tasking operating systems were common, computer games would include a Boss Key — a special keystroke that would hide the game and show something that looked like a work-related document or spreadsheet. The **Save Context** button is JDeveloper's Boss Key. It is not used to hide the application but to make sure you can get back to where you were as soon as you are done with the boss' urgent task.

Code reviews

Oracle Team Productivity Center also offers to handle your code reviews. This functionality works on files waiting to be checked in to your version control system, so it works well with a centralized system where only completed, tested code is checked into version control. It does not really match a typical workflow with a distributed version control system like Git, where you commit locally all the time.

If you decide to work with OTPC code review, your workflow will typically involve the following:

- Creating a code review
- Selecting reviewers for a code review
- Finding a code review to work on
- Commenting on a code review (including adding attachments)

You work with code review by navigating to **Team | Code Reviews**. This brings up the **Code Reviews** tab in the left-hand side of the JDeveloper window. You can create a code review from this window with the little triangle to the right of the code review dropdown or from the **Reviews** tab of a work item. Once you have created a code review, you can add reviewers.

You can search for code reviews, comment on them, add attachments, and so on. *Chapter 2, Estimating the Effort*, of the Developing Applications with Oracle Team Productivity Center manual (`http://docs.oracle.com/middleware/1212/ jdev/TPCUG/working_tpc.htm`) explains the code review features in Oracle Team Productivity Center in detail.

Viewing build status

If you have connected Oracle Team Productivity Center to your build system, you can see the build status by navigating to **Team | Builds**. The **Builds** window shown in the main work area of JDeveloper will show your various builds and the status of each one of them.

Chat

JDeveloper also has a chat client built in. As mentioned earlier, only open this window while you have explicitly decided that you are in the Work or Recharge mode. Having the chat open will negate any attempt of establishing the Focus mode.

You find this feature under **Team | Chat**. The first time you connect to chat, you will be asked to define a connection to an external chat server. You can connect with any XMPP/Jabber talk client, for example, Google Talk or HipChat.

Once you are connected, you see your team members as well as buddies from this chat server with an icon showing the status just as with other chat clients.

Reading news

Oracle Team Productivity Center even includes a **News** panel in which you read an RSS directly within JDeveloper. As you might expect, this is an anti-productivity feature ensuring constant distraction and less productivity. Only activate this feature while you are in the Recharge mode (and even then, you recharge better by getting away from your screen).

Summary

You have installed Oracle Team Productivity Center and integrated it with the new Jira issue repository you will be using for the XDM project as well as the Git repository where you will be storing all your code.

Everybody on the team has been defined as users in Oracle Team Productivity Center, so it was easy to connect each development workstation to Jira and Git. Each developer can now work directly with your Jira work items from within JDeveloper and can easily get new code from Git and commit changes.

Back from the excellent kick-off pizza party last night, you and the rest of the XDM team are ready to start writing the first production code for DMC Solutions' brand-new enterprise application. Let's move on to the next chapter where we'll start creating the common code elements and templates for the application.

5
Preparing to Build

If you have children, you might be making gingerbread figures for Christmas. Your artistic children are likely to be handcrafting each figure individually — but you, as an efficiency-oriented adult, are probably using a cookie cutter to produce a whole batch of almost identical Santas.

When you need to create many similar objects efficiently, you use a template (similar to your cookie cutter). When you need to create dozens of task flows and hundreds of screens, all with some common elements, you use the ADF cookie cutters: task flow templates and page templates for the frontend view part and framework extension classes for the backend Business Component part.

Creating common workspaces

All of the templates and framework extension classes go into a common workspace. If you are using a modular architecture, this will be the Application Common Workspace. If you are using an enterprise architecture, you will be creating your enterprise common objects in the Enterprise Common Workspace and the application common objects in the Application Common Workspace based on the enterprise common objects.

 For simplicity, the examples in this chapter describe a modular architecture.

To create a common workspace, choose **File** | **New** | **Application** and then **ADF Fusion Web Application** and perform the following steps:

1. In step 1 of the wizard, name your workspace with your application's abbreviation as the prefix and set the **Application Package Prefix** field to your project's base package. For the XDM application in this book, we call the XdmCommon workspace and set the base package to com.dmcsol.xdm, as shown in the following screenshot:

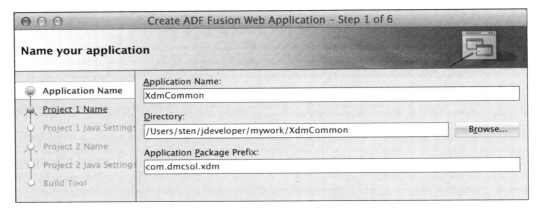

2. In step 2 of the wizard, name your model project CommonModel.

3. In step 3, you can leave the default package name (it is com.dmcsol.xdm.model in the example used in this book).

4. In step 4 of the wizard, name your user interface project CommonView.

5. In step 5, you can leave the default package name (it is com.dmcsol.xdm.view in the example used in this book).

6. Finally, in step 6, you are asked to choose a build environment. We will return to how to build the application in *Chapter 11, Packaging and Delivery*. For now, leave the default setting of **Use JDeveloper's default build tools**. Then, click on **Finish**.

You now have a `CommonModel` project for the Business Components that will be common to the whole application and a `CommonView` project for common user interface elements such as templates.

To create the last project in the Application Common Workspace (for your framework's extension classes), navigate to **File | New | Project**, and then choose **ADF Model Project**. Name your project `CommonCode` and set the default package to your application base package followed by `common` (for example, `com.dmcsol.xdm.common`). Then, click on **Finish** to create the project.

 You create the `CommonCode` project as an **ADF Model** project in order to include the ADF Business Component classes that you will be extending when creating the framework extension classes.

Working with task flow templates

You will be using bounded task flows to implement the use cases or user stories in your application, so you will probably be building quite a few of them. They are likely to share some common functionalities such as error handling.

Therefore, you should base all your bounded task flows on **task flow templates** that can contain all the common functionalities.

Always use task flow templates

Even if you don't know of any common functionality, you might want to use it in all your bounded task flows and base them on a template anyway. In that way, you have the possibility to add something later if you find a need for it during development.

Task flow templates can be nested within one another. If you are using the enterprise architecture described in *Chapter 3, Getting Organized*, you create an enterprise task flow template in your Enterprise Common Workspace and then create an application-specific task flow template in your Application Common Workspace based on the enterprise template. All the task flows in your subsystems are then based on the application common template, incorporating the elements from both Enterprise and Application Common Workspaces.

Creating a task flow template

In a modular architecture, your application task flow template goes into the CommonView project in the Application Common Workspace.

To create a task flow template, select the CommonView project, navigate to **File | New | From Gallery**, and then navigate to **Web Tier | JSF/Facelets | ADF Task Flow Template**. Give your template a name that includes the name of your application. For the example used in this book, use xdm-task-flow-template.xml, as shown in the following screenshot:

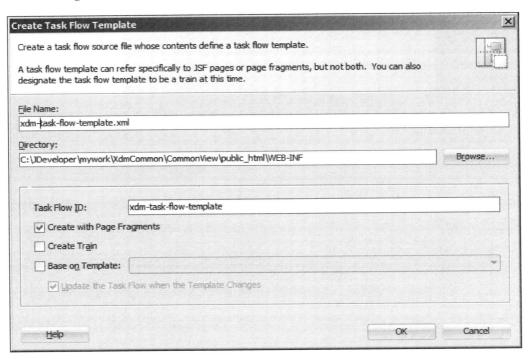

Note that the default directory is public_html\WEB-INF. The files placed here are not made accessible to a web browser, so the user cannot access your template directly.

You will normally have to check the checkbox, **Create with Page Fragments**. Do not choose **Create Train** for your task flow template.

> A **train** is a special type of task flow consisting of sequential steps similar to the JDeveloper wizards. You do not want to define your template as a train because that will turn all of the task flows based on the template into trains.

Remember that there are two types of ADF applications:

- Rich Internet Applications
- Classic web applications

Rich Internet Applications (RIA) use page fragments in dynamic regions on pages — this allows us to swap one page fragment out and another one in, making your ADF application feel like a desktop application.

If your users want a classic web application, where you navigate from one web page to another, your application should use pages instead of page fragments. In this case, do not check the **Create with Page Fragments** checkbox. Your template will then create task flows based on pages instead.

Beware of the browser's Back button

If your application uses page fragments, the entire application is typically going to consist of only one web page. The content of this page is then dynamically swapped as the user works with the application. In this case, the browser's **Back** button will not take you to the previous screen in the application, but to the last website you visited before you entered the application.

Contents of your task flow template

For your task flow template, consider the following elements:

- An exception handler
- The initializer and finalizer code

An exception handler

Each task flow can have one exception handler, the activity automatically invoked by the ADF framework in case of unhandled exceptions in your code. The exception handler is marked with a red exclamation mark. In a simple application, your exception handler will simply be a page showing a friendly message informing the user that something went wrong in the application. In a more sophisticated application, your exception handler can be a Router or Method Call component that examines the error, logs it, attempts to remedy it, and advises the user on how to proceed.

Always have an exception handler

You should always have an exception handler. If you don't and an exception occurs in your code, your users will see the ugly Java exception stack.

In the XDM application, the exception handler will simply be an error page. To create this page, drag a **View** activity onto the template from the **Components** window. Give it a name, for example, `exceptionPage`, right-click on the page, and navigate to **Mark Activity | Exception Handler**, as shown in the following screenshot:

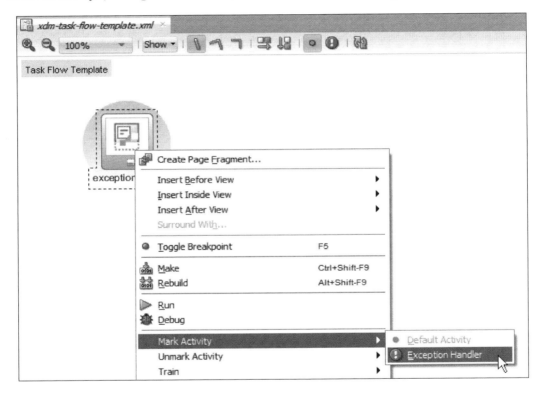

Note that by default, the first **View** activity in a task flow becomes **Default Activity** (the first thing to happen in the task flow). We do not want our exception handling to be the default for every task flow that we base on the template, so you should right-click on `exceptionPage` and navigate to **Unmark Activity | Default Activity**.

Initializers and finalizers

If you want to run a specific code before and after the execution of a task flow, write Java methods for doing what you want and then refer to these in the task flow (view the task flow in the **Overview** mode instead of the **Diagram** mode and choose the **General** subtab).

You might have to initialize the managed beans, or you might want some common logging code to be executed whenever you enter and exit the task flows. If you base your task flows on a task flow template, you have a place to add this code if you want.

Creating several levels of templates

If you are using the enterprise architecture described in *Chapter 3, Getting Organized*, or you know that your application will contain a number of specific subtypes of task flows, you can create a task flow template hierarchy. When creating task flows in the **Create Task Flow Template** dialog, you will base it on another task flow, check the **Base on Template** checkbox, and select the template on which you want to base your new template.

Your structure becomes easier to manage only if you define each element (for example, the exception handler) at one level. However, it is possible to define the exception handler in both the enterprise and application templates. Reasonably enough, in this case, the application exception handler takes precedence over the enterprise exception handler.

Using task flow templates

When you create a task flow based on a template, pay attention to the **Update the Task Flow when the Template Changes** checkbox. This one should always be checked because this *links* your task flow to the template. If this checkbox is not checked, your new task flow will receive a *copy* of the elements in the template, but later changes to the template will not affect the existing task flows. Normally, you want the changes made to your template to affect all the task flows based on the template, so be sure to check this checkbox.

Working with page templates

Just as you should never build a task flow that is not based on a task flow template, you should never build a page that is not based on a **page template**. Page templates are always referenced (never copied), so any change you make to a page template will affect all of the pages based on the template.

JDeveloper comes with two advanced templates called **Oracle Three Column Layout** and **Oracle Dynamic Tabs Shell**. You can examine these to see what an enterprise template might look like.

Creating a page template

To create a page template, select the CommonView project in your Application Common Workspace. Navigate to **File** | **New** | **From Gallery** (or press *Ctrl + N*) and then navigate to **Web Tier** | **JSF/Facelets** | **ADF Page Template**.

In step 1 of the **Create a Page Template** wizard, name your template that includes your application abbreviation (for example, XdmPageTemplate.jsf). Set **Document Type** to **Facelets** and add \WEB-INF to the end of the directory. Remember that the files in the WEB-INF subdirectory cannot be accessed directly from a browser. There is no need for your user to be able to snoop around in your page templates.

Use facelets

You should set **Document Type** to **Facelets** for both your template and your pages. Facelets documents tend to render slightly faster because they are optimized for JSF (whereas JSPX is backward compatible with JSP pages).

Your dialog should look something similar to the following screenshot:

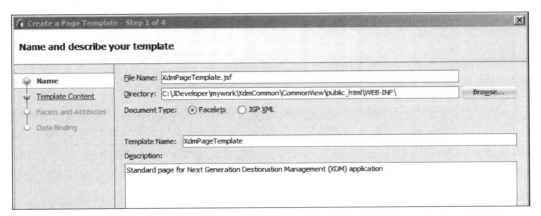

In step 2 of the page template wizard, you are given the following three options:

- **Blank Template**
- **Copy Existing Template**
- **Copy Quick Start Layout**

If you are already familiar with a JSF layout wizard with several projects under your belt, you might want to use the blank template to create your own layout from scratch, thus manually adding the layout components from the component palette.

However, if you are not already familiar with the JSF page layout, you can take a shortcut by selecting **Copy Quick Start Layout**. This will present you with a number of prebuilt layouts to choose from, as shown in the following screenshot:

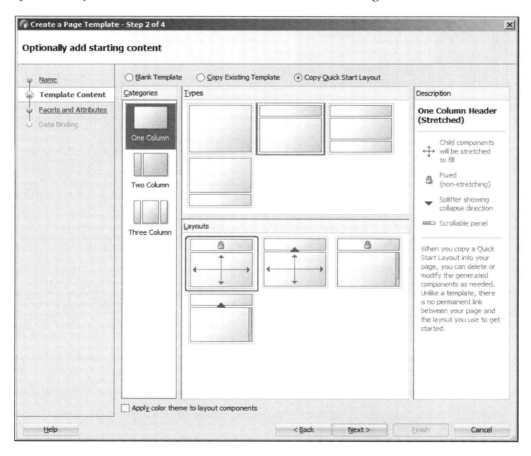

For the example used in this book, select the layout as shown in the preceding screenshot.

If you are using the enterprise architecture, you may want to produce one or more common enterprise page templates in your Enterprise Common Workspace. You then need to deploy your Enterprise Common View project as an ADF Library as described in the next section and reference that library in your Application Common View project. This will make your enterprise page templates appear under **Copy Existing Template** so that you can create an application-specific page template based on the enterprise template.

 This option only copies the template file itself. If you have an advanced template that uses managed beans, you will have to copy the class files and bean configurations into the project yourself.

As part of your requirements-gathering process, you should have produced sketches of your user interface so that you already know which layout you need. Start by selecting a category (one-, two-, or three-column layout) in the left-hand column. Then choose a type, and finally choose a layout. You should use a layout where your main area is stretchable (one with the crossed arrows symbol) in order to make the best use of the available browser area.

The layout you chose here is not fixed — it's simply a good starting point that you can further customize later as you gain experience with the JSF layout.

Using layout containers

In order to make the most of the available screen area, you should always start your layout with a stretchable container. In JDeveloper 11.1.1.7 and 12*c*, you should always start with **Panel Grid Layout**. Look at your desired layout, find the smallest area you need, and define the number of rows and columns in your grid layout accordingly. You can easily make the cells in the grid span across several rows or columns.

 One layout to rule them all

Panel Grid Layout is easy to use, flexible, and provides the best runtime performance. Always use this component if it is available in the version of JDeveloper that you use. If you are upgrading your application from an earlier version of JDeveloper where Panel Grid Layout was not available, consider simplifying your layouts by switching to Panel Grid Layout.

If you are working with an older version of JDeveloper without access to this powerful and universal layout component, you should start with a component that stretches itself and the child components inside it—normally, a **Panel Stretch Layout** or a **Panel Splitter** component. Inside this outer container, use other layout containers as necessary until you achieve the layout you wish. Components that stretch (for example, a **Table** component) should be placed inside a container that stretches its children, while components that do not stretch (for example, normal input fields) should be placed inside a layout component that stretches itself but does not stretch its children (for example, **Panel Group Layout** and **Panel Form Layout**).

Working with facets

In the JSF terminology, a **facet** is an area where components can be placed. Facets are used in two places:

- In the JSF layout components that JDeveloper offers
- In your template that must contain at least one facet

Defining template facets

When you are building a template, step 3 in the **Create a Page Template** wizard allows you to define your own facets, as shown in the following screenshot:

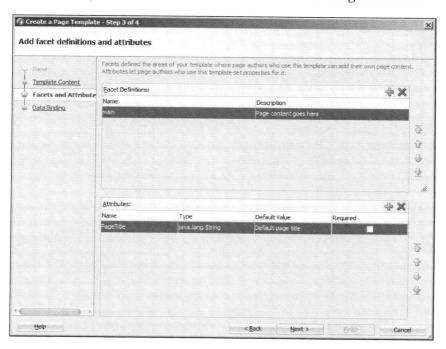

By clicking on the plus sign next to **Facet Definitions**, you can define the facets you wish to make available to the programmer using the template. In the preceding example, there is only one place for content—a facet called `main`. When you start placing content on your page template, you decide where the programmer using the template can place content by adding a `FacetRef` component. We will return to this a little later.

Understanding component facets

When you use a layout component from **Component Palette**, you will see that the layout components also have facets. These are defined as part of the component and are shown in both the **Structure** panel and the main window on the **Design** tab, as shown in the following screenshot:

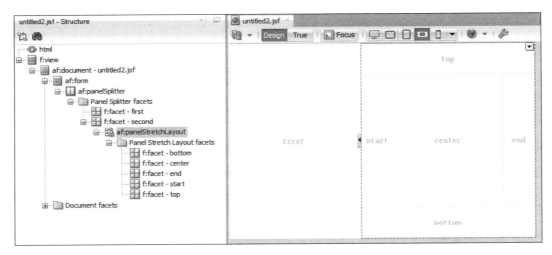

The preceding example page contains a **Panel Splitter** component. As you can see from the **Structure** Panel, the splitter contains two facets called `first` and `second`. In the second facet, another layout component (a **Panel Stretch Layout** component) has been dropped. This is a more complex component showing five facets where you can place contents (`top`, `start`, `center`, `end`, and `bottom`).

Defining template attributes

When defining a template, you can also define **template attributes**. This is done in the lower half of step 3 of the **Create a Page Template** dialog shown in the *Defining template facets* subsection. Template attributes are like parameters for the template — each page that uses the template can set different values. These are normally used to:

- Place page-specific information in template areas
- Create different layouts based on the same template

A page developer can only place his own components inside the defined facets when building a page based on a template. For example, if you want to display the name of the current page as part of a page header (which is not a facet but is defined in the template), you can use an attribute. For the example used in this book, create a single attribute called `PageTitle` of the type `java.lang.String`.

The other use of attributes is to define the parameters for the layout components that you use in the template. For example, you might use an expression language to define whether a specific accordion component is collapsed or expanded or to define the position of the splitter in a Panel Splitter component. To achieve this, you use an expression language reference to set a property value for a layout component.

Setting page template attributes

When you are creating a JSF page based on a template that uses attributes, you can set the attributes in the **Properties** window when the `af:pageTemplate` tag on the page is selected. If you can't select this from the **Design** view of the page, change to **Source** view or use the **Structure** window to find the `af:pageTemplate` element.

Adding content to the page template

When you are done with the page template wizard, your page template opens in the **Design** view.

If you chose the default layout illustrated previously, your page will contain a panel grid layout with two rows, each with one cell. In the **Structure** window, it looks similar to the following screenshot:

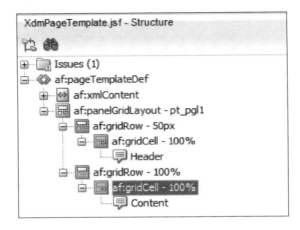

We will use the upper grid cell for a page header and the lower one for the page content. To build the header, place an OutputText component (from the **Text and Selection** section) in the upper grid cell. Set some Style attributes in the **Properties** window to make the text larger, and set the Value property to #{attrs.PageTitle}. This piece of expression language points to the PageTitle attribute that we had defined when creating the page template.

To define where the content will go, place a **Facet Definition** value (from the **Layout** section) in the lower grid cell. If you can't find it, just search for facet in the search box at the top of the **Components** window. When you drop on the page, you will be prompted for a facet name. As you have only defined one facet (main), there is only one possible selection. However, if your page template contains many facets, this is where you define which facet is used where on the page.

When programmers use the page template, they can only change the attributes (effectively setting the page header) and place their content inside the facet that you have just defined.

Framework extension classes

In addition to the page flow templates and page templates that are used for the frontend part of the application, you also need another kind of template for the backend Business Components.

The ADF framework uses eight base classes for Business Components. The four most important ones are as follows:

- `EntityImpl`: This class corresponds to one row of data and contains methods to create a row, set attribute values, and perform database operations.
- `ViewObjectImpl`: This class corresponds to the view object query. The methods in this class allow you to set a bind variable, modify the WHERE clause, and execute the query.
- `ViewRowImpl`: This class corresponds to the result set from a query and contains a collection of pointers to the actual data stored in the `EntityImpl` objects.
- `ApplicationModuleImpl`: This class is an instance of an application module; different users will have different instances. Methods in this class handle database transactions.

The ADF framework uses the following four additional classes internally:

- `EntityCache`: This class implements the cache for data retrieved from the database
- `EntityDefImpl`: This class is the factory for producing entity objects of a specific type
- `ViewDefImpl`: This class holds the definition of a view object
- `ApplicationModuleDefImpl`: This class holds the definition of an application module

These classes allow you to change the way ADF works at the fundamental level—you would not want to change this.

The following section will show how some of these classes are used and explain why you should create your own framework classes and how. A complete documentation of these classes can be found in the Javadoc that you can access from JDeveloper.

Understanding how Java classes are used in ADF

In *Chapter 1, The ADF Proof of Concept*, you saw that the Business Components that are central to your enterprise application are implemented in XML with an optional Java component. If you don't define your own Java component, the framework will simply create an instance of the standard Oracle-supplied Java class. This Java class then reads the XML definition of the object you have defined and does all the necessary work.

Every time you choose to generate a Java class for one of your Business Components (entity objects, view objects, or application modules), these will be based on the Oracle-supplied classes by default. If you look at the Java code you generate, for example, for an entity object, part of what you see is something like this:

```
...
import oracle.jbo.server.EntityImpl
...
Public class TasksImpl extends EntityImpl {
...
  public void remove() {
    super.remove();
  }
...
}
```

The keyword `extends` means that your `TasksImpl` class (implementing the `Tasks` entity object) is based on `EntityImpl`, that is, the `EntityImpl` class is the **superclass** of `TasksImpl`. The `import` statement defines the `EntityImpl` object, that is, the Oracle-supplied class, `oracle.jbo.server.EntityImpl`, in this case.

You will notice that some of the methods in this class contain a call to the corresponding method in the superclass. For example, `super.remove()` in the `remove()` method.

Some Java required

Have you ever seen an implementation of large enterprise applications such as Oracle E-Business Suite or SAP Business Suite that were not customized? Me neither.

Given the cost of customization and the pain involved when upgrading a heavily customized "standard" solution, why do organizations still do it?

They do it because it is impossible to build a standard system that will meet every need of the organization. Similarly, it is impossible for an Oracle Application Development Framework to directly meet every requirement in your enterprise application. That's why we have an option to create Java classes: to implement the specific functionality that is not built in the framework.

The place for framework extension classes

By default, when you generate a Java class for a Business Component, it will directly extend a class from the `oracle.jbo.server` package. You don't want this because you might want to change or extend the way the ADF framework does things.

If you want to change the way in which the data is stored in a single entity object, you can just change that one Java class. But, if you are making same kind of change to multiple objects, good programming practices dictate that you should make this change only once. This might be the case if you want all the entity objects to call a PL/SQL API package instead of accessing the table directly. In an object-oriented language, this change should be made in the superclass that your objects inherit from. However, if you inherit directly from the Oracle-supplied classes, you can't change the superclass without invalidating all the claims supported by Oracle.

That's why you need to place your own framework extension classes between the Oracle-supplied classes and your own implementations, as shown in the following screenshot:

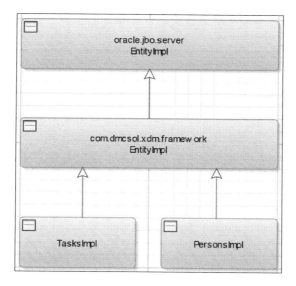

In this way, all of your own implementation classes inherit from a class under your own control. For example, your `TasksImpl` class will extend your own `com.dmcsol.xdm.framework.EntityImpl` class.

Multilayer framework extension

If you have decided to use the enterprise model, you will be creating two layers of framework extension classes: one that will be common to all ADF applications, thus extending the Oracle-supplied classes, and the other that will be specific framework extensions for each application, thus extending your own common extension class.

Creating framework extension classes

The concept of framework extension illustrates the beauty of object-oriented programming. You simply have to create an empty class extending the Oracle-supplied class. All of the methods from the Oracle-supplied superclass are automatically available and will be executed at runtime. When you decide that you need to implement a specific functionality in your framework classes, you simply need to add the relevant methods and they will automatically override the method from the superclass.

Your framework extension classes go into the `CommonCode` project in the Application Common Workspace. However, before you create these classes, you need to initialize the project for Business Components. To do this, right-click on the project, choose **Project Properties**, and then select **ADF Business Components**. Check the **Initialize Project for Business Components** checkbox and click on **OK**. This attaches the necessary libraries to the project.

Select the `CommonCode` project and press *Ctrl + N* (or *Command + N* on Mac) to bring up the **New Gallery** dialog. Navigate to **General | Java | Class**. Give your class the same name as the Oracle class you extend (for example, `EntityImpl`) and place it in your framework package in the `<company base>.<project>.framework` syntax, for example, `com.dmcsol.xdm.common.framework`. Extend the relevant Oracle class (for example, `oracle.jbo.server.EntityImpl`). Set **Access Modifiers** to **public** and uncheck all the checkboxes, as shown in the following screenshot:

Click on **OK** to create the class. It will be really simple, as shown in the following code:

```
package com.dmcsol.xdm.common.framework;

public class EntityImpl extends oracle.jbo.server.EntityImpl {
}
```

You don't have to add any content into this class right now. If you later find that you need to override a method (for example, the doDML() method that is called every time ADF issues an INSERT, UPDATE, or DELETE query to the database), right-click inside the class and navigate to **Source | Override Methods** from the context menu, as shown in the following screenshot:

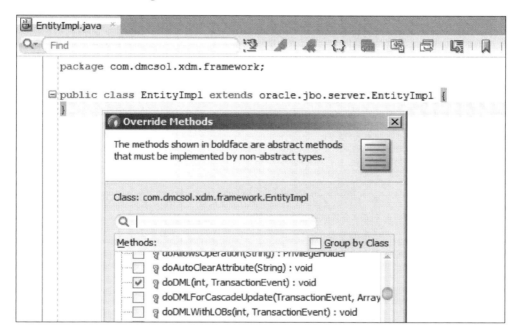

From the **Override Methods** dialog, you can check the checkboxes for the method you want to override. Repeat the preceding procedure for the remaining three ADF Business Component base classes so that you have your own version of the following classes:

- EntityImpl
- ViewObjectImpl
- ViewRowImpl
- ApplicationModuleImpl

Do not override `EntityCache`, `EntityDefImpl`, `ViewDefImpl`, and `ApplicationModuleDefImpl` unless you are very familiar with ADF and are sure that you understand the implications of changing them.

Using framework extension classes

Once you have created your own version of the four important classes, you must set up JDeveloper to use your classes instead of the Oracle-supplied classes. The easiest way to configure JDeveloper in order to use your own classes for all the projects is by navigating to **Tools | Preferences**, and then **Business Components | Base Classes**. In the dialog box, fill in the name of your own classes for the four important base classes as follows:

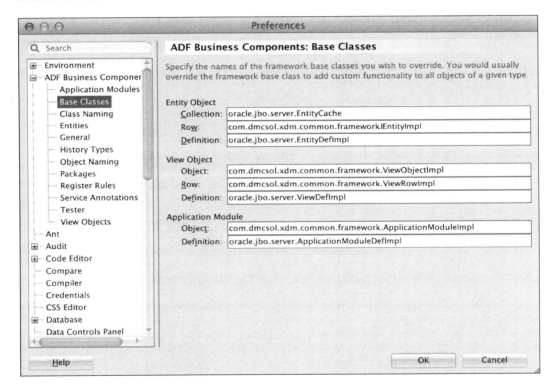

This will cause JDeveloper to always use your framework extension classes whenever you generate Java classes for an ADF Business Component.

If you are working on multiple projects, some of which use different framework extension classes, you can also define the base classes at the project level for your model project (under **Project Properties**).

If you have an existing Business Component that you want to "re-fit" from the standard Oracle class to your own framework extension class, you can choose the Java subtab for the component, click on the pencil icon to bring up the **Select Java Options** dialog, and click on the **Classes Extend** button to set the base class for your Business Component.

Packaging your common code

The output of the three projects in the common workspace needs to be packaged into ADF Libraries so that they can be made available to the developers working on the individual subsystems that your enterprise application will consist of.

To deploy a project to an ADF Library, select the project and press *Ctrl + N* to bring up the **New Gallery** dialog. Navigate to **General | Deployment Profiles** and select **ADF Library JAR File**. Give your ADF Library a name (use the project name prefixed with `adflib` and then the name of your project, for example, `adflibXdmCommonCode`) and click on **OK**. You don't need to make any selections in the **Edit ADF Library JAR Deployment Profile Properties** dialog — simply click on **OK** to finish creating your deployment profile.

Once you have a deployment profile, you can right-click on your project, choose **Deploy**, and then the name of your deployment profile. You only need to click on **Next** and then click on **Finish** to perform the actual deployment that creates the ADF Library file.

The ADF Library file is created in a new directory called `deploy` that will be created under your project (for example, `C:\JDeveloper\mywork\XdmCommonCode\CommonCode\deploy`). The file name is the same as the name of your deployment profile (for example, `adflibXdmCommonCode`) as shown in the following screenshot:

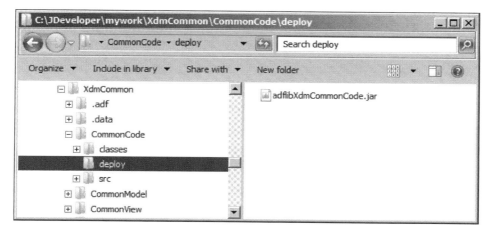

Keeping your ADF Libraries under control

It is a good idea to copy your ADF Libraries from the `deploy` directories of each project to one common library directory and import them into your version control system. In this way, the latest approved and tested libraries are available to all the developers on the project, while the teams working on the common workspaces are free to build, test, and commit code without disrupting work on other projects.

Summary

This was the final piece of preparation for building your enterprise application. Now you have the templates and framework classes that you need, all packaged nicely in ADF Libraries and ready for use. In the next chapter, we will test if it all works by rebuilding the XDM Proof of Concept functionality using all the correct enterprise methods, tools, and templates.

6

Building the Enterprise Application

Finally! We are back to real programming! With the infrastructure in place and our tools set up correctly, we're ready to start building our real enterprise application. In this chapter, you will be implementing two subsystems containing the two use cases we prototyped in the Proof of Concept in *Chapter 1*, *The ADF Proof of Concept*, and you will be collecting them into a completed enterprise application.

Decorate the project room

The room where your team is working should be decorated. Not with Christmas ornaments, but with something infinitely more useful: the data model. Even if you have not used JDeveloper to define your data model, you can use JDeveloper to create a database diagram.

Print out the entire data model for your system in a size large enough to be able to read every column in every table. Unless you work in the construction industry, you probably don't have a printer large enough to fit everything on one sheet—go to your local print shop or get out the scissors and scotch tape.

Structuring your code

Your enterprise application is going to consist of hundreds of objects: entity objects, view objects, application modules, task flows, page fragments, and many others. It is imperative that you keep everything in a logical structure. A good structure also allows you to partition work between the many people who will be working on your team, and ensures that everyone can find what they need.

Using workspaces

Remember from *Chapter 3, Getting Organized*, we divided all but the simplest applications into a number of workspaces. In recent versions, JDeveloper has unfortunately started using the Word application for what used to be called workspace. While it is correct that you need a workspace to build an application, the opposite is not true—you will have many workspaces that are not applications.

 If you look at the definition created in the filesystem, you will find that the extension for the workspace definition file is actually still .jws (which used to mean Java workspace). So, whenever you see JDeveloper use the word application, think of the workspace.

There is no need to try to keep your entire enterprise application in one JDeveloper application. Using ADF Libraries, it is easy to combine separate workspaces, and having a number of smaller development teams working on separate subsystems ensures proper modularity of your enterprise application.

The workspace hierarchy

Your workspaces will be arranged in a hierarchy, as described in *Chapter 3, Getting Organized*, and the individual workspaces at lower levels will use the workspaces at higher levels. In this chapter, we will use modular architecture, as shown in the following figure:

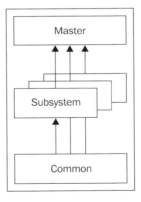

You already built the **Application Common Workspace** in *Chapter 5, Preparing to Build*. This workspace contains the **Common Model** project (still empty), the **Common View** project (with the page flow and page templates), and the **Common Code** project (containing your framework extension classes).

We will create some Business Components in the Common Model project in this chapter and build two subsystems and a master application. When we start customizing the application appearance by developing a custom skin in *Chapter 8, Changing the Appearance*, the stylesheet and other UI artifacts from this process will also go into the Common View project.

Creating a workspace

Whenever you need a new subsystem workspace, navigate to **File | New | Application | ADF Fusion Web Application**.

Name the workspace in accordance with your naming standards. If your company domain name is dmcsol.com and your project abbreviation is xdm (the next-generation destination management), all of your project code should be placed in subpackages under com.dmcsol.xdm. The code for your individual task flows go into subpackages named after the subsystem that the task flow implements. For example, you might consider the Task Overview and Edit use case (UC008) subsystem and place all of the code for this in a package named com.dmcsol.xdm.uc008. Refer to *Chapter 3, Getting Organized*, for more on package naming.

When you create a workspace of the **ADF Fusion Web Application** type, the JDeveloper wizard will automatically create two projects inside your workspace. By default, these are called Model and ViewController. As these project names are used in various configuration files, you should change the project names to reflect the subsystem you are implementing. For example, for the task management subsystem, you could choose TaskMgrModel and TaskMgrView.

The model project gets .model added to the package name, and the view project gets .view added for a total package name, for example, com.dmcsol.xdm.taskmgr.view. There is no need to change these subpackage names.

Separate names for separate tasks

It is important that you use separate package and project names for separate task flows. If you accidentally use the same name in two different task flows, you will experience mysterious errors once you combine them into an enterprise application. This is caused by the metadata and class-naming conflicts.

Working with ADF Libraries

ADF Libraries are built from projects inside workspaces, so each workspace will produce one or more ADF Libraries for other workspaces to use. This section suggests a procedure for working productively with ADF Libraries, but if you have another method that works, that's fine too.

> **Version control outside JDeveloper**
>
> As the ADF Libraries that you produced don't show up in the Application Navigator in JDeveloper, it is easiest to version control them outside JDeveloper. The Tortoise tools (TortoiseSVN and TortoiseGit) integrate with Windows Explorer when you right-click on the version control.

The ADF Library workflow

The ADF Library workflow is created in the following way:

1. The developer builds components in a workspace and performs his or her own testing.

2. When the developer is satisfied, he or she creates an ADF Library from within JDeveloper. He or she then goes outside JDeveloper, navigates to the `deploy` folder inside his or her project, and adds it to the source code repository.

3. The Build/Deployment Manager gets the entire workspace from the source code repository and copies the ADF Library to a common ADF Library folder in his or her local filesystem.

4. The Build/Development Manager works with the test team to test the ADF Library file. When satisfied, he or she commits the common library folder to the source code repository.

5. Developers check out the common library folder from the source code repository to a directory on their local filesystem. They decide on a common directory name that everybody uses (for example, `C:\JDeveloper\mywork\XdmLib`).

6. Developers create a filesystem connection to the common library folder on their local machine, as described in the following section.

Using ADF Libraries

Because ADF Libraries are simply JAR files, it is possible to just add them to your JDeveloper projects by navigating to **Project Properties | Libraries and Classpath | Add JAR/Directory**. If you use this method, you must add the individual JAR files, not just the directory.

However, you get a better overview of your ADF Libraries if you create a filesystem connection to the directory containing your JAR files. To do this, open the **Resources** window and click on the **New** button. Then, navigate to **IDE Connections | File System**, as shown in the following screenshot:

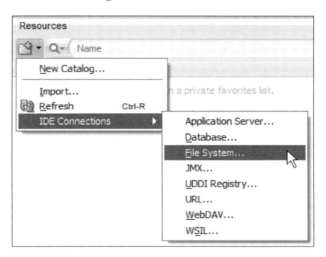

Give your connection a name (XdmLib for the sample project in this book) and point to your library directory (for example, C:\JDeveloper\XdmLib). The directory must exist before you can create the connection.

Now, the **Resources** window will show you the available libraries from all workspaces under the **IDE Connections** heading. To actually use a library in a project, you simply select a project in the **Applications** window, right-click on the individual library in the **Resources** window, and choose **Add to Project**. Alternatively, you can drag the library from the **Resources** window onto the project in the **Applications** window.

Building the Common Model

As discussed previously, in a modular architecture, your ADF application should be based on a Common Workspace with three common projects, which are as follows:

- Common Code
- Common View
- Common Model

In *Chapter 4, Productive Teamwork*, you created the first version of this workspace and put content into the Common Code and Common View projects — now, we'll put some content into the Common Model project.

This project will contain all of the entity objects used in the entire application, as well as the view objects used for common lists of values used throughout the application. The Common Model project can also include other view objects if you can identity the view objects that will be used in several places in the application.

Specialized view objects for each screen will go into the subsystem workspaces that we will build later in this chapter.

Use framework extension classes

If you did not set up JDeveloper to use your own framework extension classes when you built them in *Chapter 5, Preparing to Build*, please do so now. Navigate to **Tools | Preferences** and select **Base Classes** in **ADF Business Components**. For the four types of objects where you created your own classes (`EntityImpl`, `ViewObjectImpl`, `ViewRowImpl`, and `ApplicationModuleImpl`), change from `oracle.jbo.server` to the package name of your own classes (for example, `com.dmcsol.xdm.common.framework`). This tells JDeveloper that every ADF Business Object built now onwards should be based on your own classes.

Then, open the **Resource Palette** and find your shared ADF Libraries. Right-click on the **Common Code** library (for example, `adflibXdmCommonCode`) and choose **Add to Project**.

Entity objects

In an ADF application, you normally have one entity object for every table in your application. Since these entity objects can be re-used by many different view objects, it makes sense to develop them once in the Common Model project and then deploy them to all other parts of the application in the form of an ADF Library.

You can define the validation rules on your entity objects as well. The validation placed here will always be executed, no matter which view object uses the data.

Validation in the database

Remember that the only way to make sure that specific validation is always executed is to place it in the database. If your data might be changed by other systems not going through the ADF Business Components, critical data validation logic should be implemented in the database as well as in the entity object.

If your database contains foreign keys defining the relationship between tables, the **Business Components from Tables** wizard in JDeveloper will build all of your entity objects and associations. If you do not have foreign keys in the database, the wizard can only create the entity objects—you will have to add all the associations manually (navigate to **File** | **New** | **From Gallery** and then to **Business Tier** | **ADF Business Components** | **Association**).

As entity objects can't be tested in isolation, you should also generate default view objects (one for each entity object) and one application module. This allows you to test your entity objects through the **ADF Model Tester** built into JDeveloper. Your default view objects should be named with the suffix, DefaultVO, to make it clear that they are not intended for use in the application; similarly, your test application module should have the prefix, Test.

To create your entity objects, default view objects, and application module, perform the following steps:

1. Select the CommonModel project and press *Ctrl + N* (*cmd + N* on Mac) to bring up the **New Gallery**. Navigate to **Business Tier** | **ADF Business Components** | **Business Components from Tables**.

2. Create a connection to the database where your tables exist. Make sure you document your choice so that everybody uses the same connection name. For the example in this book, call your connection Xdm.

3. In the first step of the **Create Business Components From Tables** wizard, click on the **Query** button to find all your tables. Move them to the **Selected** box and click on **Next**.

4. In the second step of the wizard, move all the entity objects to the **Selected** column. This generates default view objects for all your entity objects.

5. Just click on **Next** in the third step of the wizard.

6. In the fourth step, deselect the **Add to Application Module** checkbox. We don't want the default application module from this wizard because it includes our view objects in every conceivable combination, and that's unnecessary here. Then, simply click on **Finish** to close the wizard and produce all the entity objects, associations, and default view objects.

7. In the **Applications** window, expand the model node and then the view node. Select the link node, press *Delete*, and confirm the deletion. This removes all the unnecessary view links that the wizard built for us.

8. Press *Ctrl + N* and navigate to **Business Tier | ADF Business Components | Application Module**. Name the application module TestXdmCommonModel and click on **Next**. In the second step, expand the tree in the left-hand box and add all the ...DefaultVO view objects. Then, click on **Finish** to close the wizard.

You need an application module in order to test your Common Model entity objects inside the Common Model project, but you don't want this application module showing up in the **Data Control** panel when somebody is using the Common Model library in a subsystem. To avoid this, set the **Library Private** property for the TestXdmCommonModel application module to **true**, as shown in the following screenshot:

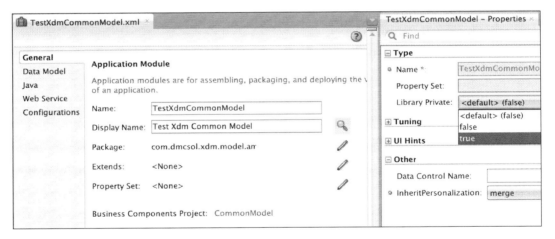

The preceding procedure creates one entity object for every table with the same name as the table, one default view object for every entity object (simply containing all the attributes in the entity object), and one application module containing all of your default view objects. The purpose of the default view objects and application module is only to allow you to test the entity objects using the ADF model tester — these default view objects should not be used in the production application.

Primary key generation

It is a good idea to let a database trigger create the primary key value for all tables with numeric keys—the sample XDM database script contains sequences and triggers that do this for the XDM_PERSONS, XDM_PROGRAMMES, and XDM_TASKS tables. While using trigger-supplied ID values like this, you need to tell the ADF framework to expect that the value for the ID columns will be changed when a record is created in the database. To do this, open each of the entity objects for these tables, choose the **Attributes** subtab in the left-hand side, select the ID attribute, and set the **Type** to **DBSequence**, as shown in the following screenshot:

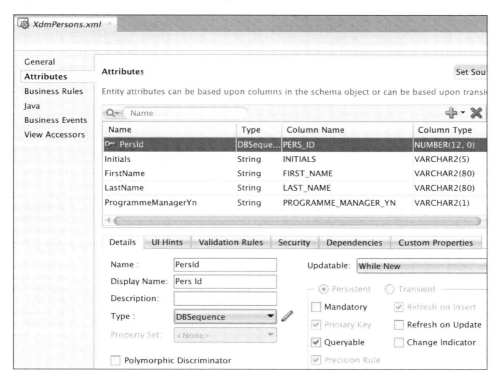

Business rules

The preceding procedure creates simple entity objects containing only a few simple business rules derived from the database ADF will automatically make an attribute mandatory if the column is mandatory in the database, and will add a length limitation based on the database column definition.

If your application needs any additional business rules, these should be added to the entity objects in the Common Model workspace. This is done on the **Overview** tab under the **Business Rules** subtab in each entity object.

Handling PL/SQL Business Rules

The business rules that you might have implemented as CHECK constraints in the database are not automatically picked up by JDeveloper — the tool has no way of translating PL/SQL database logic into ADF business rules. Functionally, it is enough to do the validation in the database, but you can provide the user with better error messages if you also implement the most important business rules in ADF.

User interface strings

You should also define the default labels used for the attributes of your entity objects here in the Common Model. This is done by selecting an attribute on the **Attributes** subtab, choosing the **UI Hints** tab below the attributes, and setting up the **Label** control hint. The label set here becomes the default label wherever the attribute is used.

The user interface strings defined under **Control Hints** are stored in a resource bundle — refer to *Appendix, Internationalization,* for more information about resource bundles and how to use them to translate your application.

Common View objects

Your application is almost certain to contain some view objects that can be shared among different task flows. The view objects used for drop-down list boxes and groups of radio buttons fall into this category; there might also be other common data objects used throughout the application. Therefore, it makes sense to place them in the Common Model.

When all of the entity objects and default view objects have been built, the team in charge of the Common Model must look through all the UI sketches for the entire application to determine which value list view objects are necessary.

In this chapter, we will only consider two use cases: UC008 Task Overview and Edit and UC104 Person Task Timeline. You can find the user interface sketches further along in the chapter. Looking at these sketches, the team responsible for the Common Model decides that they need to implement three value list view objects, which are as follows:

- ServiceLOV
- ProgrammeLOV
- ProgrammeManagerLOV

The procedure for creating these is as follows:

1. In the **CommonModel** project of the **XdmCommon** workspace, create a new view object called ServiceLOV (use the suffix LOV for view objects intended for lists of values). Place it in the lov subpackage under view to keep the LOVs separate from the other view objects, as shown in the following screenshot:

2. Choose to base it on the **Elements** entity object and deselect the **Updatable** checkbox. Deselecting this checkbox tells the ADF framework that it does not need to worry about the application changing the data in this view object, thus allowing ADF various performance optimizations.

3. Choose the ElemKey and Description attributes (an LOV view object should include the ID or key attribute as well as any identifying attributes that the user of the LOV view object might want to display).

4. In step 5, add an **Order By** clause (description).

5. Click on **Finish**.

6. Repeat steps 1-5 for ProgrammeLOV (based on XdmProgramme, the ProgId and Name attributes, and ordered by name).

7. Repeat steps 1-5 for `ProgrammeManagerLOV` (based on `XdmPersons`, the `PersId` and `Initials` attributes, but with a **Where** criteria limiting the LOV view object to those persons where `PROGRAMME_MANAGER_YN = 'Y'`, is ordered by `initials`).

8. Create a new application module called `XdmLovService`. In the data model step of the wizard, add the three ...`LOV` view objects.

Testing the Common Model

You would normally not create test cases for entity objects that simply perform the create, read, update, and delete operations and implement the default business rules. However, if you have defined additional business rules, you need to test these.

Depending on your testing strategy, you might decide to write unit tests to check your validation rules programmatically, or you might check them manually. Creating default view objects and a `TestXdmCommonModel` application module allows you to run the application module in the ADF Model Tester. Here, you can change data to verify any validation you have added to your entity objects.

Similarly, you need to test the value list view objects you created and added to the ...`LovService` application module either with unit test cases or manually. We'll discuss testing strategies in more detail in *Chapter 7, Testing Your Application*.

Exporting an ADF Library

Once you have defined and tested all of the entity objects and view objects you need, you need to deploy them to an ADF Library that can be included in other workspaces. To do this, perform the following steps:

1. Choose the **CommonModel** project in your Common Model workspace.

2. Navigate to **File | New** and then select **Deployment Profiles** (under **General**).

3. Choose **ADF Library JAR File**.

4. Give your deployment profile a name that includes the prefix, `adflib`, your project abbreviation, and **CommonModel**, for example, `afdlibXdmCommonModel`. This will be the name of the JAR file that this deployment profile will build.

5. In the **Edit ADF Library JAR Deployment Profile Properties** dialog, select
    Connections and choose **Connection Name Only**, as shown in the following
    screenshot. Selecting this radio button ensures that only the name of the
    database connection is deployed in the ADF Library. If we don't select this,
    all of the connection details, such as server, port, and database, will become
    part of our library, thus making it unusable in a different environment:

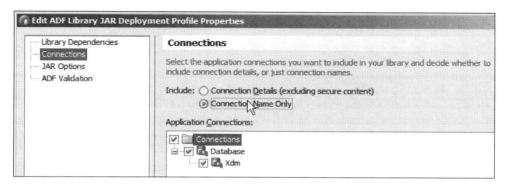

6. Click on **OK** a couple of times to close the wizard.

7. Right-click on your **CommonModel** project and navigate to **Deploy |
    XdmCommonModel**. Click on **Finish** to generate your ADF Library JAR file.

Now, your Common Model has been packaged up into a JAR file. You can find
it in the deploy subdirectory of your project. If you point to the **CommonModel**
project without clicking, you will see a pop up telling you the location of the project
definition file. The directory part of this will be something similar to `C:\JDeveloper\`
`mywork\XdmCommon\CommonModel`. If you go to that directory, you will find a deploy
subdirectory, and inside that, you will find your JAR file.

As described in the earlier section on working with ADF Libraries, you must
manually add this deploy directory to your source control system so that your
Build/Deployment manager can pick it up and have it tested and distributed.

For the purposes of the example in this chapter, you can take the role of a
Build/Deployment manager and copy your `afdlibXdmCommonModel.jar` file
from `C:\JDeveloper\mywork\XdmCommonModel\CommonModel\deploy` to
`C:\JDeveloper\XdmLib`.

Organizing the work

A climber on an expedition to Mount Everest doesn't just step out of his tent one morning in the base camp, pick up his rucksack, and head for the mountain. He starts out by carefully planning the stages of his climb, splitting the total task into smaller subtasks. This allows him to focus on task at hand and give his full concentration to climbing through the dangerous Khumbu Icefall at 18,000 feet, without worrying about the Hillary Step at 28,840 feet just below the summit.

While enterprise ADF development might lack the glory (and danger) of climbing Mount Everest, the idea of concentrating on the one task at hand still applies. Especially while you're new to ADF development, concentrate on one task to avoid being overwhelmed by the full complexity of the whole application. This is another reason to build your enterprise application as a number of separate subsystems.

Preconditions

Just like the Mount Everest climber, you need skills, tools, and favorable conditions. You have built up your skills by taking classes, reading books and blogs, doing exercises, and building smaller applications. You have set up your tools, as described in *Chapter 4, Productive Teamwork*. The last precondition is favorable conditions.

To the Himalayan climber, favorable conditions mean good, stable weather. To an ADF developer, favorable conditions mean good, stable user requirements. If you don't have good requirements, your odds of success decrease—just like those of a climber starting out in unsettled weather.

Good user requirements include the following aspects:

- A textual description of the purpose of the user case.

- A description of all the relevant business rules.

- Sketches of all screens, annotated with the requirements not obvious from the visual appearance. For example, if the UI sketch shows a drop-down list box, it must be annotated with a data source providing the values on the list.

Decorate the project room

Hang all the UI sketches you have on the walls of your project room, together with any graphical mockups showing colors and common elements. As you start building real screens, print these out and hang them on the wall, as well. Having these visual elements in front of everyone improves the consistency of your user interface.

Development tasks

If you are using a task tracking system, such as Jira, you are likely to be assigned a fairly coarse-grained task from the **Work Breakdown Structure** (**WBS**) the project manager has constructed—something similar to "Implement Task Overview and Edit."

Tasks at this level of granularity must be split into useful subtasks, so a developer can work on them in an efficient and effective manner. With Jira and many other task tracking solutions, you can split a task into subtasks.

Remember that you can identify one task as the **Active Work Item**—JDeveloper will automatically suggest that you link this item to each Subversion commit, allowing you to track code commits against tasks.

You will normally need the following subtasks:

- Create Business Components
- Implement Business Logic
- Create task flows
- Review task flow
- Create page fragments
- Implement UI logic
- Define UI test
- Review UI test

Use this list as a starting point, add additional subtasks if your specific use case calls for them, and remove any that are not relevant.

Creating Business Components

Your Common Model project will already contain all the entity objects as well as view objects for the value lists. While developing the subsystem, you only need to define the view objects specific to the subsystem and an application module.

Building view objects, view links, and the application module

To determine which view objects you need, look at the user interface sketch. Each separate block of data on your user interface sketch indicates a potential view object, and any blocks of data with a master-detail connection between them indicate a view link between the blocks.

One view object can be used in multiple places, even on separate tabs or pages if you want all data blocks to refer to the same record. For example, you only need one customer view object even if you display the customer name on one tab and the address information for that customer on another tab. On the other hand, if you have one tab showing customer names and another tab where the user can page through customer addresses independent of the selection on the first tab, you need two view objects.

Remember that you can combine data from multiple entity objects in one view object. This means that you don't need to create a view link just to retrieve a value from another table—you only need a view link if you want to display a master-detail relationship.

 In the famous SCOTT schema that has been delivered with almost all versions of the Oracle database, there is a table EMP with a foreign key pointing to the DEPT table. The EMP table contains the department number but not the department name. If you wish to show employees together with the department name, you base your view object on both the Emp and Dept entity objects, and select the necessary attributes from the Emp entity object and the department name (Dname) attribute from the Dept entity object. A view link is not necessary for this.

If your user interface includes value lists, you need to determine which view object can deliver the data you need (both the code/key and the value displayed to the user). Most value lists will be based on Common View objects that are used throughout the application. These should be part of the Common Model that you include in your subsystem workspace.

If you find that you need a value list that is not in the Common Model, consider if this value list is really unique to the task flow you are implementing. If you are sure this is the case, go ahead and build it in your subsystem workspace. However, if you are not sure that you'll be the only one ever using that value list, talk to the team in charge of the Common workspace to get your value list view object included in the Common Model for everyone to use.

Your view objects might also include named view criteria, bind variables, and so on.

When you are done building view objects, create an application module for your subsystem.

Implementing Business Logic

The team building the Common Model might already have implemented some Business Logic as **Business Rules** in the entity objects. The remaining Business Logic goes into your view objects and application module. How to program ADF Business Logic is outside the scope of this book—refer to *Chapter 4, Adding Business Logic*, of the book *Developing Web Applications with ADF Essentials, Sten E. Vesterli, Packt Publishing*, for some typical examples. An Internet search will also quickly uncover many ADF programming resources on the Oracle Technology Network and elsewhere.

Remember the database

Some Business Logic is better implemented as stored procedures in the database, especially if it involves processing many records. It is much faster to send an instruction to the database to do something to thousands of records than it is to retrieve all of them to the middle tier, process them, and send them back. If you are a Java programmer and are not familiar with the capabilities of the database, remember to talk to the database developers in the team to make sure the Business Logic is implemented in the right place.

Testing your Business Components

Once your view object is complete, test it through the ADF Model Tester. Depending on your test strategy, you might also want to write JUnit test cases that verify your view criteria; we'll discuss testing in detail in *Chapter 7, Testing Your Application*. Only write test cases for complicated stuff—you can trust the ADF framework to retrieve the data you specify.

Creating task flows

The frontend part of the application should be built with **bounded task flows**. You will most often be using **page fragments** in your task flows in order to give your application a modern, rich Internet application feel. However, it is also possible to use full pages in your task flows for a classic Web feel of page-by-page navigation.

A bounded task flow can contain screens, define transitions between them, and even include calls to code or other bounded task flows. It has well-defined entry and exit points, and you can pass parameters to the task flow. As a bounded task flow is a complete, self-contained piece of functionality, the same task flow can be used in several places in the application.

If you decide to use page fragments instead of whole pages, you can embed your task flow in a region on a page. When you are navigating through the task flow, only the content of the region changes – the contents of the page outside the region are not redrawn. This makes your ADF application look and feel like a desktop application instead of a series of web pages. If you decide to use full pages instead, you will be calling task flows but won't be able to embed them as regions in other pages.

You need to include a task flow view in your task flow for every screen your user requirements call for—but you might need additional views. It is common to create separate search pages for the user to select data before you display it; otherwise, there might be overview pages before you show all the details.

Don't create pages for warnings, confirmation messages, and other pop-up style information. In older web applications, you might be presented with a page telling you that the record you requested to be deleted has indeed been deleted. With ADF, you can easily create real pop-up dialogs; you don't need to create separate pages in order to present this type of information to the user.

Draw **Control Flow Cases** for all valid transitions from one page to another. If some transitions need to be possible from every page or from many pages, remember that there is a **Wildcard Control Flow Rule** that you can use to avoid cluttering up your task flow diagram with unnecessary arrows.

Finally, add any other elements you need, such as method calls (to execute code between pages), routers (to conditionally go from one page or another), calls to other task flows, and so on.

Reviewing the task flows

Once you have built all the task flows, have someone else review them. The reviewer should preferably be an expert user—if this is not possible, get another team member to perform this review.

Agile ADF programming

Modern Agile programming dispenses with some of the documentation that traditional software development uses. Instead, the programmers on the Agile team work closely together with real users to ensure that they deliver what the users want. Even if you're not using an Agile software development method, you can achieve some of its benefits by asking your users for feedback often.

The task flow diagrams are very visual, and you might believe it to be immediately understandable to an end user. However, don't just e-mail it to the user. Sit down with a user (or use a screen-sharing and voice-call tool, such as **Go To Meeting**) to present your page flow to the user. This allows you to explain any objects in the flow that are not obvious to a non-programmer (method calls, routers, and so on), as well as gather important feedback.

Of course, some of your task flows will consist of only one or two page fragments — in such cases, no review is necessary.

Creating the page fragments

With the page flow built and reviewed, you can start implementing the page fragments that make up the flow.

Before you start programming, talk to the other team members, stroll around the project room, and have a look at all the other pages and page fragments used in the application (you did decorate your project room, didn't you?). This allows you to identify what similar elements exist in the application and where you might be able to collaborate with another team member on a re-usable page fragment.

Implementing UI logic

By now, you have already implemented the application Business Logic in entity objects, view objects, application modules, or the database. However, you might still have a bit of programming to do if the ADF user interface components don't meet your requirements out of the box. This part of the application is the user interface logic and is implemented in separate Java classes that are then registered in the task flow as **Managed Beans**. How to program user interface logic is outside the scope of this book, but there is an introduction in *Chapter 4, Adding Business Logic*, of the book *Developing Web Applications with ADF Essentials, Sten E. Vesterli, Packt Publishing*.

Defining the UI test

The final development task is to define how to test what you've built. Some people advocate test-driven development, where the test is built before the code — however, this approach is not useful for user interface code. First, the user interface is likely to go through a number of iterations before settling in the final form and second, the automated UI test tools work best if you record a session from a running application.

If your project is using an automated user interface testing tool, such as Selenium, a tester should record the test cases as the final step in the development process. If you test the user interface manually, the tester needs to write a test script and check this document into your Subversion repository together with the code.

Reviewing the UI test

Irrespective of whether your test is automated or manual, someone else must review the test documentation.

For automated tests, this is simply a matter of having a tester run your script and possibly suggesting additional test cases (did you remember to test all of the error conditions? Your professional tester colleague will).

For manual tests, someone who does not know the task flow you are implementing must run your test. The developer who has been working on a task flow for days is very likely to accidentally skip some setup or intermediate steps because he is so familiar with the requirements and the solution.

Implementing the task management subsystem

The Task Overview and Edit use case (UC008) is part of the task management subsystem of the XDM application. In the example in this chapter, we will only build the UC008 use case from this subsystem. Later in this chapter, we will build the scheduling subsystem, again by implementing only one use case (Person Task Timeline, UC104). Finally, we will integrate these two subsystems together in a master application. In a real-life application, each subsystem will, of course, contain more than these simple one-screen use cases.

In this section, we will briefly go over the building of the Business Components and screens—you can refer back to *Chapter 1*, *The ADF Proof of Concept*, for more detailed descriptions.

Setting up a new workspace

Create a new **ADF Fusion Web Application** named after your subsystem using a package name under your project base package, followed by the subsystem abbreviation.

For UC008 in the XDM application, use the application name, `XdmTaskMgr`, and package name, `com.dmcsol.xdm.taskmgr`. Remember to rename the model and view projects to `TaskMgrModel` and `TaskMgrView`, respectively, as shown in the following screenshot. In step 6, leave the default **Use JDeveloper's default build tools** setting:

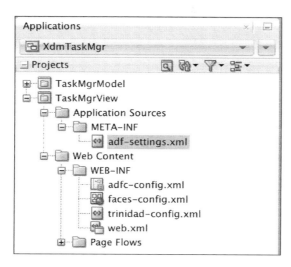

You have the option to select a build tool when you create a workspace, but you can also select and set up the build procedure later. We will return to choosing a build tool in *Chapter 11, Packaging and Delivery*.

Getting the libraries

The model project in this subsystem needs the Common Code library for the framework extension classes and the Common Model library for the entity objects. The view project in the subsystem needs the Common Model library for the value list view objects and the Common View library for the templates.

To include these ADF Libraries in the projects in your subsystem workspace, first select the `TaskMgrModel` project and open the `XdmLib` node in the **Resources** window. Right-click on **adflibXdmCommonCode** and choose **Add to Project**. In a similar way, add `adflibXdmCommonModel` to the `TaskMgrModel` project and add `adflibXdmCommonCode`, `adflibXdmCommonModel`, and `adflibXdmCommonView` to the `TaskMgrView` project.

Creating Business Components

You'll be getting the entity objects from the Common Model project—now, you just need to figure out which view objects you need. To determine this, look at the following screen design:

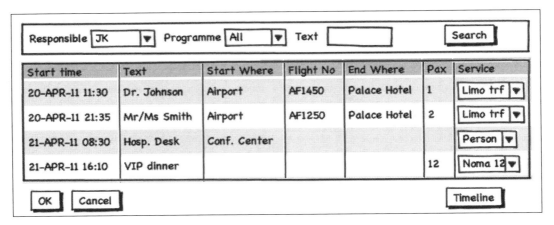

In this case, the screen design is just a mockup, a sketch showing the approximate layout and contents of the screen (and not all fields). In addition to the sketch, the following additional information is given. The full list of fields to be shown in the table includes the following:

- Start time and date (mandatory)
- Text (mandatory)
- Start location (mandatory)
- Flight no. (optional)
- End date and time (optional)
- End location (optional)
- No. of persons (optional)
- Service (mandatory)
- Comments (optional)

The list of services comes from the total catalog of elements. The list of persons responsible (filter criteria) shows only those persons marked as programme managers. The list of programmes (filter criteria) shows all programmes.

The screen has two boxes, which often indicate two view objects. However, a closer examination reveals that the top-most box doesn't really contain any data—it's just a search criteria. So, you need one view object showing tasks, including all the required columns.

Your screen shows three value lists, but the team in charge of the Common Model should already have built ...LOV view objects for these. If you find that you need value list view objects that you cannot find in the Common Model project, ask the Common Model team to add them so that they can be used across the entire application.

Starting work

If you are using the **Oracle Team Productivity Center (OTPC)**, as described in *Chapter 4*, *Productive Teamwork*, the first thing to do while starting work on a new part of the application is to set the active task. Go to the **Team Navigator** and run a query against your task repository. Find the task that specifies Business Components for the Task Overview and Edit use case, right-click on it, and choose **Make Active**. Also, open the task (listed at the top under the **Work Items** header in the **Team Navigator**) and change the status to **Start Progress** or something similar.

If you are not using OTPC, open your task management system and indicate that you have started working on it.

Building the main view object

To build the main view object, select the `TaskMgrModel` project in your subsystem workspace and press *Ctrl + N* to bring up the **New Gallery**. Navigate to **Business Tier | ADF Business Components | View Object**. The first time you work with the model project, you will be asked to define a database connection. Define a connection named `Xdm` pointing to the database schema where your XDM database objects can be found and set the **SQL Platform** to **Oracle** and the **Data Type Map** to **Java Extended for Oracle**. The procedure to create the main view object is as follows:

1. Give your view object a name (for example, `TaskVO`), leave **Data Source** at **Entity object**, and click on **Next**.

2. In step 2 of the wizard, all of the entity objects from the common model workspace should be available in the left-hand box.

No entity objects?

If you don't see any entity objects available, you might have forgotten to include the Common Model ADF Library in the model project of your subsystem workspace.

3. Select the `XdmTasks` entity object, as shown in the following screenshot:

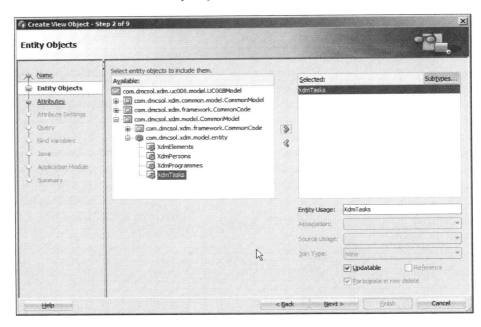

4. In step 3, select all the necessary attributes and refer to the list of attributes a couple of pages back, under the screen mockup. Your screen should look as follows:

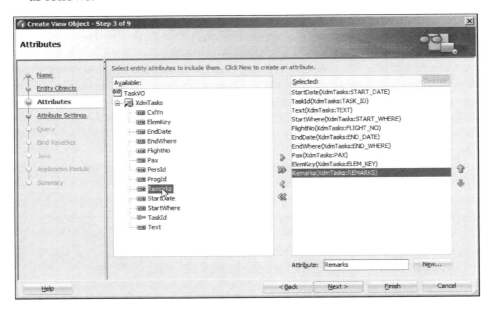

5. In step 5, select an **Order By** condition (`start_date`), and in step 6, define the bind variables like you did in *Chapter 1, The ADF Proof of Concept*, (`pResponsible`, `pProgramme`, and `pText`). Go back to step 5 of the wizard and add the following `Where` clause:

    ```
    (:pResponsible is null or PERS_ID = :pResponsible)
    and (:pProgramme is null or PROG_ID = :pProgramme)
    and (:pText is null or upper(TEXT) like '%' || upper(:pText) ||
    '%')
    ```

6. You can click on the **Test and Explain** button to validate your query and even execute it with specific bind variable values. Then, click on **Finish** to create the `TaskVO` view object.

7. As in *Chapter 1, The ADF Proof of Concept*, you must also define a list of values for the service (`ElemKey`). Open the newly created `TaskVO` view object, go to the **Attributes** subtab, and choose the `ElemKey` attribute. Create a new list of values with the `ServiceLOV` data source (from the `com.dmcsol.xdm.model.view.lov` package):

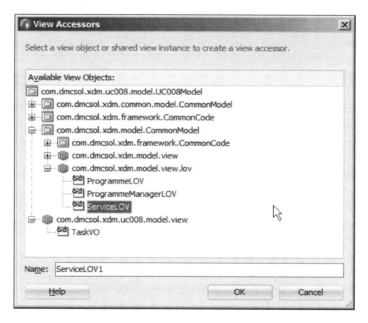

8. Use `ElemKey` as **List Attribute** and on the **UI Hints** tab, choose to display the `Description` attribute and uncheck the **Include No Selection** checkbox.

9. As in *Chapter 1, The ADF Proof of Concept*, set the format for the `StartDate` and `EndDate` attributes to **Simple Date** and the format mask to `dd-MMM-yy HH:mm` (on the **UI Hints** tab).

Building the application module

In order to make the `TaskVO` view object available to the UI developers, it must be part of an application module. Create an application module with the same name as the subsystem workspace, for example, `XdmTaskMgrService`, and include the `TaskVO` view object in the data model.

Testing your Business Components

To test your view object, right-click on the application module and choose **Run** to start the **ADF Model Tester** application to check that the correct data is shown, sorted as desired, and that you see value lists with the right values. In an enterprise project, you might decide to automate this testing with JUnit test cases. We'll get back to testing in *Chapter 7, Testing Your Application*.

 Don't worry if the filtering based on bind variables doesn't work in the ADF Model Tester. Some versions of JDeveloper 12*c* have a bug; this means that the bind variable values are not used in the query in the ADF Model Tester.

Checking in your code

When you have tested your Business Components, it's time to check them into your version control system. In this chapter, we use Git as an example.

To check your subsystem workspace into Git, navigate to **Team | Version Application | Git** to start the **Import to Git** wizard.

In step 2 of the wizard, remember to set the **Destination Directory** to a new directory with the same name as the workspace in your local Git repository folder (`C:\gitrepos\enterpriseadf\XdmUC008`). On Mac or Linux, the directory names are different, as shown in the following screenshot:

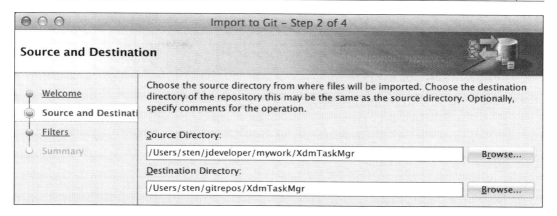

All of the objects in the **Applications** window should now have the little round "Git: No Change" marker on their icons, as shown in the following screenshot:

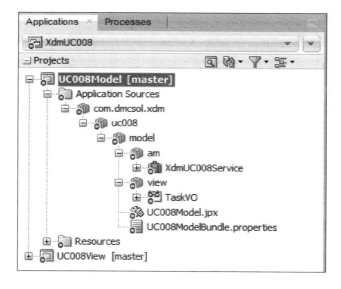

Finishing the tasks

Once the code is successfully checked in to your source code repository, mark the relevant subtask resolved. If you are using Oracle Team Productivity Center, you can click on the **Active Work Item** (at the top of the **Work Items** list in the **Team Navigator**) to open the issue within JDeveloper.

 Note that when using Git, as described here, your version control commit only goes into the local repository. We'll push our changes to the central repository later in the chapter.

Creating the task flow

With the Business Components complete, we can consider the task flow—which pages the user will see. In the Proof of Concept in *Chapter 1, The ADF Proof of Concept*, we illustrated the concept of task flows by creating a task flow containing both UC008 and UC104. As discussed in *Chapter 2, Estimating the Effort*, a real enterprise application uses many separate bounded task flows—a simple use case might have only one task flow, while a complex use case can have a dozen or more.

Our screen layout for this use case doesn't call for more than one screen—but we will still be building the bounded task flow to serve as a container for this use case. This gives us a uniform structure and the flexibility to add more screens later. In a web application, a use case will often include separate search screens, but in this case, the search capability is included directly on the page.

To build the task flow, select the `TaskMgrView` project in the `XdmTaskMgr` workspace, press *Ctrl + N*, and navigate to **Web Tier | JSF/Facelets | ADF Task Flow**. Give your task flow a name, for example, `task-overview-edit-flow`. Make sure that **Create as a Bounded Task Flow** is checked and also check **Base on Template**, as shown in the following screenshot. If the list of templates does not contain the template from the Common View workspace, you probably forgot to include the Common View library in the project:

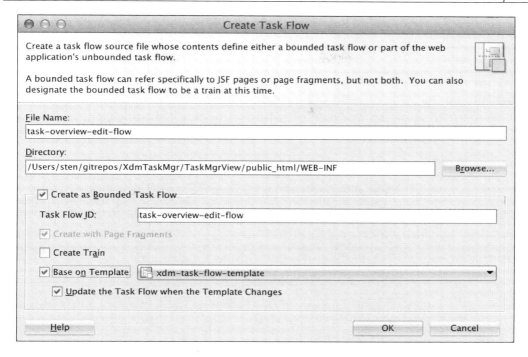

Task flows can either copy the content of the template or refer to it. This is controlled by the **Update the Task Flow when the Template Changes** checkbox. If your template contains common functionality, such as error handling, you should leave this checkbox checked.

In the task flow editor, simply drop in a single **View** component from the **Components** window and call it `taskOverviewEdit`. Mark it as the default activity.

Creating the page fragment

To create the tasks page fragment, double-click on the `taskOverviewEdit` icon in the page flow to call up the **Create ADF Page Fragment** dialog. Set **Document Type** to **Facelets**.

Most ADF applications are **Rich Internet Applications (RIA)** with only a few pages and a number of bounded task flows using page fragments. Your page or pages will be based on your page template, but your fragments are normally not based on a template.

Select **Copy Quick Start Layout** and a **One Column** layout with three sections, as shown in the following screenshot:

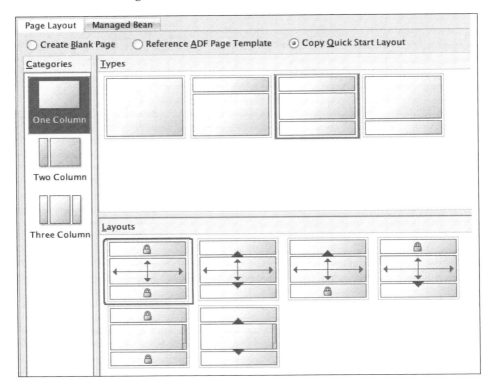

This matches our requirements for a search panel at the top, the results table in the middle, and the **OK/Cancel** buttons at the bottom. If you come to JDeveloper 12*c* or 11.1.1.7 from an earlier version, you will not have been using the powerful **Panel Grid Layout** component. In this case, use a quick start layout a number of times to get a feel of the modern, best practice in the ADF layout.

Data table

From the **Data Controls** panel in the left-hand side of the JDeveloper window, open the data control for your application module. Drag in the TasksVO1 view object instance and drop it onto the center of the page. In the popup menu, select **Table/List View | ADF Table**.

In the **Create Table** dialog, the ElemKey attribute should be shown with an **ADF Select One Choice** component—this is because a list of values has been defined for this attribute in the view object. Remove the TaskId column from the table. Allow the user to sort data in the table by checking the **Enable Sorting** checkbox.

The gridCell in the **Panel Grid Layout** component is set to stretch itself to fill all available space and will attempt to stretch the table, as well. However, the table will not stretch unless you set the **ColumnStretching** property. Click on the af:column with the Text header and make a note of its ID (in the **Property Inspector**, it will be something such as **c2**). Then, select the table (it's the easiest to do this in the **Structure Panel** in the lower-left corner) and set the ColumnStretching property to the ID of the Text column (**column:c2**).

Search panel

The next part to build is the search panel above the data table. Since the fields and buttons we will be using for the search panel do not work well if you try to stretch them, we need to place them into a container that does not stretch its contents.

The non-stretch adapter

To convert between the stretchable layout containers that make up the outer part of your layout and the non-stretchable components that show your data, you use a **Panel Group Layout**. This component is special in that it will stretch itself (so, it fits into a component that stretches its content), but it does not stretch its contents. You can consider the **Panel Group Layout** to be an adapter between stretchable and non-stretchable components.

Drag a **Panel Group Layout** in from the **Components** window (**Layout** section) and drop it onto the top cell of the panel grid layout. Set the **Layout** property to **Horizontal** to make the fields and buttons appear on the same line.

Then, build the search panel, like you did in *Chapter 1, The ADF Proof of Concept*, using the following steps:

1. Expand the **Operations** node under the TaskVO1 view object instance in the **Data Controls** panel. Open the **ExecuteWithParams** operation fully. Drag the pResponsible parameter onto the **Panel Group Layout** and drop it as a **Single Selection in ADF Select One Choice**. In the **Edit List Binding** dialog, leave **Base Data Source** at **variables** and add a new **List Data Source** based on ProgrammeManagerLOV1 in the XdmLovServiceDataControl. Choose **Initials** in the **Display Attribute** dropdown and set **"No Selection" Item to Blank Item (First of List)**. Then, click on **OK**. Use the **Property Inspector** to set the **Label** property to Responsible.

If you don't see the ...LOV data sources, maybe you forgot to include the **adflibXdmCommonModel** library in your view project.

2. Next, drag the `pProgramme` parameter onto **Panel Group Layout** next to the `pResponsible` dropdown as a **Single Selection** in **ADF Select One Choice**. Again, leave the **Base Data Source** unchanged and add a new **List Data Source** based on the `ProgrammeLOV1` view object instance. Use `ProgId` as **List Attribute** and set **Display Attribute** to `Name`. Set **"No Selection" Item** to **Blank Item (First of List)** and click on **OK**. Finally, set the **Label** property to `Programme`.

3. From the list of parameters, drop the `pName` parameter next to the `pProgramme` parameter. In the popup menu, select **Text | ADF Input Text w/ Label**. Set the **Label** property to `Text`.

4. Finally, drag the **ExecuteWithParams** operation (the node with the little green gearwheel icon) onto the page inside **Panel Group Layout** next to the three search criteria as **Operation** in **ADF Button**. This is a built-in operation that all view objects automatically offer—it executes a query on the view object it belongs to with the current value of the bind variables. In the **Property Inspector**, change the **Text** property to `Search`.

Translatable applications

For simplicity, we're defining user interface texts directly in the components here. If there is the slightest chance that your enterprise application will ever need to be translated into another language, you should use **Resource Bundles** to define your user interface texts. Refer to *Appendix, Internationalization*, for more on creating translatable applications.

Fixing the bindings

As we saw in *Chapter 1, The ADF Proof of Concept*, some versions of JDeveloper set an inappropriate default when you create a list binding for a parameter like we did for `pResponsible` and `pProgramme`.

To check and fix this, click on the **Bindings** tab at the bottom of the `taskOverviewEdit` window. You will see a graphical representation of the binding layer, as shown in the following section. Click on the hyperlink next to **Page Definition File** to go to that file. In the source of that file, search for instances of `SelectItemValueMode="ListObject"` (inside the `<list>` tags) and delete them. There are probably two of these; if you don't find any, it just means that you have a newer version of JDeveloper that sets the right value by default.

Running the page

As your task flow is now based on page fragments, it cannot be run directly — you need to create a test page to run it.

Press *Ctrl + N* and navigate to **Web Tier | JSF/Facelets | Page**. Give the page a name, such as TestTaskOverviewEdit.jsf. In the **Directory** field, add \testpages at the end in order to place your test page in a directory separate from the rest of the application. You can base this test page on your page template to get a feel of how your final page will look.

When the page opens in the editor, open the **Page Flows** node to see your task-edit-overview-flow page flow. Drag it onto the content facet on the page and drop it as a **Region**. You should see a ghosted (grayed-out) image of the first view in your task flow. Right-click on the page and choose **Run** to see your task flow and page fragment in action.

Regions and dynamic regions

There are two ways to include a page flow using page fragments in a page: as a **static region** (just called **Region** on the context menu), or as a **dynamic region**. If you use a static region, your page will always include exactly the bounded task flow you dropped onto the page. If you use a dynamic region, the ADF framework decides at runtime which task flow should be shown in the region. This allows you to swap out parts of the screen without the rest of the page refreshing to give your application a modern, rich Internet application feel.

Now, you should be able to filter data based on the drop-down lists and what you enter in the search field. Every time you click on the search button, the table should update to show only the records that satisfy the criteria.

OK and Cancel buttons

The final elements you need to put on the page are the OK and Cancel buttons at the bottom below the table (we won't be adding the "Timeline" button that was used as an illustration of page flow navigation in *Chapter 1, The ADF Proof of Concept*). These buttons will execute the **Commit** and **Rollback** actions that ADF provides at the application module level, as shown in the following screenshot:

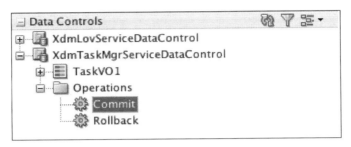

Before you drag these operations onto the page fragment, drop in a **Panel Group Layout** onto the bottom cell of the **Panel Grid Layout**. Set the **Layout** property to **Horizontal**.

Then, drag the **Commit** and **Rollback** operations from XdmTaskMgrServiceDataControl onto the **Panel Group Layout** as ADF buttons. For both buttons, change the **Text** property (to OK and Cancel) and clear the **Disabled** property to ensure that both buttons are always active.

You can now run the page again and check that your buttons are placed correctly. Make some changes to the data and click on **OK**. Use the **Database Navigator** panel or a database tool to verify that your changes are committed to the database.

Checking in your code

When you look at the Application Navigator, you will see that the nodes are marked with different version markers, not just the round, unmodified ones, as shown in the following screenshot:

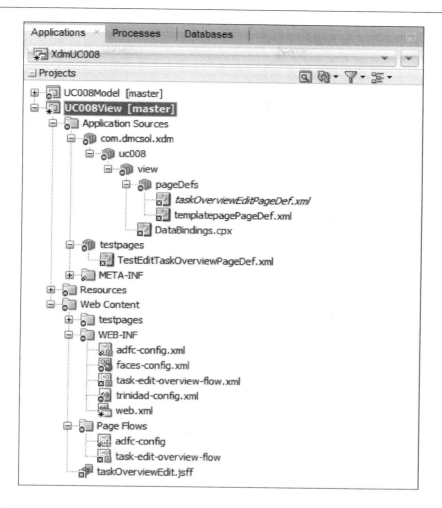

Some files are modified (marked with an *) and the others are new and as yet unversioned (marked with a **x**).

> **Versioning new files**
>
> Remember that you should have checked the **Automatically Add New Files on Commit Working Tree** checkbox (under **Tools | Preferences | Versioning | Git | General**). If you didn't do this, new files will not be automatically added to Git. There is a similar checkbox for Subversion.

If the **Pending Changes** panel is not shown (it appears below the main editing window by default), navigate to **Window | Team | Pending Changes (Git)**, as shown in the following screenshot:

You will see a number of modified files on the **Outgoing** tab and some new files on the **Candidates** tab. When you navigate to **Team | Git | Commit All** and leave the checkbox **Commit non-staged files** checkbox checked, both the files from **Outgoing** and **Candidates** are committed to your local Git repository.

When you have checked in the UI code, you can mark the task as complete (you did select an **Active Work Item**, didn't you?).

Remember that enterprise development also includes creating the following test scripts:

- A manual test script for a human to execute
- An automated test script using a tool such as Selenium

We'll discuss testing in more detail in the next chapter.

Deploying the task management subsystem

The final task is to deploy your subsystem as an ADF Library like you have done several times earlier. The library for a subsystem is created from the View project—JDeveloper automatically registers that the View project depends on the Model project, so all the necessary objects from the Model project are included automatically.

Select the `TaskMgrView` project and create a new **Deployment Profile** of the **ADF Library JAR File** type. Give the deployment profile a name that includes your project abbreviation and the subsystem name, for example, `adflibXdmTaskMgr`. In **Edit ADF Library JAR Deployment Profile Properties**, choose to deploy **Connection Name Only**, like we did previously for the Common Model library.

This setting ensures that the individual subsystems don't include connection details but will use the connection defined in the master application.

Then, right-click on the `TaskMgrView` project and deploy it to this profile.

Implementing the scheduling subsystem

As an example of another subsystem, we will implement the scheduling subsystem. For the purposes of this book, we will only be implementing the second use case you saw in *Chapter 1, The ADF Proof of Concept*, and the timeline showing the allocation of persons to tasks (UC104). In a real-life application, each subsystem contains multiple use cases.

Setting up a new workspace

Again, we set up a separate subsystem workspace by navigating to **File | New | Application** and then selecting **Applications** in **ADF Fusion Web Application**. Each subsystem is implemented in a separate workspace, thus allowing you to divide the application between many team members without the implementation of one subsystem getting in the way of another.

Give your workspace a name that starts with the abbreviation for your enterprise application, followed by the subsystem's name. For the scheduling subsystem in the XDM application, use `XdmSched` and the package name, `com.dmcsol.xdm.sched`. Name the model project `SchedModel` and the view/controller project `SchedView`. Leave the default setting for the build tool.

Getting the libraries

Select the `SchedModel` project and add the `adflibXdmCommonCode` and `adflibXdmCommonModel` ADF Libraries. Then, select the `SchedView` project and add `adflibXdmCommonCode`, `adflibXdmCommonModel`, and `adflibXdmCommonView`.

Creating Business Components

To determine the view objects you need, you look at the screen for the person task timeline, as shown in the following screenshot:

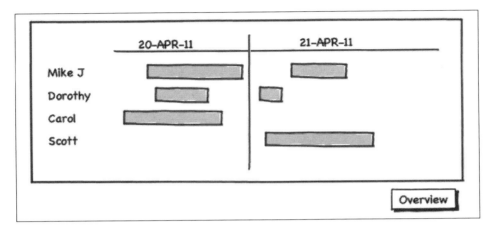

It's not immediately obvious which view objects we need for a component like this. One useful way of looking at the data is to think of **iterators** — what are the data sets that we must be looping through in order to build the screen.

For the preceding screen, it is clear that we must be looping over persons as we go down the left-hand column. That means we'll need a `Person` view object. Additionally, we must be looping over tasks as we go across to build up the sequence of tasks for each person. Therefore, we need a `Task` view object, as well.

Building the persons' view object

We can see that we'll need a view object showing persons — just the first and last name is necessary, and since we won't be changing data from this screen, the view object can be read-only.

Tell the framework what you know

When you know that you will not have to update data through a view object, tell the ADF framework by deselecting the **Updatable** checkbox. The more information you give ADF, the better it can manage performance for you.

Right-click on the `SchedModel` project and navigate to **New | View Object**. Define a database connection, `Xdm`, as you did for the task management subsystem. Give a name, such as `PersonVO`, and leave **Data Source** at **Entity object**.

Add the XdmPersons entity object and deselect the **Updatable** checkbox. Add the FirstName and LastName attributes (the PersonId is automatically included) and order by last_name, first_name.

Building the tasks view object

Create another view object and give it the name TaskVO. Base it on the XdmTasks entity object and again deselect **Updatable**. You just need the PersId, StartDate, and EndDate attributes (the TaskId is automatically included). Add a Where clause so that the view object will only show tasks with both a start and an end date using the following code:

```
start_date is not null and end_date is not null
```

Building the master-detail link

As tasks and persons are related, you also need to define the relationship in the form of a view link. Right-click on the **SchedModel** project and navigate to **New | View Link**. Give your view link the name PersonTaskLink.

In step 2 of the wizard, expand the PersonVO node on the left-hand side and choose the PersId attribute on the left-hand side of the link. On the right-hand side, expand the TaskVO node and again choose PersId, this time on the right-hand side of the link. Then, click on **Add**, **Next**, and **Finish**.

Building the MinMaxDate view object

As you might remember from *Chapter 1, The ADF Proof of Concept*, the **Gantt** chart component doesn't automatically scale to the time data it presents, so you have to set the **startTime** and **endTime** attributes. To retrieve these values, we will create an SQL Query view object.

Create a view object, give it the name MinMaxDateVO and set the **Data Source** to **SQL Query**. In step 2, enter the following query:

```
Select min(start_date) - 1 as min_start_date
,      max(end_date) + 1 as max_end_date
from   xdm_tasks
```

Click on **Next** several times and then on **Finish**. This creates a view object with one row containing a MinStartDate attribute one day before the earliest start date in the table, and a MaxEndDate attribute one day after the latest end date. You will receive a message about the view object having no key attribute. That's OK, since the view object will only ever contain one row—you don't have to define a key attribute.

As the Gantt chart component requires the start and end dates to be instances of `java.util.Date` (and not the default `java.sql.Date`), we need to create a Java class for this view object to perform this conversion. Choose the **Java** subtab in the view object and click on the pencil icon to generate a Java class for this view object. Check the **Generate View Row Class** checkbox and check **Include accessors**, as shown in the following screenshot:

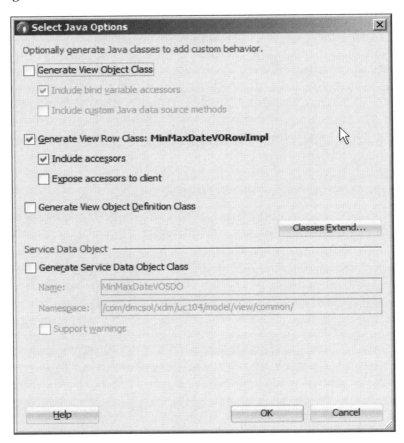

When you click on **OK**, the `MinMaxDateVORowImpl.java` class is created. Open this class and change the `getMinStartDate()` and `getMaxEndDate()` methods to look like the following code:

```
...
/**
 * Gets the attribute value for the calculated attribute
```

```
 * MinStartDate.
 * @return the MinStartDate
 */
public java.util.Date getMinStartDate() {
  return (java.util.Date)getAttributeInternal(MINSTARTDATE);
}
...
/**
 * Gets the attribute value for the calculated attribute
 * MaxEndDate.
 * @return the MaxEndDate
 */
public java.util.Date getMaxEndDate() {
  return (java.util.Date)getAttributeInternal(MAXENDDATE);
}
...
```

In the preceding code, the signature of these two methods has been changed to return a `java.util.Date` instead of the default `java.sql.Date`, and a class cast has been added to convert the `java.sql.Date` attribute value to `java.util.Date`.

Building the application module

Create an application module called `XdmSchedService` to collect the data model for the timeline screen.

In step 2 of the wizard, first select the `PersonVO` view object on the left-hand side. Correct the **New View Instance** field to `Person` and click on the **>** button to add a view object instance to the application module. Then, select the new `Person` view instance on the right-hand side and the node `TaskVO via PersonTaskLink` on the left-hand side. In the **New View Instance** field, change the value to `PersonTaskVO` and click on the **>** button to create a new view instance as a child of `Person`. Remember that you need to point to `TaskVO` via a link to get a detailed view—if you just choose the `TaskVO` without using the link, there would be no relationship between persons and tasks, and the Gantt chart component wouldn't work. Also, add the `MinMaxDateVO` view object and then click on **Finish** to close the wizard.

Testing your Business Components

To test your application module, you can right-click on the XdmSchedService application module node in the Application Navigator and choose **Run** from the context menu. In the ADF Model Tester, double-click on the view link to see the master and detail records together as shown in the following screenshot:

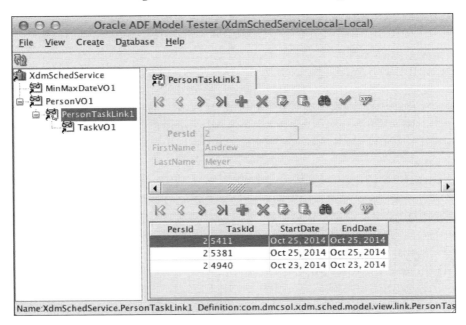

Finishing the tasks

The final step after your own test is, as always, to check the code into your source code repository. Since this is a new subsystem workspace, you'll have navigate to **Team | Version Application** and run the import wizard. Remember to create a new destination directory for this workspace in your version control system. Then, mark the corresponding task as resolved.

Building the task flow

Even though the UC104 person task timeline uses only one screen, you should still create a one-page bounded task flow for it.

Indicate that you have started on the task; go to the SchedView project in the XdmSched workspace, and create a new ADF task flow. Give it a name, for example, person-timeline-flow. The task flow should be based on xdm-task-flow-template.

In the task flow editor, simple drop in a single **View** component from the **Component Palette** and call it `personTimeline`. Mark it as the default activity.

Then, check in your code and mark this task as complete.

Building the page

To create the scheduled tasks page fragment, double-click on the `personTimeline` in the task flow. Again, use a quick start layout, this time **One Column** without a header or footer stretched, as shown in the following screenshot:

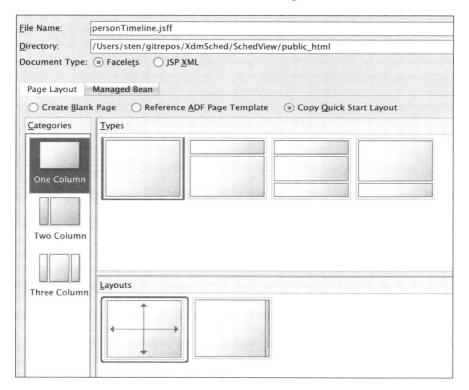

Adding a Gantt chart component

As you might remember from *Chapter 1, The ADF Proof of Concept*, the component that implements the graphic representation of tasks assigned to persons is a Gantt chart of the type scheduling.

To create the page, open the `XdmSchedServiceDataControl` node, drag the `PersonsVO1` view instance onto the **center** facet. In the pop-up menu, choose **Gantt | Scheduling**. The **Create Scheduling Gantt** dialog appears, as shown in the following screenshot:

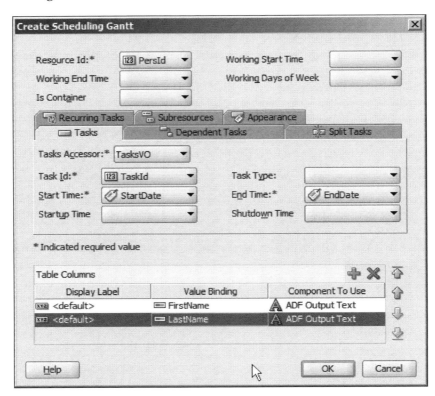

Set the fields in this dialog as follows:

- **Resource Id**: `PersId`
- **Tasks Accessor**: `Task`
- **Task Id**: `TaskId`
- **Start Time**: `StartDate`
- **End Time**: `EndDate`

Under **Table Columns**, remove the extra `PersId` column, leaving only the **FirstName** and **LastName**. Then, click on **OK** to see a graphical representation of a scheduling Gantt chart.

Defining the start and end time

The `MinStartDate` and `MaxEndDate` attributes can be found in the **Data Control Panel** under the `MinMaxDate` view instance, but you cannot simply drag them onto the attribute we need. We'll have to create a binding manually. To do this, change to the **Bindings** tab, as shown in the following screenshot:

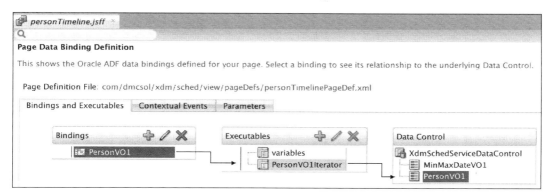

Click on the plus sign next to **Bindings** and choose to create an **attributeValues** binding. In the **Create Attribute Binding** dialog, click on the plus sign to create a new **Data Source** and select the `MinMaxDateVO1` view object instance. Then, select the `MinStartDate` attribute, as shown in the following screenshot:

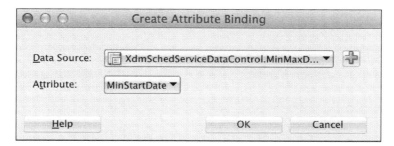

Add another **attributeValues binding** with `MinMaxDate` as **Data Source** and `MaxEndDate` as **Attribute**.

With the bindings for the start and end date created, click on the **Design** tab to return to the person timeline page fragment and select the `dvt:schedulingGantt` component in the **Structure** window. Then, click on the little gearwheel next to the **StartTime** attribute and choose the expression builder. Open **ADF Bindings** and then the **bindings** node. Select the **MinStartDate** attribute and then **inputValue**, as shown in the following screenshot:

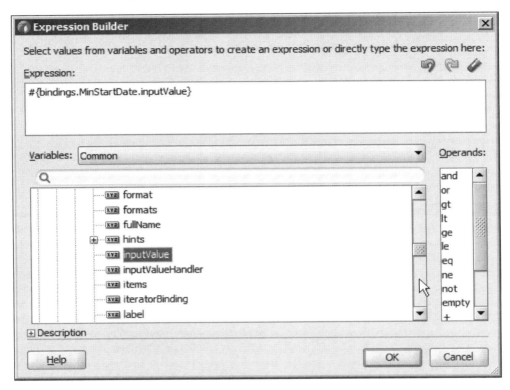

Set the **EndTime** property to `#{bindings.MaxEndDate.inputValue}` in a similar way as to `StartDate` in the preceding paragraph.

At runtime, the Gantt chart component will retrieve the start and end dates from the binding, which connects the component to the `MinMaxDate` view object.

Running the page

Just like the Task Overview and Edit task flow, this task flow is based on page fragments and cannot be run directly. Create a new page in the view project, call it `TestPersonTimeline`, and place it in the `testpages` subdirectory of `public_html`.

When the page opens in the editor, drop the `person-timeline-flow` page flow onto the content facet on the page as a region. You can then right-click on the page and choose **Run** to see your task flow and page fragment in action.

Checking in your code

If you wish, you can call up the **Pending Changes (Git)** window before committing by navigating to **Window | Team | Pending Changes (Git)**. This will show you the new and changed files.

Navigate to **Team | Git | Commit All** to commit all of the new and changed files to your local repository. If you have the **Pending Changes** window open, you should see all of the files removed from this window after you commit.

Now, you can mark the task complete, and all that remains is to write a test script.

Deploying your scheduling subsystem

As you did for the task management subsystem, you need to deploy the scheduling subsystem as an ADF Library, this time called `adflibXdmSched`. Remember to choose **Connection Name Only** when defining the ADF Library deployment profile.

Building the master application

In this chapter, we have built two very small subsystems and deployed them as ADF Libraries—now, we will create the master application that brings the subsystems together to the final application. A real-life enterprise application will have a number of subsystems, and these will be much larger, but the same principle applies.

In addition to the task flows from the subsystems, the master application will contain the following aspects:

- The master application page
- A dynamic region for the task flows
- A menu for selecting task flows
- A bit of user interface code to tie everything together

Setting up the master workspace

Create a new application workspace of the **Custom Application** type, name it XdmMaster, and assign an application package prefix of com.dmcsol.xdm. Also, name the project XdmMaster and include the following technologies:

- **ADF Business Components**
- **ADF Faces**
- **HTML and CSS**

JDeveloper will automatically add a number of other technologies that these depend on.

When you have created the application workspace, right-click on the **XdmMaster** project, choose **Project Properties** in **Java EE Application**, and shorten the content of the **Java EE Web Application Name** and **Java EE Web Context Root** fields to just Xdm.

Getting the libraries

As described in the section on the ADF Library workflow at the beginning of this chapter, the Build/Deployment manager collects the subsystem workspaces, has them tested, and releases them for use. For the purposes of the example in this chapter, take the role of the Build/Deployment manager and copy C:\JDeveloper\ mywork\XdmTaskMgr\TaskMgrView\deploy\adflibXdmTaskMgr.jar to your ADF Library directory (for example, C:\gitrepos\enterpriseadf\XdmLib). Also, copy C:\JDeveloper\mywork\XdmSched\SchedView\deploy\adflibXdmSched.jar to this directory.

You should now have five ADF Libraries showing in your **Resources** palette under **XdmLib**, as shown in the following screenshot:

Add them all to the `XdmMaster` project in the `XdmMaster` workspace.

Now, open the **Application Resources** heading in the **Application Navigator**. You will see that it contains a database connection called `Xdm`, but it is marked with a red **x**, as shown in the following screenshot:

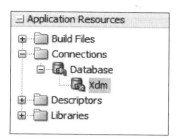

This is because the ADF Libraries you have added contain an XDM connection, but you only included the name while creating the ADF Library. Here, in the master application, you must define the connection properties. You do this by right-clicking on the connection, choosing **Properties**, and filling in the dialog box with the necessary connection information.

Creating the master page

An ADF enterprise application will contain many bounded task flows, each containing many page fragments—but it will have few pages, possibly only one. You need one page for every direct access point your application needs—if you want three different entry points to the application with three different URLs, you need three pages.

In the example application that we are building in this chapter, we will create only one page. Give this page the name `Xdm`, choose **Facelets**, and choose to base it on `XdmPageTemplate`.

With the new page selected, go to the **Structure** window and expand the structure until you see the `af:pageTemplate` node. Among the properties in the **Properties** window, you should see the **pageTitle** variable that you defined in the page template. Set the value to `Next Generation Destination Management`, as shown in the following screenshot:

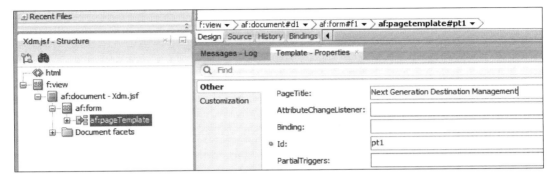

Creating the layout

Drop a **Panel Grid Layout** component on the `main` facet of the page. We need just one column and two rows: one row for the menu and one for the page content. You don't need to change any of the settings in the second step of the **Create Panel Grid Layout** wizard.

Adding the menu

To build the menu, first drop a **Menu Bar** component on the top cell (from the **Menus and Toolbars** section). Then, drop a **Menu** component on the menu bar by setting the **Text** property to `Tasks`. Finally, drop two **Menu Item** components onto the `Tasks` menu by setting the **Text** property to `Overview/Edit` and `Timeline`, respectively.

Creating a dynamic region

When you use bounded task flows on pages, they live inside **regions**. A region can be static, always displaying the same task flow; we used that for the test pages in the subsystems. A region can also be dynamic—this means that the region content is determined by an expression that is evaluated at runtime. By changing the value of the expression, you can make a dynamic region show different task flows.

To create a dynamic region on the master application page, open the **Resources** window and then the `adflibXdmTaskMgr` library. Expand the **ADF Task Flows** node and drag the `task-edit-overview-flow` onto the lower cell of the **Panel Grid Layout** on the page and drop it as a **Dynamic Region**, as shown in the following screenshot:

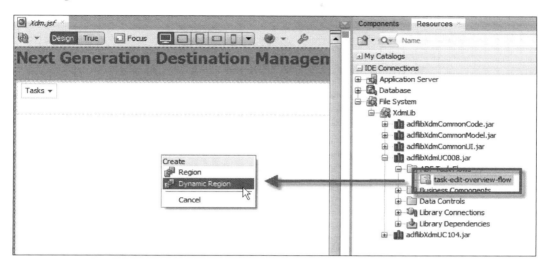

You will be prompted to select or create a managed bean that will provide the URL to the task flow to be displayed in the dynamic region. Click on the plus sign to create a new managed bean and fill in the **Create Managed Bean** dialog, as shown in the following screenshot:

Click on **OK** twice to create the bean and then select it. You can also just click on **OK** in the **Edit Task Flow Binding** dialog — if your task flow had taken parameters, this dialog would be where you'd define values for these parameters.

The preceding steps will execute the following four tasks:

- Create a new Java class with the package and name you specified
- Define the Java class as a managed bean in the unbounded task flow (in the `adfc-config.xml` file)
- Create a task flow binding in the data bindings for the page (`XdmPageDef.xml`)
- Set the **Value** attribute of the dynamic region to point to the task flow binding

Managed beans

Managed beans are Java classes that are instantiated by the JSF framework as needed. JSF enforces separation between user interface components and user interface logic — the JSF page contains the components, and the managed beans contain the user interface logic.

Understanding the dynamic region

If you run the page now, you'll see the Task Overview and Edit task flow. Let's follow the execution flow to understand how these pieces fit together.

1. Whenever the ADF framework has to show the page containing the dynamic region, it will execute the task flow binding indicated by the **Value** attribute of the dynamic region component. In the XDM example, this value is `#{bindings.dynamicRegion1.regionModel}`.

2. If you click on the **Bindings** tab on the `Xdm.jsf` page, you will see the task flow binding called `dynamicRegion1`. If you select this binding and look in the **Properties** window, you can read the `taskFlowId` attribute to see where the task flow for the binding comes from. In the XDM example, this is `${viewScope.PageSwitcherBean.dynamicTaskFlowId}`.

3. This is a reference to a managed bean defined on the unbounded task flow. If you open the `adfc-config.xml` file, go to the **Overview** tab, and then the **Managed Beans** subtab, you will find a bean with a scope of **View** and the name `PageSwitcherBean`. On this screen, you can also see the actual class implementing the managed bean. In the XDM example, this is `com.dmcsol.xdm.beans.PageSwitcher`.

4. If you open this class, you will see that it has a `getDynamicTaskFlowId` method corresponding to the binding you found in step 2 earlier. Whatever this method returns is used to look up the task flow to be displayed in the dynamic region.

Additional code for task flow switching

To switch between different task flows inside the dynamic region, we need some way of making the `getDynamicTaskFlowId()` method return different values and some way of setting these values. The solution we'll implement consists of four parts, which are as follows:

*   Another managed bean to store the value across page requests
*   A way to access this second bean from the first
*   A way to set values in this second bean from the user interface
*   A way to make the region redraw itself when needed

Storing the selected task flow value

The existing managed bean has a scope of **View**. This is a short scope only valid for as long as the current view is shown on the screen, so it cannot store the selected task flow as the user is working with the application. Instead, we need a managed bean with a scope that endures for as long as the page is open — the **page flow** scope. Values in a page flow scoped managed bean endure until the page flow is done, so such a bean can store the selected task flow.

To store the selected task flow, create a new Java class called `UiState` in the `com.dmcsol.xdm.beans` package. At the most basic level, this bean only needs to store a reference to the currently selected task flow; this can be done with the following code:

```
package com.dmcsol.xdm.beans;

public class UiState {
  private String currentTF = "/WEB-INF/task-edit-overview-flow.
xml#task-edit-overview-flow";

  public void setCurrentTF(String s) {
    currentTF = s;
  }

  public String getCurrentTF() {
    return currentTF;
  }
}
```

This class must be added to the unbounded task flow as a managed bean. To do this, open the `adfc-config.xml` file (under **Web Content / WEB-INF**), choose the **Overview** tab, and then the **Managed Beans** subtab. Click on the green plus sign at the top and add a new managed bean with the name, `UiStateBean`, class `com.dmcsol.xdm.beans.UiState`, and scope, **pageFlow**.

This chapter uses the simplest possible example to illustrate the use of dynamic regions, and the `UiState` class simply stores a **Java String** value. Obviously, this is not a robust solution that breaks as soon as a string is misspelled. In a real enterprise application, all task flows should be stored in a data structure, and a key should be used to look up the task flow.

Accessing the session bean from the backing bean

We can use the JSF functionality of **Managed Properties** to make the `UiState` session bean available to the `PageSwitcher` backing bean. To do this, change the `PageSwitcher` class to look like the following code:

```
package com.dmcsol.xdm.beans;

import oracle.adf.controller.TaskFlowId;

public class PageSwitcher implements Serializable {
  private UiState currentUiState;

  public TaskFlowId getDynamicTaskFlowId() {
    return TaskFlowId.parse(
      currentUiState.getCurrentTF());
  }

  public void setUiState(UiState state) {
    currentUiState = state;
  }
}
```

This class now has a private variable of the `UiState` class and a corresponding `setUiState` method. We can ask JSF to automatically set `UiState` whenever the `PageSwitcherBean` is instantiated by defining a **Managed Property**. In the `adfc-config.xml` file on the **Managed Beans** subtab, first select the `PageSwitcherBean` at the top and then click on the green plus sign at the bottom of the window. The managed property name should be `uiState` (matching the `setUiState()` method), the class should be `com.dmcsol.xdm.beans.UiState`, and the value should be `#{UiStateBean}`, as shown in the following screenshot:

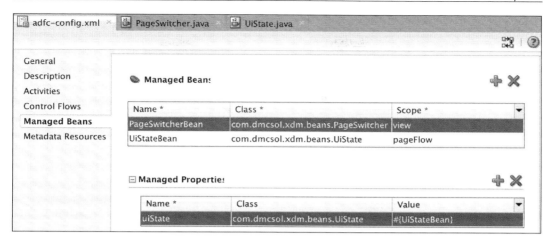

Setting up the task flow values

The final thing we need is to set the `UiState` value to select one or the other task flows. This can be done with a **Set Property Listener** operation that you can drag in from the **Component Palette**. In the XDM user interface, the switching of task flows is done with `af:commandMenuItem` elements, but the other command elements, such as buttons and links, can also be used.

To set the value, select the page and expand the tree in the **Structure** window until you see the menu items. Then, go to the **Components** window and open the **Operations** node. Find the **Set Property Listener** operation and drag it onto the `af:commandMenuItem`, as shown in the following screenshot:

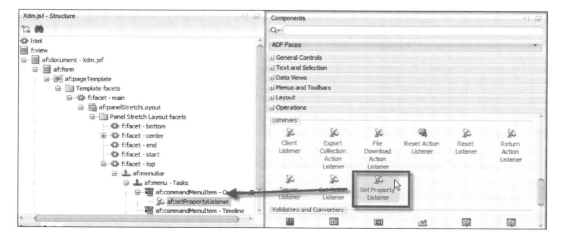

In the **Insert Set Property Listener** dialog, set the **From** property to #{'/WEB-INF/
task-overview-edit-flow.xml#task-overview-edit-flow'}, the **To** property to
#{pageFlowScope.UiStateBean.currentTF}, and the **Type** to action, as shown in
the following screenshot:

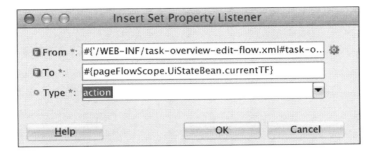

Repeat this for the timeline command menu item, only set **From** to #{'/WEB-INF/
person-timeline-flow.xml#person-timeline-flow'}.

These two property listener components will assign literal values (in the **From**
fields) to the currentTF attribute in the UiStateBean. Again, this only serves as
the simplest possible example of how to use a dynamic region—a real enterprise
application would store the actual task flow URLs in some central repository
(for example, a database table).

Making the region redraw itself

The final part of the solution is to find a way to make the region redraw itself as
needed. The ADF framework makes this very simple—all you need to do is to
set the **PartialTriggers** property on the region component. The **PartialTriggers**
property on a component is a list of all of the other components that can trigger
a refresh of that component.

Select the region and click on the little gearwheel next to the **PartialTriggers** property
and choose **Edit**. This opens a dialog box where you can define the components that
should trigger a redrawing of the region. Select the two commandMenuItem elements
and move them to the right-hand side, as shown in the following screenshot:

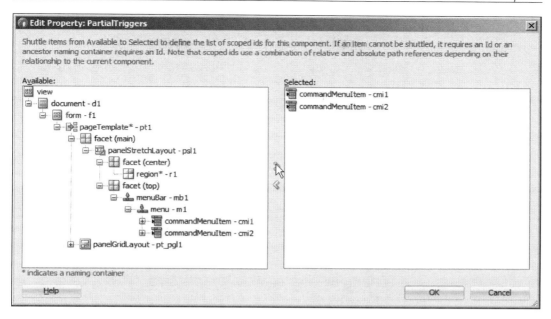

In this way, whenever a user selects either of the menu items, the dynamic region component is instructed to redraw itself, thus reflecting any change to the current task flow in the `UiState` bean. Only the region will be refreshed, not the entire page.

Now, you can right-click anywhere on the `xdm` page and choose **Run** to see your enterprise application in action. When you select a menu item, the task flow reference is set in the variable, the region refreshes, and the selected task flow from one of the subsystems will automatically appear.

Checking in your code

Navigate to **Team | Version Application Git** to add the master application to your local repository. Now would also be a good time to push your local changes to your central Git repository by navigating to **Team | Git | Push**.

Now, you can mark the task as complete, and all that remains is to write a test script.

Summary

In this chapter, you have added content to the Common Model to supplement the Common Code and Common View projects you built in the Common Workspace in *Chapter 5, Preparing to Build*. Using the ADF Libraries created from these three base projects, you have developed two subsystems by implementing the two use cases you first saw in *Chapter 1, The ADF Proof of Concept*.

You have used bounded task flows with page fragments to build well-defined, re-usable blocks of functionality that can easily be combined into a larger master application. You have seen how to use a proper enterprise methodology including task tracking to focus your work and a central source repository.

You have deployed your subsystems as ADF Libraries and combined them in a master application, including both a menu and a dynamic region with all necessary supporting code to make your enterprise application look like a desktop application and not just like a series of web pages. With this knowledge, you can build additional subsystems and add them to your master application until you have implemented all the requirements.

One thing that we skipped over in this chapter, though, is the testing. That'll be the subject of the following chapter.

7
Testing Your Application

After years of study, when a scientist finally discovers a promising chemical compound with the potential to cure cancer, does he or she crank up the pill-making machine right away? Of course not! He or she has already tested on cell cultures and lab animals for years, and an approved drug is still years away. The potential new drugs go through a rigorous and strictly regulated testing program, starting with just a few humans and leading up to large-scale Phase III clinical trials with hundreds of patients.

Your enterprise application is not likely to be subject to the same regulatory requirements, but that is no excuse for you to go from in vitro testing to full-scale deployment. You also need to test your application through several phases and not simply dump it untested on your unsuspecting users.

The holy grail of software testing

The purpose of software testing is to ensure that the software meets the requirements. Manual software testing can achieve this, but a manual test introduces a degree of variability into a process that should be strictly uniform; the tester might forget a test step or might miss an answer, thus deviating from the correct one.

That's why you should aim for as high a degree of **automated testing** as possible. If your test is run by a computer, it will be run the same way every time, and the computer won't miss small errors.

Initial tests

In the pharmaceutical business, a new drug candidate is first subjected to Phase I testing on a small number of healthy patients to test that the drug is safe for humans and works in the human body the way the models predict.

In your enterprise project, you similarly subject your code to initial, simple tests in order to ensure that each part of your code works the way you intend it to. These tests are often called **unit tests** because they test the smallest possible unit of work. Good tools for this are JUnit (`http://junit.org`) and TestNG (`http://testng.org`).

Keep testing

Your unit tests must be stored together with the application source code, so they can be run again after each change made to the application. If the requirements change, you should update the unit tests accordingly, and you should add additional unit tests when a new functionality is added.

Working with JUnit

JUnit is a unit testing framework for Java. Two things that you need to know about JUnit are as follows:

* It is used to test Java code
* The test cases are written in Java

Your test cases use annotations and some classes that are part of the JUnit framework, and you use other classes in the JUnit framework to actually run your tests.

With JUnit, you create **test classes** containing **test methods**. Inside these test methods, you place **assertions**, statements that "assert" what should happen. If your assertion is correct, the test is considered passed; otherwise it is considered failed.

There is a JUnit extension for JDeveloper to help you write and run unit tests. For licensing reasons, JUnit is not delivered with JDeveloper, but you can easily install it using **Check for Updates** under the **Help** section. You find the JUnit extension under Official Oracle Extensions and Updates—when you choose **BC4J JUnit Integration**, you will automatically be prompted to also include **JUnit Integration** (BC4J, Business Components for Java, is the old name for ADF Business Components). You have to accept the JUnit license when installing this extension.

Using JUnit to test code

JUnit excels at testing code. The classic example in *JUnit Cookbook* (http://junit. sourceforge.net/doc/cookbook/cookbook.htm) tests a Java class for adding monetary amounts in multiple currencies.

If you have a class that does something simple like this, it is easy to write unit tests. However, an ADF application is much more complicated, so it can be harder to identify what to test.

Writing good unit tests

If you google "good unit tests", you will find many people offering ideas about what constitutes a good unit test. A good unit test probably has the following characteristics:

- It tests one thing
- It can run in isolation
- It is easy to run
- It runs quickly

Your unit tests should test one unit of work — the smallest bit of code that makes sense to test in isolation. A small unit test points out exactly where the error is, while the failure of a big unit test just leads to more debugging.

Your unit tests should be able to run in isolation and in any order. To a unit testing purist, a unit test should not depend on external resources such as databases — that is probably a bit unrealistic for an enterprise ADF application. Nevertheless, your unit tests should preferably set up their own test data so that they can be run and rerun at any time and not depend on someone remembering to run a test-data-building script beforehand. This also allows the test to run as part of an automated build process.

Your unit tests should be easy to run; this is achieved using the JUnit framework in JDeveloper, where you can simply run your test class and get feedback directly in JDeveloper by using **JUnit Test Runner**.

Your unit tests should run fast, so you will actually run them and not be tempted to skip testing because it will hold up your work.

The unit testing ADF applications

It follow from this criteria that it is not easy to write a good unit test for your user interface. However, that doesn't matter—we'll leave user interface testing for later.

The functionality you should test during this phase is all the Java code you have written, depending on the following factors:

- If your framework extension classes have any content (we built them empty in *Chapter 5, Preparing to Build*), you need test cases to verify that they work as intended
- If your view objects or entity objects contain custom methods, you must test these functionalities
- If you have written and published custom methods in your application modules, you need to test these functionalities

Don't test ADF itself

You don't need to test the ADF framework itself—Oracle has already done that. This means that if you have defined an entity object on a table and a view object on the entity object, you don't need to test that the view object actually retrieves the rows in the underlying table. This is a standard ADF functionality, and while testing it doesn't hurt, it does squander resources that could be used better.

Preparing for unit testing

As an example of how to set up unit testing, we will implement unit testing of the common model (in the XdmCommon workspace). We will keep our unit testing in a separate project in the workspace to avoid cluttering up the real Common Model project with test artifacts.

Setting up a test project

Open the common workspace and navigate to **File | New | Project**. Select **Custom Project**, give the project the name `TestModel`, and click on **Finish** to create the project. The wizard doesn't prompt you for the default package name for Java code created in this project, so you need to right-click on the `TestModel` project, choose **Project Properties**, and then select **Project Source Paths** in the tree to the left. At the bottom right of the dialog, set **Default Package** to `com.dmcsol.xdm.model.test`, as shown in the following screenshot:

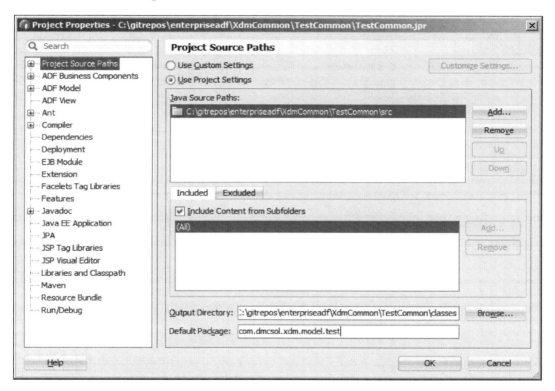

Adding default testing

Now, select the `TestModel` project, navigate to **File | New | From Gallery**, and then navigate to **General | Unit Tests | Business Components Test Suite**, as shown in the following screenshot:

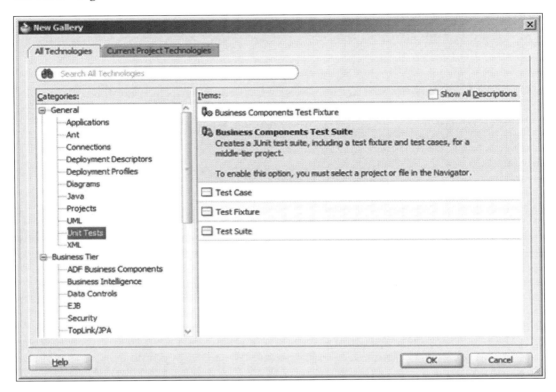

If you don't see the **Unit Tests** option, you probably did not install the **JUnit Integration** extension. If you see the **Unit Tests** option but do not see **Business Components Test Suite**, you probably did not install the **BC4J JUnit Integration** extension. You might get a warning saying that the current project does not contain any application modules—just click on **OK**.

The **JUnit ADF Business Components Test Suite Wizard** window allows you to choose the **Business Components Project** you wish to test as well as the application module. Select the **CommonModel** project and the application module you wish to test, as shown in the following screenshot:

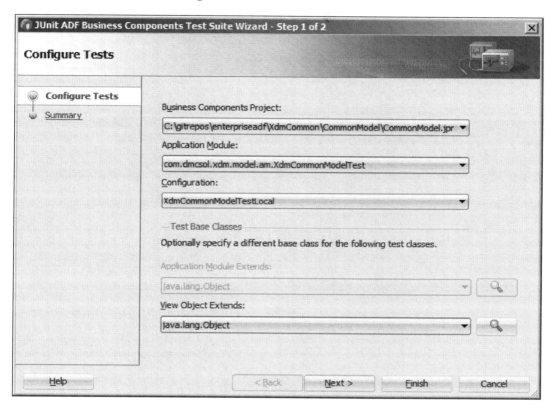

Click on **Finish** to complete the wizard.

The application navigator panel will now show many new files, as shown in the following screenshot:

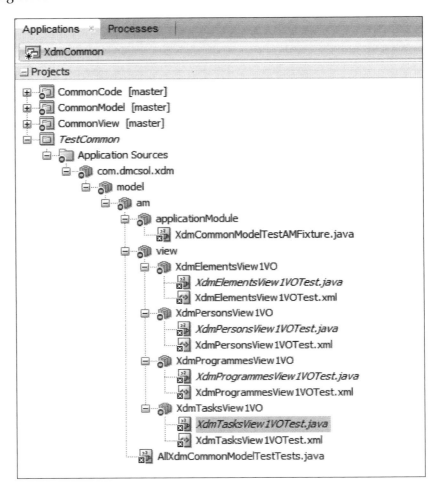

The wizard has created three kinds of objects for you. They are as follows:

- A test fixture
- A test suite
- A number of test classes

The test fixture takes care of creating an instance of the application module you wish to test. Since this is an expensive operation, it makes sense to do this only once in your test run. You can open the `XdmCommonModelTestAMFixture.java` file to see what it does — it's a standard code for programmatically accessing ADF application modules.

The test suite collects all the individual tests that make up your test suite. This class makes heavy use of Java **annotations** — the keywords prefixed with @. Annotations are a way to make metadata available for frameworks, such as JUnit, to use. For example, the `@Suite.SuiteClasses` annotation lists all the test classes that the suite must run, as shown in the following code:

```
@Suite.SuiteClasses( { XdmTasksView1Test.class,
                       XdmProgrammesView1Test.class,
                       XdmPersonView1Test.class,
                       XdmElements View1Test.class })
```

Finally, the framework has built a number of test classes — by default, one for every view object included in the application module under test. These classes also use annotations to tell JUnit what each method does and contain test methods to actually perform the test. The default test class generated for the `XdmTasksView1` view object looks as shown in the following code:

```
package com.dmcsol.xdm.model.am.view.XdmTasksView1;

import
com.dmcsol.xdm.model.am.applicationModule.XdmCommonModelTestServic
eAMFixture;

import oracle.jbo.ViewObject;

import org.junit.*;
import static org.junit.Assert.*;

public class XdmTasksView1Test {
   private XdmCommonModelTestServiceAMFixture fixture1 =
XdmCommonModelTestServiceAMFixture.getInstance();

   public XdmTasksView1Test() {
   }

   @Test
   public void testAccess() {
      ViewObject view =
fixture1.getApplicationModule().findViewObject("XdmTasksView1");
      assertNotNull(view);
```

```
    }

    @Before
    public void setUp() {
    }

    @After
    public void tearDown() {
    }
}
```

The "real" testing work happens in the test method or methods—those annotated with `@Test`. Each test method will *do* something and then *assert* that something is true. The default test discussed earlier will get the application module under test (from the `fixture1` object that is retrieved from the test fixture class) and then find a specific view object (`XdmTasksView1`). It then asserts that the view object reference is not null, that is, the application module under test does indeed contain an `XdmTasksView1` view object instance. If this is the case, the test has succeeded. If this is not the case, the test has failed.

To see the testing in action, right-click on the test suite class (`AllXdmCommonModelTestTests.java`) and choose **Run as Unit Tests**.

In the log window, you will see a new tab called **JUnit Test Runner**. In this tab, you see the tests being executed and the results summarized, as shown in the following screenshot:

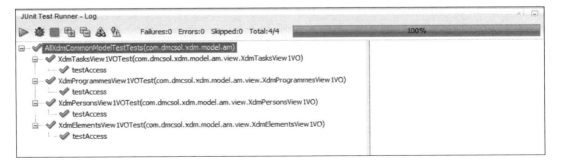

You'll see that four tests were executed (the default test for each view object used in the application module), and they all succeeded (as expected). The progress bar goes all the way to **100%** to indicate that all tests passed. If any tests fail, the progress bar does not go to **100%**.

The results of your tests are indicated as follows:

- A checkmark indicates a test passed.
- An exclamation mark indicates that a test has failed.
- An x indicates that there is a code error in the test, and it did not run.

The real unit testing example

Writing a test and watching it complete correctly complete correctly isn't really enough. You might have an error in your test that means it will always show success. You haven't really proven that your test works *until you have seen it change state*.

This is the thinking behind test-driven development where you write your tests first. As an example, we will implement the requirement that tasks are never actually deleted but only marked cancelled. In the database, this is indicated by setting the CXL_YN column to the value Y.

Adding a test case

As it must be possible to run the test in isolation, your test method can't depend on data already in the database. In this case, we will let the test method itself add the record, but you might also create a set of test data in the test fixture class.

Keep the test data separate

If you insert dummy data into your tables, you should make sure that it is easily recognized so that you can clean up any test data left over from a failed test method execution. One way of doing this is using large negative numbers for primary keys. As ADF also uses negative numbers as placeholders for DBDomain attribute values, start with something such as -1001, -1002, to avoid conflicts with the temporary keys.

Your test method must do the following:

1. Add a new Tasks record (with an ID: 1001).
2. Find the record through the view object and call the remove method.
3. Verify that the record still exists and that the CxlYn attribute now has the value Y.
4. Clean up: remove the Tasks record.

With a bit of cleanup, your XdmTasksView1 class might look as shown in the following code:

```
package com.dmcsol.xdm.model.am.view.XdmTasksDefaultVO;
import …
public static class XdmTasksDefaultVOTest {
  private static CommonModelTestServiceAMFixture fixture1 =
  CommonModelTestServiceAMFixture.getInstance();
  private static ApplicationModule am =
  fixture1.getApplicationModule();

  public Tasks1VOTest() {
  }

  @Test
  public void testAccess() {
    ViewObject view = am.findViewObject("XdmTasksView1");
    assertNotNull(view);
  }

  @Test
  public void testDelete() {
    // add a test record directly to the table
    Transaction tr = am.getTransaction();
    tr.executeCommand("INSERT INTO xdm_tasks (task_id, start_date,
    text) VALUES (-1001, sysdate, 'Test Task')");
    tr.commit();
    // find the row with ID -1001 and remove it
    ViewObject v = am.findViewObject("XdmTasksView1");
    Key k = new Key(new Object[] { -1001 });
    Row r1 = v.getRow(k);
    assertNotNull("Test row (-1001) found", r1);
    v.setCurrentRow(r1);
    v.removeCurrentRow();
    tr.commit();
    // look for the row
    v.executeQuery();
    Row r2 = v.getRow(k);
    assertNotNull("Test row (-1001) found again", r2);
    // test that CxlYn attribute is now Y, indicating deletion
    assertEquals("Test row CxlYn value is Y", "Y",
    r2.getAttribute("CxlYn"));
  }

  @Before
  public void setUp() {
  }

  @After
  public void tearDown() {
```

```
    }

    @AfterClass
    public static void deleteTestData() {
      Transaction tr = am.getTransaction();
      tr.executeCommand("DELETE FROM xdm_tasks " +
      "WHERE task_id = -1001");
      tr.commit();
    }
}
```

The `testDelete()` method is new and performs the test described. It is annotated with `@Test` so that the JUnit framework knows to run it as a test case. The method uses `executeCommand()` to issue SQL directly to the connection the application module is using and then uses `findViewObject()` to get a reference to the `XdmTasksDefaultVO` view object. An assertion checks if we did find the test row, and then we remove this row from the view object row set with `removeCurrentRow()`. It commits the transaction (to force execution of the logic in the entity object) and then re-executes the view object query to find the row again. The method asserts that the row is found and that the `CxlYn` attribute has now been set to `Y`, thus indicating a logical delete.

An extra cleanup method `deleteTestData()` has also been added and given the annotation `@AfterClass`. This means that it will run as cleanup after all the test methods in the class have been executed.

Finally, the fixture class and the application module have been moved up as private static variables to simplify the code.

When you run the test suite, you will see the `testDelete()` method fail, with an `AssertionError` message showing the text **Test row (-1001) found again**, as shown in the following screenshot. This was the text we put into the `AssertNotNull` statement and is to be expected—after all, we haven't implemented the logical delete functionality yet.

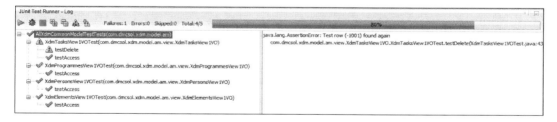

Implementing logical delete

Implementing logical delete—setting a marker on a record instead of actually deleting it—requires two changes to the entity object. They are as follows:

- Changing the remove method to set the marker
- Changing the SQL statement from a DELETE to an UPDATE statement

This is not something that can be done in metadata—you need a Java class implementing your entity object.

Open the XdmTasks entity object and choose the **Java** subtab on the left. Then, click on the little pencil icon in the top-right corner to generate Java code for this entity object. The **Select Java Options** dialog appears, as shown in the following screenshot:

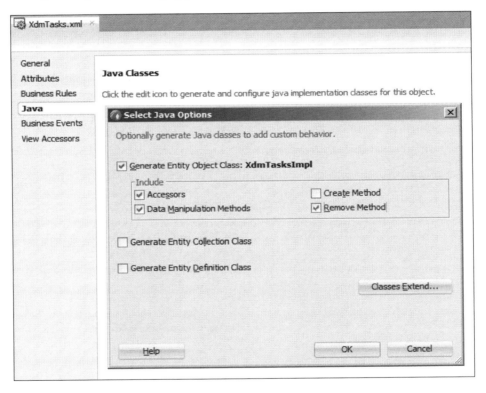

Choose to generate methods for **Accessors, Data Manipulation Methods** and **Remove Method**. It doesn't hurt to select the **Create Method** as well, or you can override this method later if you need it. When you click on **OK**, an `XdmTasksImpl.java` file is created and can be seen in the application navigator under the `XdmTasks` entity object node.

In this class, first find the `remove()` method. It is probably easier to find the method in the **Structure** panel in the bottom-left corner, where all the methods are listed in alphabetical order. Double-click on the `remove()` method to jump to that method in the main editing window. Add a `setCxlYn()` instruction, so your remove method looks like the following code:

```
public void remove() {
  // set cancel flag. doDML() will change DELETE to UPDATE
  setCxlYn("Y");
  super.remove();
}
```

This means that the `CxlYn` attribute (corresponding to the `CXL_YN` column in the database) must be set to Y, and then the normal `remove()` processing should continue.

Then, jump to the `doDML()` method. This method is invoked whenever the framework needs to execute a **data manipulation language (DML)** SQL statement against the database — INSERT, UPDATE, or DELETE. This means that it is invoked after the `remove()` method, which was discussed earlier, to actually perform the operation against the database. Change this method to look like the following code:

```
protected void doDML(int operation, TransactionEvent e) {
  if (operation == DML_DELETE) {
    super.doDML(DML_UPDATE, e);
  } else {
    super.doDML(operation, e);
  }
}
```

This code will simply intercept a DELETE command and do the normal processing associated with the UPDATE command. Since the `remove()` method already sets the marker to Y, this is all we need.

Re-testing

Now you can go back to the **TestModel** project and run the test suite
(AllXdmCommonModelTestTests) again. You should now see the progress
bar run to **100%**, thus indicating that all five tests have passed, as shown in
the following screenshot:

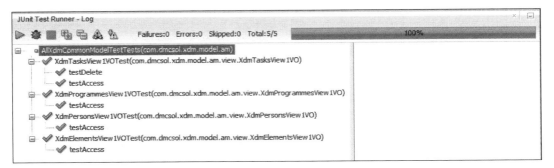

Automating unit testing

It's great that the developer has a test suite that he or she can run against the code
at all times—however, the full value of having a collection of unit tests comes if you
integrate them with an automated build process. We'll discuss automated build
process in *Chapter 11*, *Packaging and Delivery*.

User interface tests

After Phase I testing of a drug, the candidate has successfully established that it is
safe to use, and Phase II testing commences. This is performed on larger groups
of patients to test that the drug is actually effective against the ailment that it is
supposed to cure.

In your enterprise project, your next testing phase is a test of the user interface. It
tests if your application actually meets the user requirements. One tool for verifying
this is **Selenium** (www.seleniumhq.com) that we will see in action in this chapter.

What should you test?

When you test your user interface, you should have at least one test for every
non-trivial page in your application. If your requirements are formulated as use
cases, they will typically contain all the steps you need to go through in your user
interface test. If not, you will have to start by writing out a list of the steps the user
would go through when using your application so that you know what to record.

A user interface test will compare the content of the web page to the recorded assertions. For example, you could assert that a specific text is part of the page or that a field has a specific value. Generally, a user interface test tool does not test the look of the application—if you change the look of the application, for example, through skinning, as explained in *Chapter 8, Changing the Appearance*, your UI test tool should give the same result.

Again, don't test the ADF framework itself—if you've built a simple view object on a single entity object and dropped it onto a page as an ADF table without modifying it, you can trust ADF to take care of the details.

About Selenium

Selenium is an open source tool for testing web applications, including those that make heavy use of JavaScript, which ADF does. You can use Selenium in two different ways, which are as follows:

- For recording simple scripts, you can use the **Selenium IDE**
- For full test automation and advanced test scripts, you can use **Selenium WebDriver**

Selenium IDE is a Firefox plugin that allows you to record a user session in a browser, including assertions about what is expected to happen. You can then playback the recorded session to verify that your page works (or still works, after you made changes). You can even export your recorded test in a programming language for further enhancements.

Selenium WebDriver is a tool that programmatically executes test scripts by calling the browser API. You can either run Selenium WebDriver on your local machine, or you can run the Selenium server on your test/integration server as part of an automated process.

As this is not a book on Selenium, we will only cover how to record and playback a simple test script with Selenium IDE. For more information about Selenium WebDriver, refer to the Selenium documentation at `http://docs.seleniumhq.org/docs/03_webdriver.jsp`.

Installing Selenium IDE

The Selenium IDE only exists as a Firefox plugin, so you need the Firefox browser. If you don't already have it, you can download it from `http://www.firefox.com`. The Selenium IDE can be downloaded from `http://seleniumhq.org/download`. When you have accepted to install the Selenium add-ons and restarted Firefox, you'll see the **Selenium IDE** menu item on the **Tools** menu in Firefox, as shown in the following screenshot:

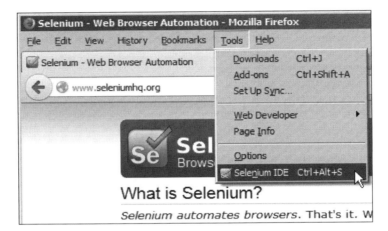

A simple test with Selenium

To record a test session with Selenium, you first need to start the application. For this example, we will test the "Task Overview and Edit" page task flow from the `XdmTaskMgr` workspace. Open this workspace and then the `TaskMgrView` project. Right-click on the `TestTaskOverviewEdit.jspx` page (under **Web Content |** `testpages`) and choose **Run**. The application starts and shows up your web browser.

Then, choose the **Selenium IDE** menu item from the **Tools** menu in Firefox. The **Selenium IDE** window appears, as shown in the following screenshot:

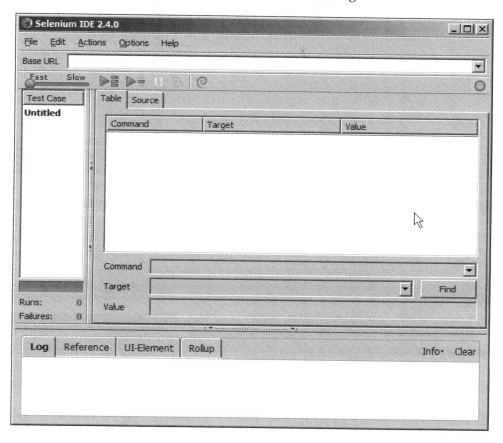

By default, it is already recording, shown by the light gray box around the red recording button in the right-hand side of the Selenium IDE window toolbar.

Go back to the browser address line and copy the page URL *without* parameters. You will probably have noticed that ADF applications have fairly long URLs—everything to the left of the question mark sign is the real URL of the page, and everything to the right are session-specific parameters that the ADF framework has added. You just want the real URL, something similar to `http://127.0.0.1:7101/XdmTaskMgr/faces/TestTaskOverviewEdit.jspx`.

Shortening the URL

If your application still has the long default JDeveloper URL, you can go to the project properties of the `TaskMgrView` project and choose the **Java EE Application** node. Change both the **Java EE Web Application Name** and **Java EE Web Context Root** fields to just the name of your workspace, for example, `XdmTaskMgr`.

Clear the browser address bar and paste in the application URL. The page loads again in the browser, but there is nothing to see in the **Selenium IDE** window. However, if you right-click anywhere on the page, you will see that the context menu in the browser has acquired a few more options, as shown in the following screenshot:

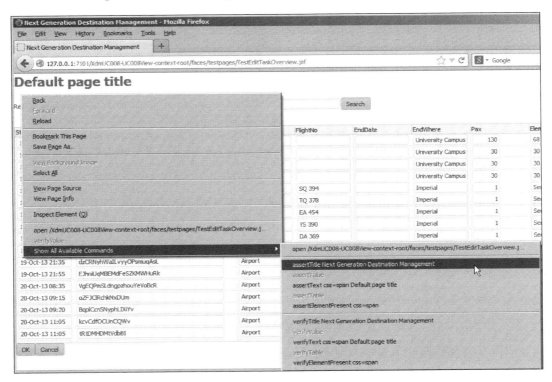

Choose **Show All Available Commands** and then the **assertTitle...** option (for example, **assertTitle Next Generation Destination Management**). This is a testing step that requires the title of the web page to have a specific value.

 The title of the web page is set through the **Title** property of the af:document tag on a page.

You should now see two commands registered in Selenium: an open command and the assertTitle you just selected, as shown in the following screenshot:

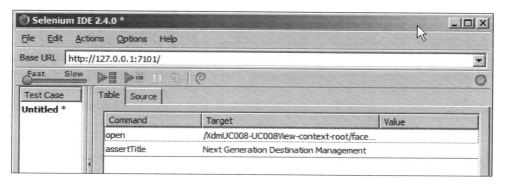

You can continue to use the application and let Selenium record your actions. If, for example, you make a selection from the **Responsible** drop-down box and click on the **Search** button, you'll see Selenium register a **select** command and two **click** commands.

If you right-click on a specific field, you'll see a number of options related to that specific field, as shown in the following screenshot:

open /XdmUC008-UC008View-context-root/faces/testpages/TestEditTaskOverview.j...
assertTitle Next Generation Destination Management
verifyValue id=pt1:r1:0:t1:0:it2::content RzyWKuVuwNQym
Show All Available Commands ►

Normally, you'll use assertValue to assert that the field has a specific value — we'll get back to these options later.

When you're happy with your test, click on the recording button in the Selenium IDE window to stop recording. For now, move the speed slider in the left-hand side of the Selenium IDE toolbar to the middle to avoid running your test faster than ADF can handle — we'll address a few of the challenges in the *Using Selenium effectively* section later in this chapter. Then, click on one of the green **Play** buttons to run your test, as shown in the following screenshot:

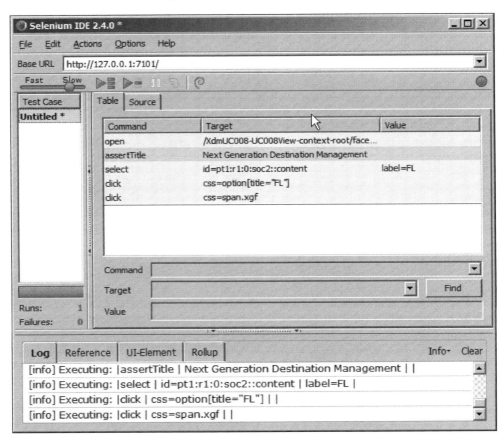

You can edit the test (for example, to update parameter values, page title, and so on) and save your test case for later use. Selenium also allows you to combine individual test cases into test suites.

Exporting your test

In a true automated testing, you would be using a tool such as Selenium WebDriver. You can export your test from the Selenium IDE to code by navigating to **File | Export Test Case As...**, as shown in the following screenshot:

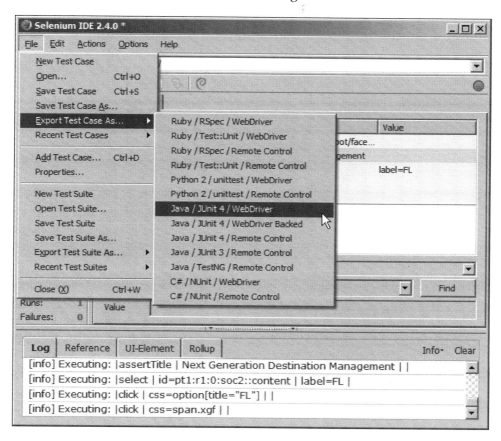

This produces a code that you can modify and run in Selenium WebDriver. Refer to the Selenium documentation for more information.

Using Selenium effectively

While a simple test, such as the one discussed in the preceding section, is fairly easy to run, Selenium is a powerful tool with many options, and ADF pushes the web browser to the limit, thus using massive amounts of JavaScript. You will need to read at least some of the Selenium documentation at `http://seleniumhq.org/docs` if you want to use Selenium to test your enterprise project.

Value checking options

Much of your application testing will concern values inside components, for example, input fields. When you right-click on a field while recording, you get the following four options:

- `assertValue`: This will record an absolute demand that the value is correct. If the field in the browser does not have the right value when you run the test, the test will be aborted.

- `verifyValue`: This will record a requirement for a specific value. If the field in the browser does not have the right value when the test is played back, it will be registered as a failure, but the test will still continue to the next test step.

- `waitForValue`: This will record a requirement for a specific value to appear before a configurable timeout. If you know the application might take several seconds to respond, you use a **waitForValue** option. If the value appears in the field before timeout, the test continues. If the timeout appears, the test is a failure. You can configure a timeout in the IDE under **Options | Options**. The default is very high (30 seconds).

- `assertElementPresent`: This will record a requirement for the existence of a specific element, but it does not check the value in the field. As long as a field with the recorded ID exists on the screen, the test is considered passed.

Lazy content delivery

When you navigate between records and assert values in an ADF application, you might experience that your Selenium test fails for no good reason. This is because ADF uses and issues a request for new data asynchronously (without refreshing the whole page), and Selenium doesn't know that it must wait for a fraction of a second for the data.

Additionally, some ADF components (such as `af:table`) have a **ContentDelivery** property that can be set to **Lazy**. This means that the page will render quickly, and the table data will be delivered in a second request to the application server. This causes the same kind of confusion where Selenium notices that the page is loaded and starts running the assertions while table data is still coming in.

You can somewhat mitigate these problems using **waitForValue** (for navigation between records) and `waitForElementPresent` (for lazy-loading components). Of course, you also need to set your timeout to a reasonable value, so you won't be waiting for 30 seconds before detecting a failure.

Testing the context menus

The Selenium IDE uses the right-click (context) menu to record the test steps, but if your application also uses a context menu, the browser context menu will never be shown. This means that you have to manually enter the test steps for context menus in the Selenium IDE window.

To test the context menu of your application itself, you use the `contextMenuAt` command in Selenium — you can look up the details in the Selenium documentation.

Verifying the item ID

If your application is going to be customized (now or sometime in the future), you should use `assertElementPresent` to verify the presence of all user interface elements. This command takes an element ID as the parameter, and the testing for that ID will catch the situation where the element ID changes.

The application will work with different component IDs, but if anybody has customized the application, the customization is tied to the component ID. Therefore, if you change the ID of a component, you break any customization made on that component. We'll return to customization in *Chapter 9, Customizing Functionality.*

Testing passivation and activation

The user interface tests you have recorded and played back have only been simulating one user, and in the following section, we will simulate many. However, there is one part of ADF testing that requires a bit of extra precaution: application module **passivation** and **activation**.

For performance reasons, ADF keeps a pool of application modules in memory. It tries to give each session the same application module that the session used during the last request; however, this might not be possible during the peak load of your application. In this case, ADF saves the application modules state in a database table, so the application module can be used by another session. This is called passivation. When the first session needs the application module again, its state is retrieved from the database, a process known as activation.

If you have made an error in your code and depend on some variable that is not persisted correctly when your application module state is stored, you will experience mysterious errors under high load.

To make sure you don't hit this problem, open your application module and select the **Configurations** tab to the left. By default, each application module has two configurations. Right-click on the one ending in ...Local and choose **Edit**. Then choose the **Pooling and Scalability** tab and *deselect* the **Enable Application Module Pooling** checkbox, as shown in the following screenshot:

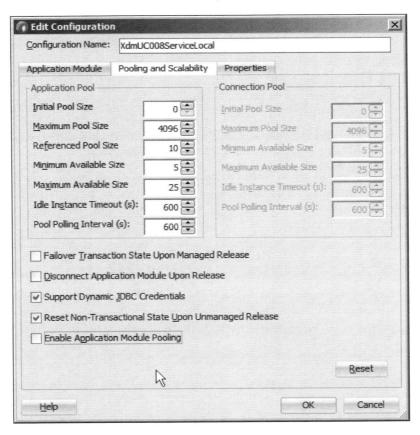

This forces the ADF framework to always store an application module state in the database between requests. Run your user interface tests again to make sure none of these tricky persistence bugs lurk in your code. They will typically show up as `NullPointerExceptions` when an object you believed had a value is suddenly empty because the application module has been passivated and reactivated.

Remember to enable the application module pooling again before deploying the application for stress/performance testing.

ADF tuning

There are many ways of tuning the application module pool and other aspects of the ADF framework. Refer to the *Oracle Fusion Middleware Performance and Tuning Guide*, which has a chapter on tuning ADF. There is also a chapter on tuning application module pools in the *Fusion Developers Guide for Oracle Application Development Framework* guide.

Stress and performance tests

When a new drug candidate has successfully completed Phase II testing and has proven that it works, he or she moves on to Phase III testing with even more people to verify that it works on a larger scale.

In your enterprise project, successfully completing user interface testing proves that the application works for an individual user—now, you need to prove that it is robust enough to handle real-life load. To do this, you can use another open source tool: **JMeter**.

Working with JMeter

JMeter is a tool for load testing web applications. Like Selenium, it records a user session and plays it back, but it does not attempt to really run the user session in the browser (like Selenium does)—it simply sends off the requests that a browser would make to the application server and measures the time it takes the application server to respond.

As it does not invoke a browser but simply sends requests and receives responses, one workstation with JMeter can simulate the load of dozens or even hundreds of real-time users.

JMeter tests are brittle

When you start working with JMeter, you will discover that there are a number of manual steps that have to be done exactly right for your test to run; even very small changes to your application necessitates revisiting and fixing your JMeter tests. Furthermore, testing ADF is not officially supported by Oracle, so you are likely to have to do a bit of troubleshooting before you get your tests to run. On the other hand, JMeter is free.

If you don't want the hassle of making JMeter run your ADF application, you can look at commercial alternatives, such as the HP LoadRunner or Oracle Application Testing Suite.

Testing application performance with JMeter

At this point in your testing, you already know that your application works the way it's supposed to. What remains is the following:

- To test that the application works with multiple concurrent users
- To test how many users your system can handle

The majority of the errors you will find during this phase of testing will be **concurrency** issues—strange things that happen when more than one user is using your application. These can slip through both the programmer's own initial tests, unit tests, and user interface tests because all of these run only one session.

Your initial stress/performance tests should be run with just a small number of simulated concurrent users—five concurrent sessions are normally enough to uncover any concurrency issues in your application.

Once you are sure that your application works with multiple users, you can scale up the load to ensure that your application meets the performance requirements.

Installing and running JMeter

You can download JMeter from `http://jakarta.apache.org/jmeter`. It is a Java application, so it requires Java 6 or a later version installed on your workstation.

To start JMeter, you simply execute the `jmeter.bat` file (on Windows) or
the `jmeter` file (on Linux). The JMeter main window appears, as shown in
the following screenshot:

A simple test with JMeter

A JMeter test plan starts with a **Thread Group**, which defines the number of
concurrent processes you will let loose on your application. To add a thread group,
right-click on the **Test Plan** node and navigate to **Add | Threads (Users) | Thread
Group**, as shown in the following screenshot:

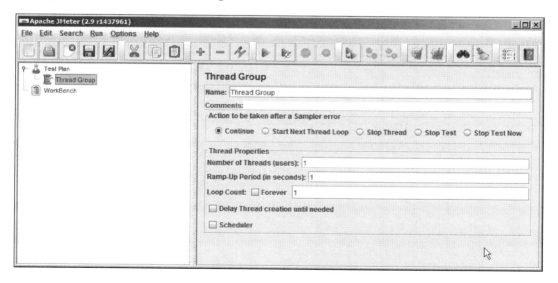

Here, you can define the number of users, the number of repetitions of your test,
and so on. While defining and testing your JMeter test script, you should use only
one user.

Once you have defined the thread group, you can start adding test elements manually by right-clicking on your thread group and choosing **Add**. However, like in Selenium, there is an easier way: recording the test.

Setting up JMeter as a proxy

To record a test, you set up JMeter as a proxy—a kind of gateway that all your web requests go through. If you work in a large corporation behind a firewall, your Internet access is likely to go through a proxy that will filter out some sites, protect them against viruses, and so on. The JMeter proxy doesn't do any of this—what it does is record every request for playback later.

To set up JMeter as a proxy, right-click on the **Workbench** node and navigate to **Add | Non-Test Elements | HTTP Proxy Server**. Enter a port that is not already in use (for example, 8080) and set the **Target Controller** to your thread group, as shown in the following screenshot. If you wish, you can exclude certain URL patterns from the capture that JMeter does. This is useful, for example, if you have browser plugins that might contact some server in the middle of your recording.

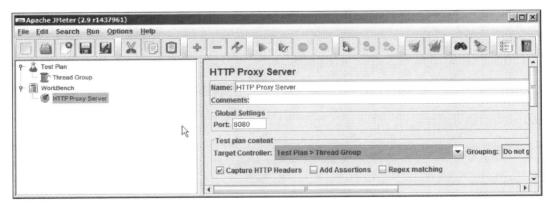

When you are done, set up your web browser to use the JMeter proxy you just configured. In Firefox, this setting hides under **Tools | Options | Advanced | Network | Settings**. Choose `localhost` as the server and the port you defined in JMeter. Check the **No Proxy for** field—it should *not* include `localhost` or `127.0.0.1`, as shown in the following screenshot:

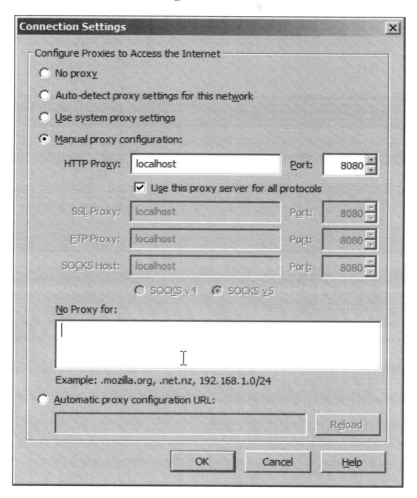

Recording a session

To start recording, click on **Start** at the bottom of the **HTTP Proxy Server** window in JMeter (you might have to click on **OK** when a Windows warning about running Java appears). Then, go to your browser and enter the URL of the page you wish to test. You'll see the page as normal in the browser. At the same time, everything is being recorded by JMeter—if you expand your thread group in JMeter, you will see that even a very simple page request might lead to multiple requests from the browser to the server, as shown in the following screenshot:

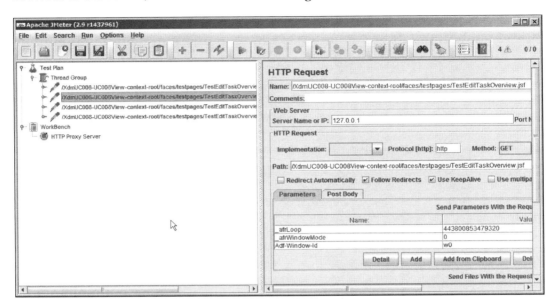

When you have recorded what you want, you can stop the JMeter proxy again. Remember to also reconfigure your browser—you can't access anything if the browser is pointing to a JMeter proxy that no longer runs.

Post-processing a recorded session

The recording shows the entire communication between the browser and the application server. If you examine the individual requests, you'll see that after the initial request, the subsequent requests include one or more parameters—either with the request or as part of the URL.

In order to replay a session, you need to modify it so that JMeter can retrieve the parameter values from one request and send them as part of the following request. This is a fairly complex procedure that in effect involves reverse engineering the ADF communication protocol.

You can find the procedure explained in an ADF Insider video by Senior Principal ADF Product Manager Chris Muir at `http://www.youtube.com/watch?v=cudvV12KgiQ`. Chris has also made a JMeter project available at `http://bit.ly/SFUKNp`.

The whole procedure involves the following:

- Adding a cookie manager and an HTTP header manager
- Defining JMeter variables to hold the values from request to request
- Extracting values from requests into the variables
- Replacing the recorded values with references to the variables

Chris' pre-built JMeter project does much of this, but this only works for some versions of ADF. You will need to google "ADF JMeter" to find the latest information about any changes to variables you have to define and the specific regular expressions you must use to extract values from the requests.

Running a recorded session

To see what actually happens during the execution, you'll need **listeners**. The prebuilt JMeter project already contains the following four listeners:

- **View Results Tree**: This listener shows the detailed responses from the web server—normally, this should show `HTTP/1.1 200 OK` to indicate a successful HTTP request
- **Graph Results**: This listener shows your response time in the form of graphics
- **View Results in Table**: This listener shows an overview with response time and status
- **Aggregate Graph**: This listener shows you the aggregated data in a table or in the form of graphics

The project also contains some JMeter assertions to check for common ADF errors.

When you have done this, you can run your recorded session by navigating to **Run | Start** and watch the results roll in.

If you run an automated build and test process, JMeter testing is normally not included in the daily build because application performance doesn't change everyday. Instead, JMeter tests are normally run through the JMeter application once a large part of the application is complete. Preferably, your stress/performance tests should be executed on a dedicated test environment similar to the production environment.

Troubleshooting JMeter sessions

If you misspell anything in your extractors or make a mistake when putting your variable names into the request, your JMeter execution will fail. JMeter can recognize some failures and mark them in the **View Results Tree** view, but others are harder to find.

In order to make sure that your JMeter test did run successfully, you need to check the log from WebLogic to make sure there are no errors. Additionally, you might find some results shown with green checkmarks in JMeter that actually cover an error—anything that contains an HTTP error 500 indicates a failure of your test. See an example of this in the following screenshot:

The Oracle alternative

If you would purchase an integrated testing solution rather than putting together these open source tools, Oracle offers **Oracle Application Testing Suite**.

The product consists of the following:

- Oracle Functional Testing for testing your application functionality (like Selenium does)

- Oracle Load Testing for testing how your application performs under load (like JMeter does)

- Oracle Test Manager for managing the test process (there is no equivalent open source tool)

You can find more information on Oracle Application Testing Suite at `http://www.oracle.com/technetwork/oem/app-test/index.html`.

Summary

Together with the test team in DMC Solutions, you have created unit tests for your Business Components and user interface tests that exercise the whole XDM application. Once the application passed these tests, you recorded a stress test and ran it to be sure that the application performs as you expect it to, even under heavy load.

Functionally, the XDM application is ready to deploy, but your boss would like you to tweak the user interface just a little before releasing the application. This is the topic of the following chapter.

8
Changing the Appearance

Henry Ford famously said:

> *"Any customer can have a car painted any color that he wants so long as it is black."*

He actually had a good reason: black paint dried quickly, thus allowing him to operate the assembly line at a higher speed.

Today, you can have your car in a large number of standard colors. You can have your web browser in any color you want—Firefox now offers more than 35,000 "personas" with different colors and images.

You probably don't want to offer your enterprise application in thousands of color schemes, but you do want to build a visually attractive application that matches the graphical identity used by your organization. If your application is going to be used by several different groups of users, for example, if it is going to be deployed to multiple customers, you want it to be easy to change the appearance of the application.

Controlling appearance

An **ADF Faces** application is a modern web application, so the technology used for controlling the look of the application is **Cascading Style Sheets (CSS)**.

The idea behind CSS is that the web page (in HTML) should contain only the structure and not information about appearance. All of the visual definitions must be kept in the style sheet, and the HTML file must refer to the style sheet. This means that the same web page can be made to look completely different by applying a different style sheet to it.

The Cascading Style Sheets basics

In order to change the appearance of your application, you need to understand some CSS basics. If you have never worked with CSS before, you should start by reading one of the many CSS tutorials available on the Internet.

To start with, let's repeat some of the basics of CSS.

The CSS layout instructions are written in the form of **rules**. Each rule is in the following form:

```
selector { property: value; }
```

The `selector` function identifies which part of the web page the rule applies to, and the `property`/`value` pairs define the styling to be applied to the selected parts.

For example, the following rule defines that all `<h1>` elements should be shown in red font:

```
h1 { color: red; }
```

One rule can include multiple selectors separated by commas, and multiple property values separated by semicolons. Therefore, it is also a valid CSS to write the following line of code to get all the `<h1>`, `<h2>`, and `<h3>` tags shown in large, red font:

```
h1, h2, h3 { color: red; font-size: x-large; }
```

If you want to apply a style with more precision than just every level 1 header, you define a **style class**, which is just a selector starting with a period, as shown in the following line of code:

```
.important { color: red; font-weight: bold }
```

To use this selector in your HTML code, you use the keyword `class` inside an HTML tag. There are three ways of using a style class. They are as follows:

- Inside an existing tag: `<h1>`
- Inside the special `<span>` tag to style the text within a paragraph
- Inside a `<div>` tag to style a whole paragraph of text

Here are examples of all the three ways:

```
<h1 class="important">Important topic</h1>
You <span class="important">must</span> remember this.
<div class="important">Important tip</div>
```

In theory, you can place your styling information directly in your HTML document using the `<style>` tag. In practice, however, you usually place your CSS instructions in a separate `.css` file and refer to it from your HTML file with a `<link>` tag, as shown in the following line of code:

```
<link href="mystyle.css" rel="stylesheet" type="text/css">
```

Styling individual components

The preceding examples can be applied to HTML elements, but styling can also be applied to JSF components. A plain JSF component could look like the following code with inline styling:

```
<h:outputFormat value="hello" style="color:red;"/>
```

It can also look like the line of code shown using a style class:

```
<h:outputFormat value="hello" styleClass="important"/>
```

ADF components use the `inlineStyle` attribute instead of just style as shown in the following line of code:

```
<af:outputFormat value="hello" inlineStyle="color:red;"/>
```

The `styleClass` attribute is the same, as shown in the following line of code:

```
<af:outputFormat value="hello" styleClass="important"/>
```

Of course, you normally won't be setting these attributes in the source code, but will be using the **StyleClass** and **InlineStyle** properties in the **Property Inspector** instead.

In both HTML and JSF, you should only use **StyleClass** so that multiple components can refer to the same style class and will reflect any change made to the style. **InlineStyle** is rarely used in real-life ADF applications; it adds to the page size (the same styling is sent for every styled element), and it is almost impossible to ensure that every occurrence is changed when the styling requirements change—as they will.

Building a style

While you are working out the styles you need in your application, you can use the **Style** section in the JDeveloper **Properties** window to define the look of your page, as shown in the following screenshot. This section shows six small subtabs with icons for font, background, border/outline, layout, table/list, and media/animation. If you enter or select a value on any of these tabs, this value will be placed into the **InlineStyle** field as a correctly formatted CSS.

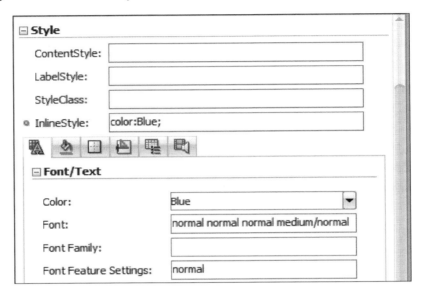

When your items look the way you want, copy the value from the **InlineStyle** field to a style class in your CSS file and set the **StyleClass** property to point to that class. If the style discussed earlier is the styling you want for a highlighted label, create a section in your CSS file, as shown in the following code:

```
.highlight {background-color:blue;}
```

Then, clear the **InlineStyle** property and set the **StyleClass** property to highlight. Once you have placed a style class into your CSS file, you can use it to style the other components in exactly the same way by simply setting the **StyleClass** property.

We'll be building the actual CSS file where you define these style classes. This is explained in the section on skinning later in this chapter.

InlineStyle and ContentStyle

Some JSF components (for example, `outputText`) are easy to style—if you set
the font color, you'll see it take effect in the JDeveloper design view and in your
application, as shown in the following screenshot:

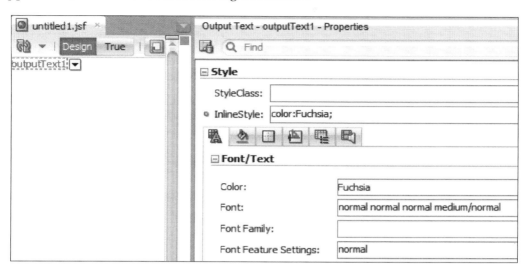

Other elements (for example, `inputText`) are harder to style. For example, if you
want to change the background color of the input field, you might try setting the
background color, as shown in the following screenshot:

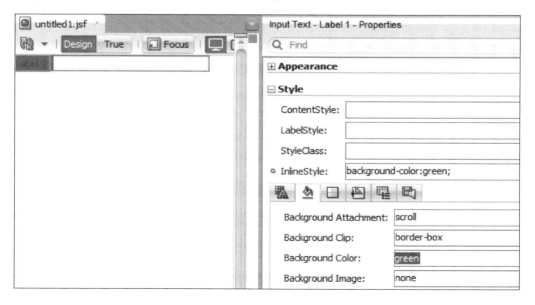

You will notice that this did *not* work the way you reasonably expected — the background behind both the label and the actual input field changes. The reason for this is that an inputText component actually consists of several HTML elements, and an inline style applies to the outermost element. In this case, the outermost element is an HTML <tr> (table row) tag, so the green background color applies to the entire row.

To help mitigate this problem, ADF offers another styling option for some components: **ContentStyle**. If you set this property, ADF tries to apply the style to the content of a component — in the case of an inputText, **ContentStyle** applies to the actual input field, as shown in the following screenshot:

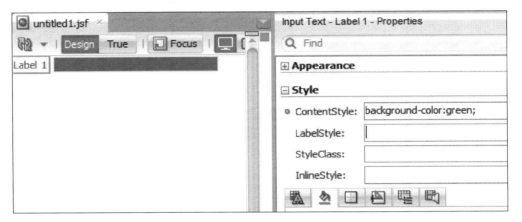

In a similar manner, you can apply styling to the label for an element by setting the **LabelStyle** property.

Unravelling the mysteries of CSS styling

As you saw in the **Input Text** example, ADF components can be quite complex, and it's not always easy to figure out which element to style to achieve the desired result. To be able to see into the complex HTML that ADF builds for you, you need a support tool such as **Firebug**. Firebug is a Firefox extension that you can download by navigating to **Tools | Add-ons** from within Firefox, or you can go to `http://getfirebug.com`.

When you have installed Firebug, you see a little Firebug icon to the far right of your Firefox window, as shown in the following screenshot:

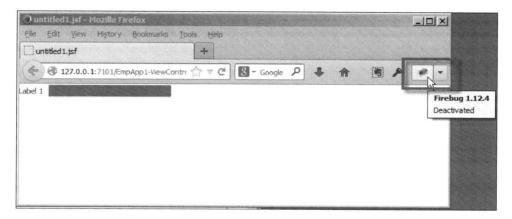

When you click on the icon to start Firebug, you'll see it take up the lower half of your Firefox browser window.

> **Only run Firebug when you need it**
>
> Firebug's detailed analysis of every page costs processing power and slows your browser down. Run Firebug only when you need it. Remember to deactivate Firebug, not just hide it.

If you click on the **Inspect** button (with a little blue arrow, second from the left in the Firebug toolbar), you place Firebug in **inspect** mode. You can now point to any element on a page and see both the HTML element and the style applied to this element, as shown in the following screenshot:

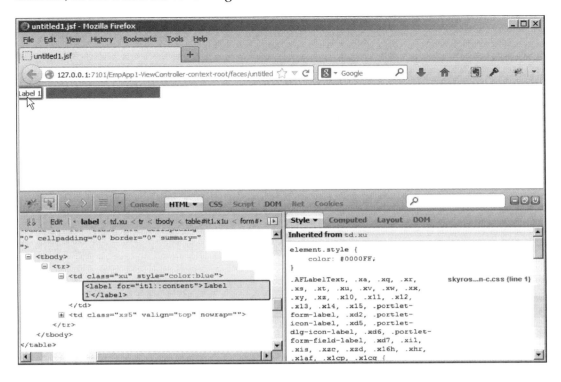

In the preceding example, the pointer is placed on the label for an input text, and the Firebug panels show that this element is styled with color: #0000FF. If you scroll down in the right-hand side **Style** panel, you can see other attributes such as font-family: Tahoma, font-size: 11px, and so on.

In order to keep the size of the HTML page smaller so that it loads faster, ADF has abbreviated all the style class names to cryptic short names such as `.x10`. While you are styling your application, you don't want this abbreviation to happen. To turn it off, you need to open the `web.xml` file (in your **View** project under **Web Content | WEB-INF**). Change to the **Overview** tab if it is not already shown, and select the **Application** subtab, as shown in the following screenshot:

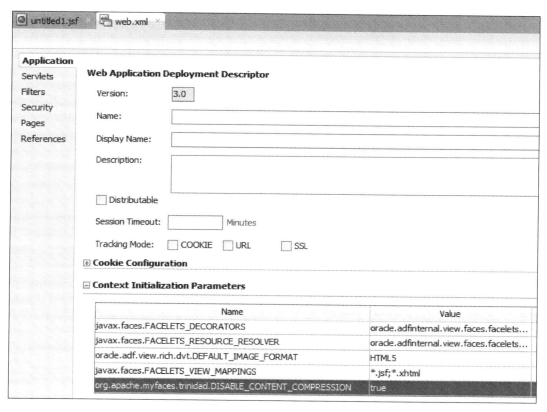

Under **Context Initialization Parameters**, add a new parameter, as shown:

- **Name**: `org.apache.myfaces.trinidad.DISABLE_CONTENT_COMPRESSION`
- **Value**: `true`

When you do this, you'll see the full human-readable style names in Firebug, as shown in the following screenshot:

```
Style ▼   Computed   Layout   DOM

Inherited from td.af_inputText_label

element.style {
    color: #0000FF;
}
.AFLabelText, .af_outputLabel, .af_inputChoice_label,        skyros...n-u.css (line 11)
.af_inputFile_label, .af_inputNumberSpinbox_label,
.af_inputText_label, .af_selectBooleanCheckbox_label,
.af_selectBooleanRadio_label, .af_inputColor_label,
.af_inputDate_label, .af_inputListOfValues_label,
.af_selectManyCheckbox_label,
.af_selectManyListbox_label, .af_selectOneChoice_label,
.af_selectOneListbox_label, .af_selectOneRadio_label,
.af_panelLabelAndMessage_label, .portlet-form-label,
.portlet-icon-label, .portlet-dlg-icon-label, .portlet-
form-field-label, .af_richTextEditor_label,
.af_codeEditor_label, .af_selectManyShuttle_label,
.af_selectOrderShuttle_label,
.af_selectManyChoice_label,
.af_inputComboboxListOfValues_label,
.af_quickQuery_label, .af_inputNumberSlider_label,
.af_inputRangeSlider_label {
    color: #4F4F4F;
    font-family: Tahoma,Verdana,Helvetica,sans-serif;
    font-size: 11px;
    font-weight: normal;
    text-align: right;
}

Inherited from body.af_document

.AFFieldText, .af_outputDocument,                            skyros...n-u.css (line 8)
.af_inputChoice_content, .af_inputChoice_content-input,
.af_selectBooleanRadio_content,
```

You notice that you now get more readable names such as .af_outputLabel. You might need this information when developing your custom skin.

Getting the maximum speed

You want this compression enabled in your production application for best performance. Remember to remove the DISABLE_CONTENT_ COMPRESSION initialization parameter again before deploying your application to production.

Conditional formatting

Similar to many other properties, the style properties do not have to be set to a fixed value—you can also set them to any valid expression written in **Expression Language** (**EL**). This can be used to create conditional formatting.

In the simplest form, you can use an Expression Language **ternary operator**, which has the form `<boolean expression> ? <value if true > : <value if false>`. For example, you could set **StyleClass** to the following line of code:

```
#{bindings.Job.inputValue eq 'MANAGER' ? 'managerStyle' :
'nonManagerStyle'}
```

The preceding expression means that if the value of the `Job` attribute is equal to `MANAGER`, use the **managerStyle** style class; if not, use the **nonManagerStyle** style class. Of course, this only works if these two styles exist in your CSS.

Skinning overview

An **ADF skin** is a collection of files that together define the look and feel of the application. To a hunter, skinning is the process of removing the skin from an animal, but to an ADF developer it's the process of putting a skin onto an application.

All applications have a skin—if you don't change it, an application built with JDeveloper 12*c* uses some variation of the `skyros` skin.

When you define a custom skin, you must also choose a parent skin among the skins JDeveloper offers. This parent skin will define the look for all the components not explicitly defined in your skin.

Skinning capabilities

As you saw earlier in this chapter, there are a few options to change the style of the individual components through their properties. However, with your own custom ADF skin, you can globally change almost every visual aspect of every instance of a specific component.

To see skinning in action, you can go to `http://jdevadf.oracle.com/adf-richclient-demo`. This site is a demonstration of lots of ADF features and components, and if you choose the **Skinning** header in the accordion to the right, you are presented with a tree of skinnable components, as shown in the following screenshot:

You can click on each component to see a page where you can experiment with various ways of skinning the component.

For example, you can select the very common **InputText** component to see a page with various representations of the input text components. On the left-hand side, you see a number of **Style Selectors** that are relevant for that component. For each selector, you can check the checkbox to see an example of what the component looks like if you change that selector. In the following example, the **af | inputText:disabled::content** selector is checked, thus setting its style to `color: #00C0C0`, as shown in the following screenshot:

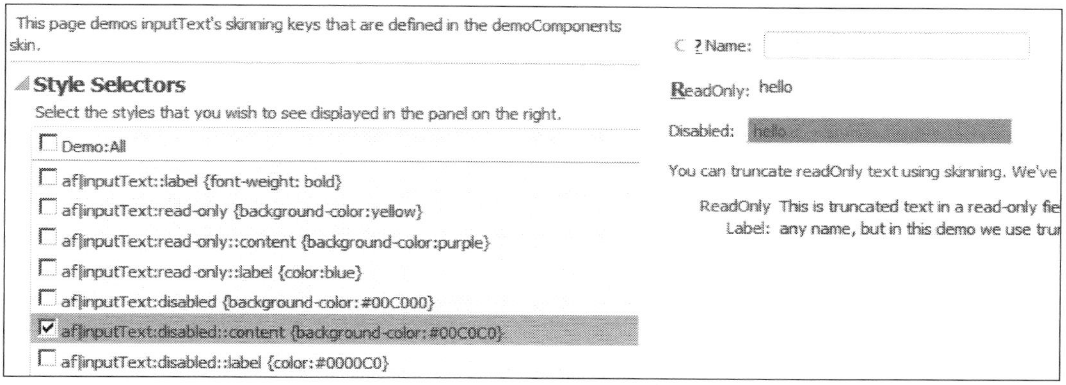

As you might be able to deduce from the **af | inputText:disabled::content** style selector, this controls what the *content* field of the *input text* component looks like when it is set to *disabled* — in the demo application, it is set to a bluish color with the color code `#00C0C0`. The example application shows various values for the selectors but doesn't really explain them. The full documentation of all the selectors can be found online, at the time of writing this book, at `http://jdevadf.oracle.com/ adf-richclient-demo/docs/skin-selectors.html`. If it's not there, search for `ADF skinning selectors`.

On the menu in the demo application, you also find a **Skin** menu that you can use to select and test all the built-in skins. This application can also be downloaded and run on your own server. At the time of writing this book, it could be found on the ADF download page at `http://www.oracle.com/technetwork/developer-tools/adf/downloads/index.html`, as shown in the following screenshot:

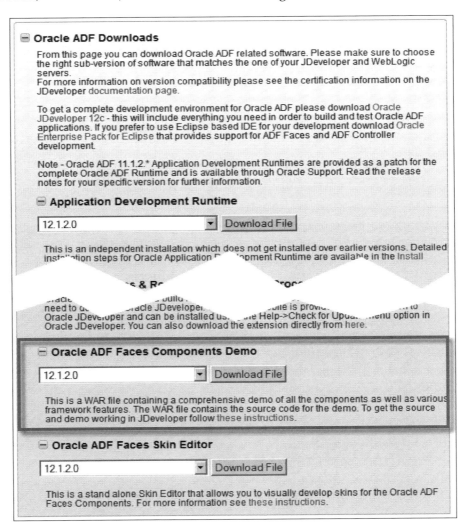

Skinning recommendations

If your graphics designer has produced sample screens showing what the application must look like, you need to find out which components you will use to implement the required look and define the look of these components in your skin.

If you don't have a detailed guideline from a graphics designer, look for some guidelines in your organization; you probably have web design guidelines for your public-facing website and/or intranet.

If you don't have any graphics guidelines, create a skin, as described later in this section, and choose to inherit from the latest `skyros` skin provided by Oracle. However, don't change anything—leave the CSS file empty. If you are a programmer, you are unlikely to be able to improve on the look that the professional graphics designers at Oracle in Redwood Shores have created.

Always wear your own skin

Creating an empty skin is similar to creating empty framework extension classes as you did in *Chapter 5, Preparing to Build*. It provides a placeholder that you can fill with content later if you need it.

The skinning process

The skinning process in ADF consists of the following steps:

1. Create a skin CSS file.
2. Optionally, provide images for your skin.
3. Optionally, create a resource bundle for your skin.
4. Package the skin in an ADF Library.
5. Import and use the skin in the application.

In JDeveloper 11*g* Release 1 (11.1.1.x) and earlier versions, this was very much a manual process. Fortunately, from 11*g* Release 2, JDeveloper has a built-in skinning editor.

Standalone skinning

If you are running JDeveloper 11*g* Release 1, don't despair. Oracle is making a standalone skinning editor available, containing the same functionality that is built into the later versions of JDeveloper. You can give this tool to your graphic designers and let them build the skin ADF Library without having to give them the complete JDeveloper product.

ADF skinning is a huge topic, and Oracle delivers a whole manual that describes skinning in complete detail. This document is called *Creating Skins with Oracle ADF Skin Editor* and can be found at `http://docs.oracle.com/middleware/1212/ skineditor/ADFSG`.

Creating a skin project

You should place your skin in a common workspace. If you are using the modular architecture described in *Chapter 3, Getting Organized*, you create your skin in the Application Common Workspace. If you are using the enterprise architecture, you create your enterprise common skin in the Application Common Workspace and then possibly create application-specific adaptations of that skin in the Application Common Workspaces.

The skin should be placed in its own project in the common workspace. Logically, it could be placed in the common UI workspace, but because the skin will often receive many small changes during certain phases of the project, it makes sense to keep it separate. Remember that changing the skin only affects the visual aspects of the application, but changing the page templates could conceivably change the functionality. By keeping the skin in a separate ADF Library, you can be sure that you do not need to perform regression testing on the application functionality after deploying a new skin.

To create your skin, open the common workspace and navigate to **File | New | Project**. Choose the **ADF ViewController** project, give the project the name `CommonSkin`, and set the package to your application's package prefix followed by `.skin` (for example, `com.dmcsol.xdm.skin`).

Skinning in practice

Now that we know what skinning is and what it can do, let's create and apply a skin to the example application.

Creating a skin CSS file

The most important part of your skin is the special ADF CSS file that defines the look of all the components you use in your application.

To create the CSS file, follow the ensuing steps:

1. Select the `CommonSkin` project and navigate to **File | New | From Gallery....** Under **Web Tier | JSF/Facelets**, choose **ADF Skin**. The **Create ADF Skin** dialog appears, as shown in the following screenshot:

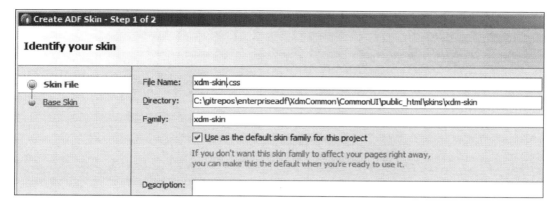

2. Give your CSS file a filename that includes `-skin` (for example, `xdm-skin. css`). You can leave the location at its default setting, and you don't have to change the value for **Family** either.

Skin families

Skins come in **families**—a collection of related skins. All skins in a family share the same family name, and each skin in the family has a unique **Skin Id** consisting of the family name and a platform suffix. You start with the `.desktop` member of the family—this is the version of the skin that will be used for normal browser access to your application. You can also define other family members, such as `.mobile`, for controlling how the application will look on a mobile device.

3. In the second step of the wizard, you have the option to select various skins to base your own skin on. As you can read from the descriptions, Oracle recommends you base your own skin on the `skyros-v1.desktop` skin for most applications. If you are building an application that will work together with fusion applications, Oracle recommends that you base your skin on `fusionFx-simple-v3.desktop`.

Once you finish the wizard, your skin is opened. JDeveloper automatically recognizes your ADF skin CSS file as a special kind of CSS and shows it in a special skinning editor window, as shown in the following screenshot:

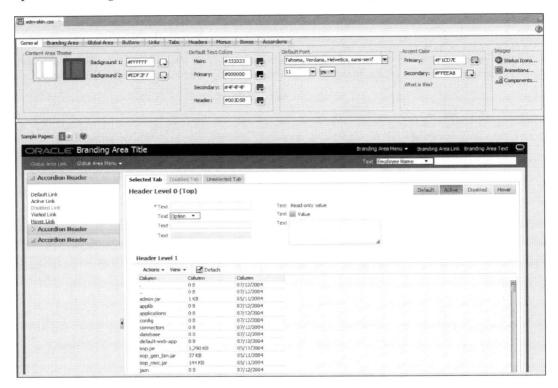

If your skin is based on the `skyros` or `fusionFX-simple` skin, the skin editor window contains a **Design** tab as well as a **Selectors** tab and a **Source** tab.

If you based your skin on another one of the Oracle-supplied skins, you will not see the **Design** tab. The **Design** tab makes it easier to make certain changes, but everything can also be done on the **Selectors** and **Source** tabs.

Working in the Design tab

The **Design** tab allows you to easily make a number of changes that apply to the whole application. The upper part of the window contains a number of tabs where you can change various values, and the lower part of this window can show some sample pages. You can click on the browser icon to open the sample page in your browser. The browsers available here are the ones that are set up in JDeveloper under **Tools | Preferences | Web Browser**.

 Update problems

Some versions of JDeveloper have contained a subtle bug. This means that you sometimes will not see the sample page update after you change the settings. The changes are shown when you close the skin and reopen it.

On the tabs here, you can change various aspects of the application, as follows:

- The **General** tab allows you to change the default font and text

- The **Branding Area** and **Global Area** tabs affect the applications that use the default templates provided by Oracle (**Oracle Three Column Layout** and **Oracle Dynamic Tabs Shell**)

- The remaining tabs allow you to change the default look of buttons, links, menus, and many other parts of your application

As you make changes, JDeveloper records your changes in the CSS file—you can always change to the **Source** tab at the bottom of the window to see the actual code JDeveloper writes.

Working in the Selectors tab

The **Selectors** tab allows you to style individual components with much more detailed control. This tab contains a tree selector to the left and a preview of the selected component to the right, as shown in the following screenshot:

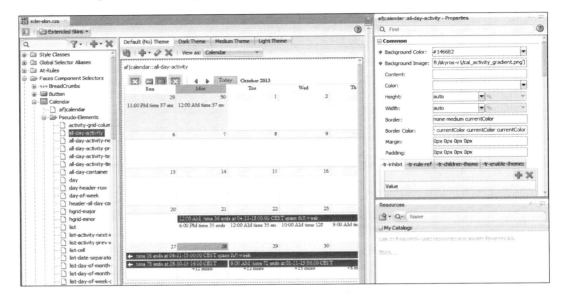

For components that can be rendered in several different ways, there are tabs to the right that can be selected to view the component with a specific **theme**, and you can also select from the **View as** drop-down list. You can change the properties for the selected component in the **Properties** window.

The tree has five top-level nodes:

- **Style Classes**
- **Global Selector Aliases**
- **At-rules**
- **Faces Component Selectors**
- **Data Visualizations Component Selectors**

Style Classes

The **Style Classes** are built-in styles intended for your use in the `StyleClass` attribute—these do no affect any components.

If you need to define your own styles classes, you can click on the plus sign above the navigator to the left and choose **New Style Class** to define a new class. It will be added to your CSS file and will show up under the **Style Classes** node. You can define the visual properties of the class using the **Property Inspector** or directly in the CSS source code by selecting the **Source** tab at the bottom of the skin editor panel.

Global Selector Aliases

The **Global Selector Aliases** are selectors that control many different components. Typically, you'd want to make these kinds of changes on the **Design** tab. However, if your skin is not based on `skyros` or `fusionFx-simple`, you don't have a **Design** tab and will have to make your global changes here.

At-Rules

At-Rules allows you to specify the style properties that will only be applied in specific environments, for example, a specific browser, platform, or locale. Defining an at-rule allows you to define, for example, that you want extra spacing if the browser is Internet Explorer. Refer to *Chapter 10* of the *Creating Skins with Oracle ADF Skin Editor 12c* manual for more information on at-rules.

Faces Component Selectors

Under the **Faces Component Selectors** node, you find all the individual ADF Faces components that you can change the visual appearance of. To change a component, expand the node corresponding to the component to see the different selectors you can control.

You can click on the component itself to set the general attributes for the component, or you can expand the **Pseudo-Elements** node to change some specific aspects. For example, if you want to change the actual field where the user enters data, you can select the **content** pseudo element. In the right-hand side of the **ADF Skin** dialog, you see the various subtypes of content styling that can apply to the component. As you select these subtypes, the **Property Inspector** shows the styling of that subtype, as shown in the following screenshot:

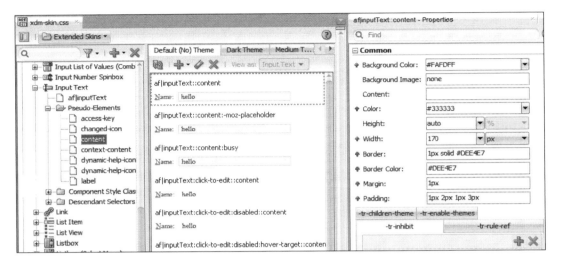

The preceding example shows the default styling of the entry field for an input text component. Notice the blue arrows that indicate a setting that is inherited from somewhere else — you can point to the arrow to see a pop up showing you where that setting inherits from.

If you want, for example, to change the border of a text field that contains a warning, scroll down among the examples of the **InputText** content to find the **af | inputText:warning::content** example and select it. In the **Property Inspector**, change the **Border** property, for example, to 4px dotted #FFFF00 to use a wider border as a series of dots in bright yellow, as shown in the following screenshot:

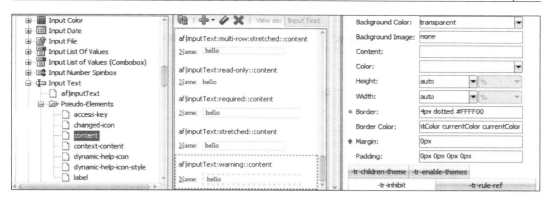

Data Visualizations Component Selectors

Finally, the **Data Visualizations Component Selectors** define the look of the various data visualization components (Gantt charts, graphs, maps, and so on.), as shown in the following screenshot:

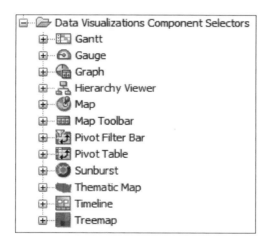

Finding the selector at runtime

If you can't find the selector you want in the skinning editor, you can create a simple JSF page in JDeveloper and drop an instance of the component you want to skin onto this page and run the page in Firefox. Then, start the Firebug add-on and inspect the element you want to skin.

The right-hand panel in Firebug shows the styling that's applied to that element—if you set `DISABLE_CONTENT_COMPRESSION` to `true`, as described earlier in this chapter, you will see a style class name such as `.af_panelFormLayout_label-cell`. This translates into the `af|panelFormLayout` component and the `label-cell` pseudo element. You can then look this up in the skinning editor and define the appearance you want.

Optionally providing images for your skin

If you want to change the images used in your application, first select the **Design** view (click on the tab at the bottom of the skin editor window). Then, select the **General** tab at the top of the window. On this tab, the right-most box is called **Images**. If you click on one of the images in this box, you get the **Replace Icons** dialog box, as shown in the following screenshot:

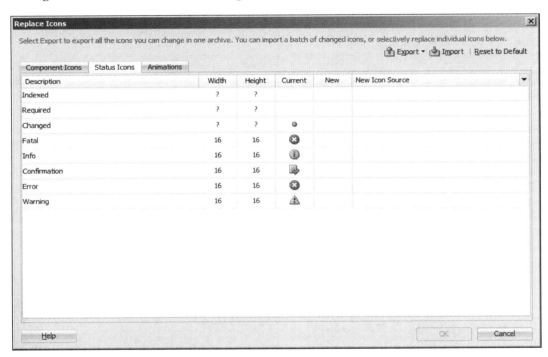

From this dialog, you can export all the images to a ZIP file. You can then open the file, replace the icons or other images you want to change, and import them again.

You can also change the images from the **Selectors** tab, but that's more complicated. It involves the following:

- Selecting a pseudo element in the tree
- Finding the image attribute (often **Content**, sometimes **Background Image**)
- Using the settings icon (a little gearwheel) next to the attribute and selecting **Copy Image**

This places a copy of the image in your project—you can copy your own image into the same directory and change the relevant attribute, or simply overwrite the standard image with your own.

Optionally creating a resource bundle for your skin

You might have noticed that many ADF components display texts that you can't set through properties, for example, the pop up help that appears if you allow sorting in an `af:table` component and point to the table header, as shown in the following screenshot:

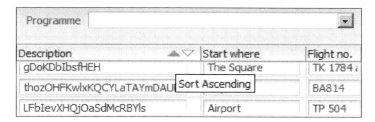

If you want to change these standard strings, you first need to go to the documentation and find the **resource string** you want to override. For table sorting, you need `af_column.TIP_SORT_ASCENDING` and `af_column.TIP_SORT_DESCENDING`.

Then, you need to open the resource bundle file that the skin editor has built for you, called `skinBundle.properties` by default, as shown in the following screenshot:

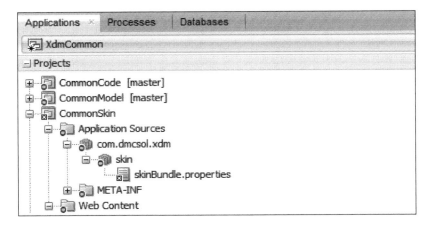

The default file contains a couple of examples, and you need to add your own resource strings to this file. It might look like the following code:

```
# This file may be used to define alternative text
# for resource strings that appear in the user
# interface of ADF Components.
# Example: To change the text that appears on the
# buttons of the af:dialog component from Ok and
# Cancel to Continue and Go Back, add the following
# to this file:
#   AF_DIALOG.LABEL_OK = Continue
#   AF_DIALOG.LABEL_CANCEL = Go Back      AF_COLUMN.TIP_SORT_ASCENDING =
First things first
AF_COLUMN.TIP_SORT_DESCENDING = The last shall be first
```

Packaging the skin

Once you are done with your skin, you need to package it into an ADF Library. To do this, you can right-click on your skin project and navigate to **Deploy | New Deployment Profile**. Choose **ADF Library JAR File** and give your deployment profile a name (for example, `adflibXdmSkin`).

In the **Edit ADF Library JAR Deployment Profile Properties** dialog that appears next, simply click on **OK**.

Then, right-click on your skin project again and choose the name of your deployment profile (for example, `adflibXdmSkin`), click on **Next** and then on **Finish**. Like for other ADF Libraries, this creates a JAR file in the `deploy` directory under your project. As a developer, you should add it to your version control system, and your build/deployment manager will pick it up and have it tested and distributed to the various subsystem teams.

Using the skin

To use the skin, you simply need to add the ADF Library to your project from the **Components** palette and change the `trinidad-config.xml` file in the project using the skin to refer to the skin in the library.

In the `trinidad-config.xml` file under **Web Content/WEB-INF** in your project, you need to change the `<skin-family>` tag to refer the skin family you defined:

```
<skin-family>xdm-skin</skin-family>
```

If you now run your application, you should see your skinning take effect, as shown in the following screenshot:

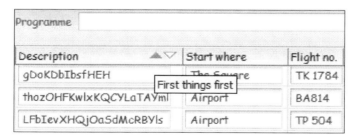

Summary

In this chapter, you've seen how ADF uses Cascading Style Sheets (CSS) for defining the appearance of components without affecting their functionality. For changing the look of an individual component, you can use inline styles, content styles, and style classes.

If you want to customize the look of the entire application, you define a skin. This used to be difficult and complex, but with the skinning editor available both as an integrated product in JDeveloper and as a standalone product, this has become much easier. You have a **Design** tab for quickly making application-wide changes and a **Selectors** tab with a tree navigator for selecting the components. You can use the **Property Inspector** to change the settings and immediately see what your component will look like. You final skin can include both global changes affecting the whole application, including the color scheme, and visual changes that affect only one specific component or even just one aspect of it.

When you are done with your application skin, you can deploy it as an ADF Library using the normal procedures for working with ADF Libraries to use it in your subsystems and master application.

Your manager is impressed with the way you can easily customize the look of the application and asks you if you can also customize the functionality. Yes, you say, using the ADF customization features. These features will be the topic of the next chapter.

9
Customizing Functionality

You've seen that you can change the way your application looks and deploy the same application to different users with a different visual appearance. But your boss at DMC Solutions would like to be able to sell the XDM application to different customers, thus offering each of them a slightly different functionality.

Fortunately, ADF makes this easy through a feature known as **customization**.

The reason for customization

Oracle ADF has customization features because they were needed for **Oracle Fusion Applications**. Oracle Fusion Applications is a suite of programs capable of handling every aspect of a large organization—personnel, finance, project management, manufacturing, logistics, and much more. As the organizations are different, Oracle has to offer a way for each customer organization to fit Oracle Fusion Applications to their requirements.

This customization functionality can also be very useful for organizations that don't use Oracle Fusion Applications. If you have two screens that work with the same data and one screen must show more fields than the other, you can create one screen with all the fields and use customization to create another version of the same screen with fewer fields for other users.

For example, the destination management application that we are using as an example in this book might have a data entry screen showing all the details of a task to a dispatcher, but only the relevant details will be shown to an airport transfer guide. The following illustration shows what the dispatcher would see on the left and what the airport transfer guide would see on the right:

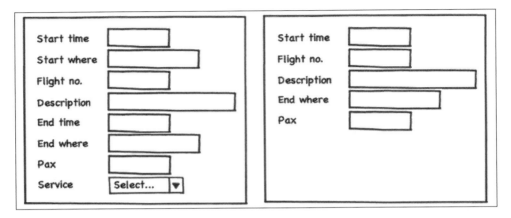

Companies such as DMC Solutions that produce software for sale realize an additional benefit from the customization features in ADF. DMC Solutions can build a base application, sell it to different customers, and customize each instance of the application to that customer without changing the base application.

The technology behind ADF customization

More and more Oracle products are using something called **Meta Data Services** (**MDS**) to store metadata. Metadata is the data that describes other pieces of information—where it came from, what it means, or how it is intended to be used. An image captured by a digital camera might include metadata about where and when the picture was taken, which camera settings were used, and so on. In the case of an ADF application, the metadata describes how the application is intended to be used.

There are three kinds of customizations in ADF, as follows:

- **Seeded customizations**: These are the customizations defined by customization developers and delivered together with the application. They stay with the application as long as it is deployed.

- **User customizations**: These customizations (sometimes called **personalizations**) are changes to the aspects of the user interface by application end users. The ADF framework offers few user customization features—for example, an ADF application can remember if a user has reordered the columns in a table. You need additional software such as Oracle WebCenter for most user customizations. User customizations are outside the scope of this book.

- **Design time at runtime customization**: This is an advanced customization of the application by application administrators and/or properly authorized end users. This requires the application developers to prepare the possible customizations as part of application development; it is complicated to program using only ADF, but Oracle WebCenter provides advanced components that make this easier. This is outside the scope of this book.

Your customization metadata is stored in either files or in a database repository. In a development environment, your customizations are stored in files, but in a production environment, you should set up your production server to store customizations in a metadata database. Refer to *Chapter 14*, *Managing the Metadata Repository*, in the *Administering Oracle Fusion Middleware* manual (`http://docs.oracle.com/middleware/1212/core/ASADM/repos.htm`) for information on managing the metadata repository.

Applying customization layers

When an ADF application is customized, the ADF framework applies one or more **customization layers** on top of the base application. Each layer has a value, and customizations are assigned to a specific customization layer and value.

The concept of multiple layers makes it possible to apply, for example, the following:

- Industry customization (customizing the application, for example, the travel industry: `industry = travel`)

- Organization customization (customizing the application for a specific travel company: `org = xyztravel`)

- Site customization (customizing the application for the Berlin office)

- Role-based customization (customizing the application for casual, normal, and advanced users)

The XDM application that DMC Solution is building could be customized in one way for ABC Travel and in another way for XYZ Travel, and XYZ Travel might decide to further customize the application for different types of users. These two customization layers are shown in the following screenshot:

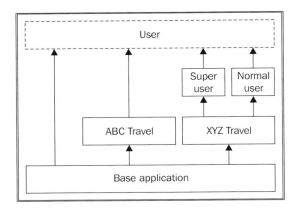

You can have as many layers as you need—Oracle Fusion Applications use many, but your applications will probably only need a few layers.

For each customization layer, the developer of the base application must provide a customization **class** that will be executed at runtime, returning a value for each customization layer. The ADF framework will then apply the customizations that the customization developer has specified for that layer/value combination. This means that the same application can appear in many different ways depending on the values returned by the customization classes and the customizations registered.

Organization layer value	Role layer value	Result
qrstravel	any	This is a base application because there are no customizations defined for QRS Travel.
abctravel	any	This application is customized for ABC Travel. As there are no role layer customizations for ABC Travel, the value of the role layer does not change the application.
xyztravel	normal	This application is customized for XYZ Travel and further customized for normal users in XYZ Travel.
xyztravel	superuser	This application is customized for XYZ Travel and further customized for superusers in XYZ Travel.

Making an application customizable

To make an application customizable, you need to do the following three things:

1. Develop a customization class for each layer of customization
2. Enable seeded customization in the application
3. Link the customization class to the application

The customization developer, who will be developing the customizations, will additionally have to set up JDeveloper correctly so that all the customization levels can be accessed. This setup is described later in the chapter.

Developing customization classes

For each layer of customization, you need to develop a customization class in a specific format — technically, it has to extend the Oracle-supplied abstract class, `oracle.mds.cust.CustomizationClass`.

A customization class has a name (returned by the `getName` method) and a `getValue` method that returns one or more values. At runtime, the ADF framework will execute the customization classes for all the layers to determine the customization value or values at each level. Additionally, the customization class has to return a short and unique prefix to be used for all customized items and a cache hint telling ADF whether this is a static or dynamic customization.

Building the classes

Your customization classes should go in the Common Code project in your Application Common Workspace because customizations are application specific. Even if you are using the enterprise architecture described in *Chapter 3, Getting Organized*, there is rarely a need for a customization class in your Enterprise Common Workspace.

A customization class is a normal Java class, that is, it is created by navigating to **File | New | Java Class**. In the **Create Java Class** dialog, give your class a name (for example, `OrgLayerCC`) and place it into a customization package (for example, `com.dmcsol.xdm.customization`). Choose `oracle.mds.cust.CustomizationClass` to extend it and check the `Implement Abstract Methods` checkbox, as shown in the following screenshot:

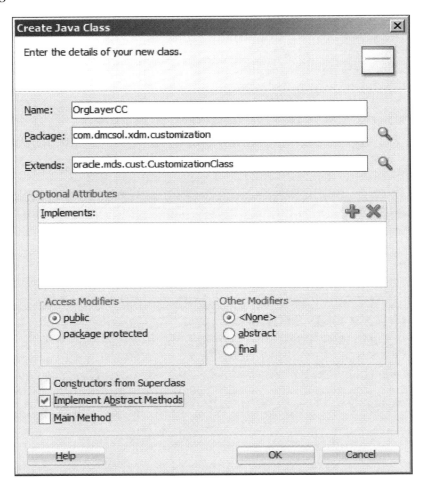

Create a similar class named `RoleLayerCC`.

Implementing the methods

As you asked JDeveloper to implement the abstract methods, your classes already contain the following three methods:

- `getCacheHint()`
- `getName()`
- `getValue(RestrictedSession, MetadataObject)`

The `getCacheHint()` method must return an `oracle.mds.cust.CacheHint` constant that tells ADF if the value of this layer is static (common for all users) or dynamic (depending on the user). The normal values here are `CacheHint.ALL_USERS` for static customizations or `CacheHint.MULTI_USER` for customizations that apply to multiple users. In the XDM application, you will use the following:

- `ALL_USERS` for `OrgLevelCC` because this customization layer will apply to all the users in the organization
- `MULTI_USER` for `RoleLevelCC` because the role-based customization will apply to multiple users but not necessarily to all the users

Refer to *Chapter 45* in ADF's *Developing Fusion Web Applications with Oracle Application Development Framework* manual for information on other possible values.

The `getName()` method simply returns the name of the customization layer.

The `getValue()` method must return an array of `String` objects. It will normally make more sense to return just one value—the application is running for exactly one organization, and you are either a normal user or a superuser. For advanced scenarios, it is possible to return multiple values; in this case, multiple customizations will be applied to the same layer. Each customization that a customization developer defines will be tied to a specific layer and value. There might be a customization that happens when `org` has the `xyztravel` value.

For the `OrgLayerCC` class, the value is static and is defined when DMC Solutions install the application for XYZ Travel, for example, in a property file. For the `RoleLayerCC` class, the value is dynamic depending on the current user and can be retrieved from the ADF security context. The `OrgLayerCC` class could look as shown in the following code snippet:

```
package com.dmcsol.xdm.customization;

import ...

public class RoleLayerCC extends CustomizationClass {
  public CacheHint getCacheHint() {
```

```
      return CacheHint.MULTI_USER;
  }

  public String getName() {
    return "role";
  }

  public String[] getValue(
    RestrictedSession restrictedSession,
      MetadataObject metadataObject) {
    String[] roleValue = new String[1];
    SecurityContext sec =
      ADFContext.getCurrent().getSecurityContext();
    if (sec.isUserInRole("superuser")) {
      roleValue[0] = "superuser";
    } else {
      roleValue[0] = "normal";
    }
    return roleValue;
  }
}
```

The GetCacheHint method returns MULTI_USER because this is a dynamic customization—it will return different values for different users.

The GetName method simply returns the name of the layer.

The GetValue method uses oracle.adf.share.security.SecurityContext to find out whether the user has the superuser role and returns the value superuser or normal.

Deploying the customization classes

As you place your customization class in the Common Code project, you need to deploy this project to an ADF Library and have the build/configuration manager copy it to your common library directory before you can use your customization classes.

Enabling seeded customization

In order to be able to customize pages, you need to tell JDeveloper to prepare for customization as you add components to the page flows and pages in your `ViewController` project.

In this chapter, we will customize the `TaskMgr` subsystem. Open the `XdmTaskMgr` workspace and choose the **Project Properties** dialog for the View project (`TaskMgrView`) in the workspace for each task flow that you want to customize. Choose **ADF View** and then check the **Enable Seeded Customizations** checkbox, as shown in the following screenshot. When you check this checkbox, JDeveloper automatically changes some project configuration files.

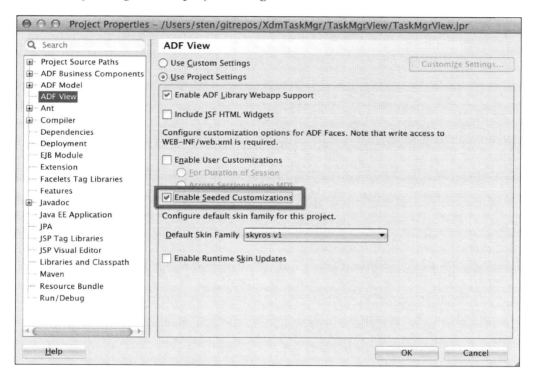

Linking the customization class to the application

The last step in preparing an application for customization is to define which customization levels you will use and in which order they will be applied. This is done in the adf-config.xml file that is found under the **Application Resources** panel in **Application Navigator**. Expand the **Descriptors** node and then expand ADF META-INF to find the adf-config.xml file, as shown in the following screenshot:

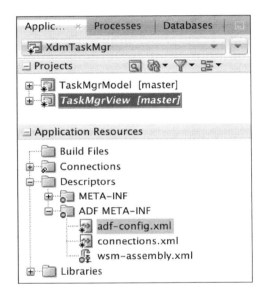

Open the adf-config file and choose the **MDS** subtab in the left-hand side of the window, as shown in the following screenshot. On this tab, you can add all of your customization classes and define the order in which they are applied (the topmost class in this dialog is applied first).

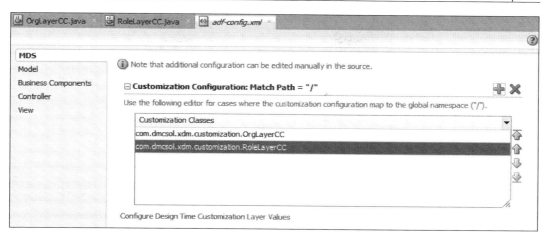

 Your customization classes defined in the common code workspace are not available until you have deployed the common code workspace to an ADF Library and have made this library available to the project in which you want to perform customization.

Configuring customization layers

When developing customizations, the customization developer must choose a layer and a value to work in—for example, developing customizations for `org = xyztravel`. However, because the layer values are returned by code at runtime, there is no way for JDeveloper to figure out which layer values are available. That's why you need to define the available customization layers and the possible values in a `CustomizationLayerValues.xml` file.

When you are developing customizations, JDeveloper will read the `adf-config.xml` file to find out which layers exist and the `CustomizationLayerValues.xml` file to find out which values are possible in each layer. The static `CustomizationLayerValues.xml` file must contain all the layers defined in the `adf-config.xml` file and should contain all the possible values that your customization class can return.

Match the XML file with the customization class

The CustomizationLayerValues.xml values are used at design time, and the customization class is called at runtime. If you leave out a value from the XML file, you will not be able to define customizations for that value. If you add a value to the XML file that will never be returned by the customization class, you might accidentally define a customization that will never be applied at runtime.

To edit the CustomizationLayerValues.xml file, click on the **Configure Design Time Customization Layer Values** link at the bottom of the **MDS** tab in the adf-config.xml file. The first time you edit the file, you get a warning about overriding the global CustomizationLayerValues.xml file. Simply acknowledge this warning and continue to your file.

You are presented with an example file containing some customization layer values and descriptive comments. For the XDM application using two customization layers of org and role, use the following code to change the file:

```
<cust-layers xmlns="http://xmlns.oracle.com/mds/dt">
  <cust-layer name="org" id-prefix="o"
      value-set-size="small">
    <cust-layer-value value="abctravel"
        display-name="ABC Travel" id-prefix="a"/>
    <cust-layer-value value="xyztravel"
        display-name="XYZ Travel" id-prefix="x"/>
  </cust-layer>
  <cust-layer name="role" id-prefix="r"
      value-set-size="small">
    <cust-layer-value value="normal"
        display-name="Normal user" id-prefix="n"/>
    <cust-layer-value value="superuser"
        display-name="Superuser" id-prefix="s"/>
  </cust-layer>
</cust-layers>
```

The name attribute of the cust-layer element must match the values returned from the getName() methods in your customization class. Similarly, the value attribute of the cust-layer-value element must match the values returned by the getValue() method in the corresponding customization class.

The id-prefix values for both layers and their values are used to ensure that each component is given a globally unique name. All the components in an ADF Faces application are given a component ID—for example, an inputText element might get the ID it3 in the base application.

With customization, however, that same element might exist in many different variations, customized in one way for one organization and in another way for another organization. To ensure that ADF can tell all of these components apart, it adds prefixes to the ID of the layers' component as specified in the following example file:

- The input component in the base application would be `it3`
- The same component customized in the `org` layer for the `abctravel` value would be `oait3` (the `o` is from the `org` ID prefix and the `a` is from the `abctravel` ID prefix)
- The same component customized in the `org` layer for the `xyztravel` value and in the `role` layer for the `superuser` value would be `oxrsit3` (`o` from `org` layer, `x` from the `xyztravel` value, `r` from the `role` layer, and `s` from the `superuser` value)

The `display-name` value is shown to the customization developers to help them select the right layer, and the `value-set-size` parameter should normally be set to `small` (this causes JDeveloper to show a drop-down box for selecting the layer value).

Using resource bundles

If you want to be able to change the text strings in the user interface, you have to use test strings from **resource bundles** and enable them for customization.

To assign a string from a resource bundle, click on the little gearwheel next to a label or text property and choose **Select Text Resource**, as shown in the following screenshot:

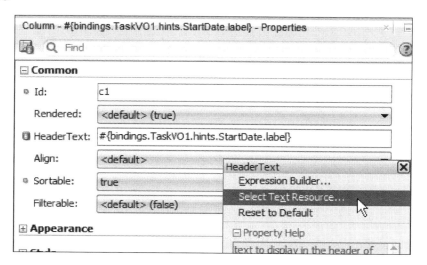

This brings up the **Select Text Resource** dialog, as follows:

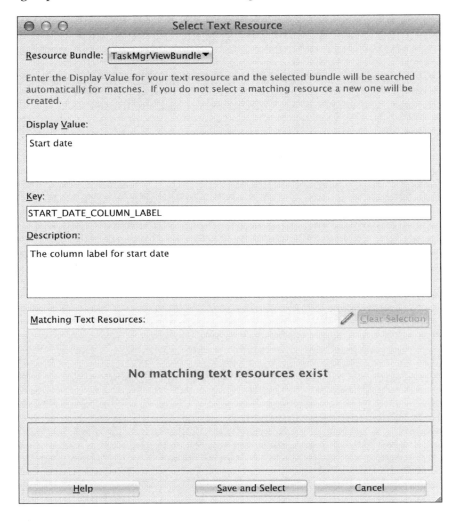

In this dialog, you can write a new text in the **Display Value** field and click on **Save and Select** to add the string to the resource bundle. You can also select an existing UI string from the **Matching Text Resources** box, in which case the button text is just **Save**.

 There is more information about internationalization in *Appendix, Internationalization*.

Allowing resource bundle customization

To enable a resource bundle for customization, you have to explicitly add it to your application. You can do this by navigating to **Application | Application Properties** and then choosing **Resource Bundles**. Click on the plus icon, navigate to your resource bundle, and click on **Open**. The resource bundle is shown in the list. Check the checkbox in the **Overridden** column, as shown in the following screenshot:

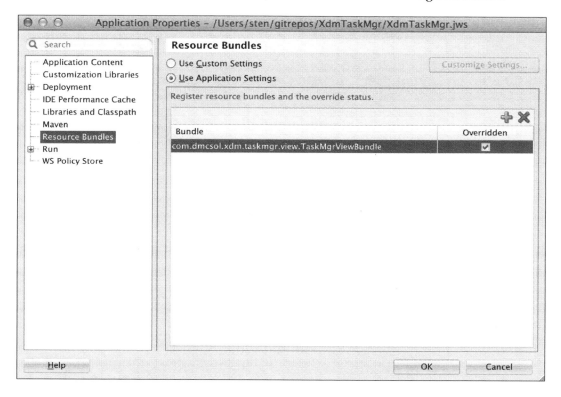

This allows customization of the text strings in that resource bundle.

Performing customization

With your application prepared for customization and JDeveloper set up correctly, you are ready to perform the actual customization.

Selecting the customization role

The first thing you need to do is run JDeveloper in a special **Customization Developer** role. To switch to this role, navigate to **Tools | Switch Roles | Customization Developer**. JDeveloper will tell you that it has to restart in order to switch roles.

You might remember that the first time you started JDeveloper, you were greeted with a role-selection dialog. If you have deselected it, you can re-enable it by navigating to **Tools | Switch Roles | Always prompt for role selection on startup**.

When JDeveloper is running in the customization mode, you will notice the new **Customization Context** panel shown at the bottom of the screen, as follows:

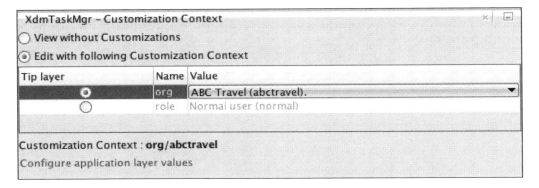

The values shown in this window come from the CustomizationLayerValues.xml file you created — the values in the **Name** column correspond to the cust-layer elements, and the values in the **Value** column correspond to the cust-layer-value elements.

When developing customizations, you are always working on a specific layer called the **Tip layer**. You select the **Tip layer** option with the radio buttons in the **Tip layer** column in the **Customization Context** panel. In the preceding illustration, the org layer is selected as the tip layer, and the **Value** column is **ABC Travel**. This means that the customizations that you make will be registered to the customization context, org/abctravel.

You see that the `role` layer value is grayed out when `org` is the tip layer. As the `org` layer is below the `role` layer, it doesn't matter what the value of `role` is when you are customizing for the organization. When you select `role` as the tip layer, the **Value** column becomes active, as shown in the following screenshot:

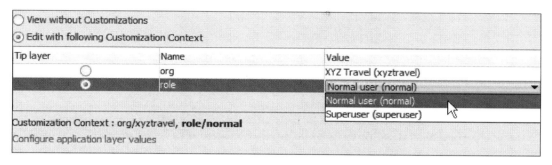

Any customizations that you register with the preceding settings will be registered in the role layer in the `org/xyztravel`, `role/normal` customization context.

If you want to see the base application, select **View without Customizations**.

Customizing Business Components

You can customize some aspects of Business Components—for example, it is possible to add or change the validation rules on entity objects. This can be useful, for example, if XYZ Travel wants to change a validation rule in the base application, but ABC Travel is happy with the base application functionality.

In this case, you select `org` as the tip layer, `XYZ Travel` as **Value** and change the validation rule as XYZ Travel requires. The base application remains unchanged, but JDeveloper has now stored a customization in the `org/xyztravel` context. When XYZ Travel is running the application, the `getValue()` method in the `OrgLayerCC` class will return `xyztravel`, the customization and modified business rule are applied. When ABC Travel is running the application, the `getValue()` method will return `abctravel`, and the unmodified validation rule from the base application is applied.

You can also customize UI hints (for example, default labels) by assigning new resource strings to them, as described in the *Customizing strings* section in this chapter.

Customizing pages

You can customize your pages and page fragments in the following ways:

- You can add new fields, buttons, and layout components
- You can remove fields
- You can reorder the existing items—reorder fields, move fields to other layout components, and so on
- You can assign new resource strings to components

In order to make a change, you have to work in the **Design** view and **Property Palette**. You can switch to the **Source** view of your page, but the source is read only when running JDeveloper in the **Customization Developer** mode.

As a simple example, imagine that ABC Travel does not require the Flight No. column and wants the StartWhere column before the Text column. Additionally, normal users should not be shown the Comment column.

To perform this customization, first choose org as the tip layer and ABC Travel as **Value**. Then, open the taskOverviewEdit.jsff page fragment and delete the FlightNo column and move the StartWhere column. Then, choose role as the tip layer and select ABC Travel as **Value** for org and Normal user as **Value** for role. JDeveloper will show a message that it has to close the customizable files. Click on **OK**, reopen the taskOverviewEdit.jsff page fragment, and delete the Remarks column.

While you were performing this customization, JDeveloper was storing your customizations as XML files with the same name as the base object. After the previous customization, your application navigator will show a couple of new files, as shown in the following screenshot:

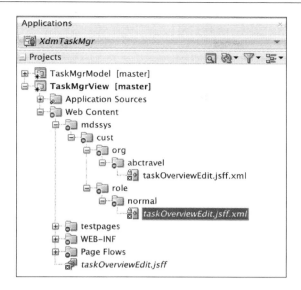

The `taskOverviewEditPage.jsff.xml` file shown under `mdssys/cust/org/ abctravel` contains the customizations that you have defined for ABC Travel, and the file under `mdssys/cust/role/normal` contains the customizations that you have defined for Normal users. These files record the changes that you have made in a compact XML format, as shown in the following code snippet:

```
<mds:customization version="12.1.2.66.68"
    xmlns:mds="http://xmlns.oracle.com/mds">
  <mds:replace node="c4"/>
  <mds:move node="c3" after="c1"/>
</mds:customization>
```

If you want to see your unmodified base application, you can select **View without Customizations** in the **Customization Context** panel.

 Notice the little human figure next to the application name in the preceding screenshot. If your application name does not show this icon, the application is not configured for customization.

Customizing strings

When customizing an application, you will find that the attributes defining the text displayed to the users are grayed out—you cannot change the Text property of a button or the Label property of a field. What you can do, however, is to assign new **resource strings** to the items using a resource bundle, as described in the *Using resource bundles* section in this chapter.

In the customization mode, click on the little settings icon in the right-hand side of the property field and choose **Select Text Resource**. In the **Select Text Resource** window (shown in the following screenshot), you can add a new string just like you did when originally developing the application.

If you add a new string while in the **Customization Developer** mode, JDeveloper will ask you to confirm that you want to add a new key to the **override bundle**. Your base application already has a resource bundle, but the changes you make while customizing are stored in a separate resource bundle that is created automatically by JDeveloper.

Your customizations are stored just like other customizations. If you are customizing for ABC Travel and changing the StartDate column's HeaderText attribute on the taskOverviewEditPage.jsff page fragment, the taskOverviewEditPage.jsff. xml file under mdssys/cust/org/abctravel will be updated to include something similar to the following code:

```
<mds:modify element="c3">
  <mds:attribute name="headerText"
      value="#{taskmgrviewBundle.WHEN_COLUMN_LABEL}"/>
</mds:modify>
```

The actual override bundle containing your custom strings and their keys is not displayed in JDeveloper. You can find it in the filesystem in the resourcebundles\xliffBundles subdirectory under the root directory of your application. For example, the override bundle for XdmTaskMgr might be found in C:\gitrepos\enterpriseadf\XdmTaskMgr\resourcebundles\xliffBundles\ XdmTaskMgrOverrideBundle.xlf.

This file is a normal XLIFF file similar to the one you might be using in your base application. If you only defined one new string, Find, it would look as shown in the following code snippet:

```
<?xml version="1.0" encoding="utf-8" ?>
<xliff version="1.1"
  xmlns="urn:oasis:names:tc:xliff:document:1.1">
  <file source-language="en" original="this" datatype="x-oracle-
    adf">
    <body>
      <trans-unit id="WHEN_COLUMN_LABEL">
        <source>When</source>
        <target/>
        <note>Customized column label for start date</note>
      </trans-unit>
    </body>
  </file>
</xliff>
```

There is more information on using resource bundles in *Appendix, Internationalization*.

Elements that cannot be customized

ADF customization works by registering changes to XML files in other XML files.

This means that you cannot customize Java code — you have to develop all your Java code in the base application. However, because you can customize attributes, it is possible to customize your application to select among different methods from the base application. For example, a button has an `ActionListener` property that can point to a method binding. If you have implemented two different methods in the base application and have created action bindings for them, you can use customization to choose one or the other method.

You also cannot customize certain configuration files, resource bundles, or security-related files. When you are running JDeveloper in the **Customization Developer** mode, **Application Navigator** will show all of these with a small padlock icon in the top-left corner of the item icon. In the following example, you can see that the `faces-config.xml`, `trinidad-config.xml`, and `web.xml` files cannot be customized:

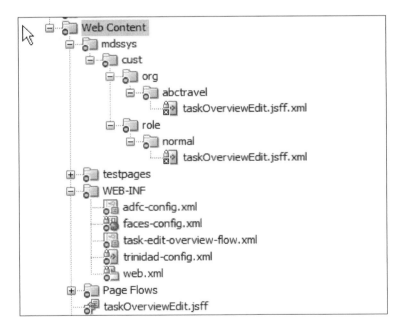

Summary

The ADF customization features are just what an independent software vendor, such as DMC Solutions, needs. The development team can build one base application, and implementation teams can customize the application for different customers in a controlled manner without affecting the base application.

You've learned how to prepare an application for customization and how to perform customization. You have also seen that your customizations are stored separately from the application so that they can be re-used even if you provide a new version of the base application.

Even if your enterprise application is not intended to be implemented for different customers, you can still use the customization features to offer different versions of screens to different users.

The following chapter will explain how to secure your application.

10

Securing Your ADF Application

Back in 2004, someone found out that you could open a high-security bicycle lock made out of hardened steel with a ballpoint pen! (Google `bike lock ballpoint pen` for more information). This was an excellent product that would resist bolt cutters, hacksaws, and crowbars—but the circular lock had a glaring weakness.

Security is like that: only as strong as the weakest link. To make certain that your enterprise ADF application is secure, you need security at many levels—your servers, your network, your application, and your data must be secure.

This chapter is only concerned with securing your enterprise ADF application using the many easy-to-use security features built into ADF. It covers the following topics:

- The security basics
- Security decisions
- Implementing ADF Security
- Securing task flows and pages
- Securing data
- Defining users, groups, and roles

The security basics

Two important parts of security are **authentication** (determining who the user is) and **authorization** (determining what the user is allowed to do). As an ADF application is a standard Java EE application and runs inside a Java EE application server, it can make use of the security features of Java EE and does not have to implement everything itself.

Authentication means knowing your user

A Java EE application server offers an approach to handle security for the applications that run inside it—this is called **container-managed security**. This approach offers several types of authentication—for an enterprise ADF application, you will always choose **Form-based authentication**. This allows the application to point to a web page (a login form) where the user can enter their username and password. You can design this login page as part of your application so that it looks like the rest of the application.

> Alternatives are **basic** or **digest** authentication; both of these depend on the browser to present a login screen. The basic authentication even sends your password unencrypted unless you use **SSL (Secure Sockets Layer)**. You might have seen this in use on basic websites—you'll simply get a dialog box with two fields for the username and password in whatever look the browser has decided to give it. You don't want this for your beautiful enterprise ADF application. Additionally, there is no way to log out of an application using the basic or digest authentication short of closing the browser.

The actual verification of the username and password is handled by the Oracle WebLogic application server using an **authentication provider**. The authentication provider connects WebLogic with some identity store—WebLogic comes with prebuilt providers for the built-in LDAP server, Oracle Internet Directory, Microsoft Active Directory, and relational databases. If none of these meet your needs, you can even program your own authentication provider. Setting up authentication providers is the responsibility of the application server administrator.

Authorization means deciding on access

While container-managed security works fine for authentication, the authorization features are a bit too basic for enterprise ADF applications. Container-managed authorization only protects specific URL patterns, but this is not enough for a modern, dynamic web application. **JavaServer Faces (JSF)** uses server-side navigation, so the same URL can represent many different parts of the application. You saw an example of this in *Chapter 6, Building the Enterprise Application*, where we used a dynamic region to swap task flows within the same page. It's obvious that a simple protection of URLs is not enough to secure our ADF application.

To achieve a more fine-grained authorization control, we turn to the **Java Authentication and Authorization Service (JAAS)**. This technology offers to protect different resource objects, not just the URL patterns. Unfortunately, JAAS-based web application authorization is not standardized across application servers, so an application using JAAS security is not portable across them.

The Oracle security solution

Because of these integration challenges, Oracle offers **Oracle Platform Security Services (OPSS)** as part of Oracle Fusion Middleware.

OPSS provides a common interface for authentication and authorization and handles the intricacies of the integration. It is used for ADF Security as well as in many other Oracle products.

So, even though the underlying technology can be quite complex, the application developer is presented with a simple, secure solution: ADF Security.

But wait, there's more!

ADF Security makes it easy to build a secure application, but this one chapter cannot address every security issue. Every organization should appoint a security officer with the responsibility to ensure the correct level of security considering your data, users, and threat environment.

Alternative security

This chapter describes the usual way of implementing security in an ADF application based on the full ADF license and running it on Oracle WebLogic. As this solution depends on some specific WebLogic features, it does not work if you are running the free ADF Essentials on another JEE server, such as GlassFish. However, there are other security solutions for JEE application servers—for a description of how to implement security in ADF Essentials using Apache Shiro, refer to *Chapter 7, Securing an ADF Essentials Application*, of the book *Developing Web Applications with Oracle ADF Essentials, Packt Publishing*.

Security decisions

The first security decision is whether you need to secure the application. Since the focus of this book is on enterprise applications, we assume that you need to secure it. If you don't need security, feel free to skip to the next and final chapter on packaging and deploying your application.

Performing authentication

In an enterprise setting, you will normally already have an identity management infrastructure of some kind in place—Microsoft Active Directory, an LDAP-server like Oracle Internet Directory, or some other solution. We don't want each application to handle its own users but do want it to integrate with the existing identity infrastructure. This means that all of the applications should delegate the *authentication* to the application server, and the application server must be integrated with the existing authentication mechanism.

Performing authorization

However, you cannot delegate the *authorization*. Only the application developer knows the requirements and what pages, task flows, and data elements need to be accessible to different categories of users. So, as part of your application design, you must identify the **application roles**—logical groupings of users to whom you can give detailed access rights. You should be able to identify these roles from your application's requirements; if not, you need to go back to your end users to determine the roles that the application needs. For example, the destination management application that we use in this book needs the following roles: `OperationsStaff`, `AdminStaff`, `EventResponsible`, `Finance`, and `Manager`.

Where to implement security

If you are structuring your enterprise application development as recommended in *Chapter 3, Getting Organized*, you will be keeping all of your entity objects in a common model workspace using a number of subsystem workspaces and will be collecting all of this in one or more **master workspaces**. As you only want to define your application roles once in the application, you apply security in the master workspace to cover the whole application.

Implementing ADF Security

If you were to set up ADF Security manually, you would be editing half a dozen complex XML files with complex interdependencies. Fortunately, JDeveloper offers to do all of the hard work for you through the **Configure ADF Security** wizard.

To secure your ADF application, simply navigate to **Application** | **Secure** | **Configure ADF Security**.

Selecting a security model

In the first step of the wizard, you are asked to select a security model, as shown in the following screenshot:

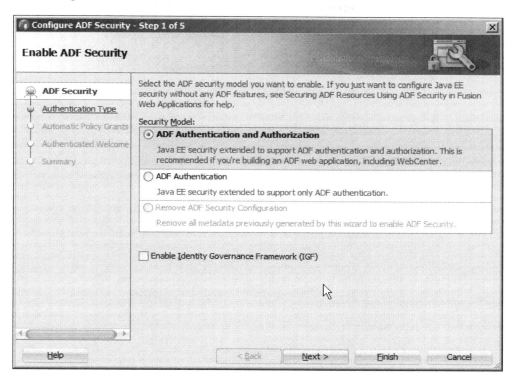

Normally, you'll always select **ADF Authentication and Authorization**. Even if your application does not distinguish between authenticated users, you still want to use ADF authorization to define which parts are accessible to anonymous users and which parts are accessible to authenticated users.

Selecting the authentication type

Next, you are asked to choose the authentication type. You have several options, but as described earlier, you'd normally select **Form-Based Authentication** in order to be able to control the login form displayed to the user, as shown in the following screenshot:

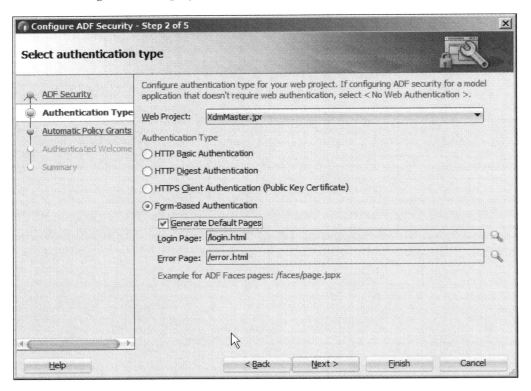

To demonstrate how form-based login works, you can ask JDeveloper to produce a default login page (and an error page, if the authentication fails). In a real-life enterprise application, you would not use these default HTML pages but build a .jspx login and error pages as part of your application instead. Once you have examined the simple HTML pages and read the help topics about using your own .jspx pages as login and error pages, you can build the proper .jspx login and error pages and run the wizard again to set your application to use these pages.

For the examples used in this chapter, check the **Generate Default Pages** checkbox.

Selecting how to grant access

In the third step of the wizard, you can decide how much access you want to grant to your task flows and pages, as shown in the following screenshot. By default, securing your ADF application will secure all the task flows and pages. This means that after you are done with the ADF Security wizard, you do not have access to any pages until you create test users and roles.

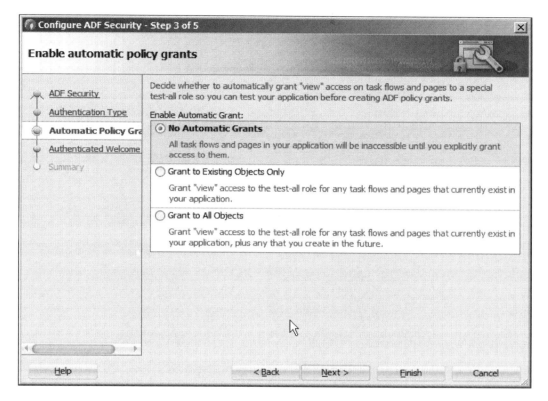

The most secure option is **No Automatic Grants**, which means that you will have to explicitly grant access to all of the task flows and pages. The other two alternatives will grant access to a special `test-all` role either for all of the existing task flows and pages or for all of the existing and future task flows and pages. These two options are useful if you add security at a later stage in the project when your testers are already testing the application — by granting your testers the `test-all` role, you are not locking them out while you configure security for your application. If you choose this approach, be sure to check that you have removed grants to the `test-all` role before your application goes into production — there is a **Show ...** checkbox with test-all grants only in the security dialog to help you find these grants.

Select a common welcome page

The last decision you need to make is whether you will automatically direct your users to a common welcome page after their successful login, as shown in the following screenshot:

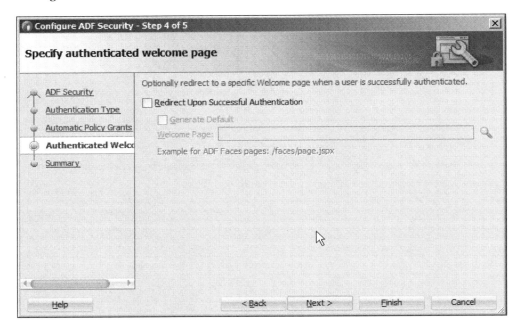

This matters because the ADF Security framework will automatically intercept attempts to access a protected page and send the user to a login page. There are two possible options:

- If you do not check the Redirect Upon Successful Authentication checkbox, your user will be sent to the requested page after your successful login
- If you do check this checkbox, your user will be sent to the common welcome page after login

If you decide to redirect to a common start page, you should use the search icon to select an existing page in your application.

When you click on **Next** on this page, you are shown a summary of all of the security XML files that will be changed. You don't have to worry about these because JDeveloper will configure them correctly based on your choices in the wizard. Simply click on **Finish** to close the wizard and apply security to your application.

Application roles

The application developer is the person who understands the requirements and the pages, task flows, and entity objects that will be needed in the application. Therefore, it is up to the developer to determine the different roles that a user might have while working with the application.

The whole XDM application will make use of the following five roles:

- Admin Staff
- Operations Staff
- Finance
- Event Responsible
- Manager

As we haven't built the whole application in this book, we will only define Event Responsible and Operations Staff here. Navigate to **Application | Secure | Application Roles** to open the application's security configuration stored in the `jazn-data.xml` file. JDeveloper recognizes this file as part of the security configuration and presents you with a nice overview tab—but you can click on the **Source** tab to see the raw XML data.

Click on the plus sign next to **Roles** and choose **Add New Role**. If a submenu appears, choose **Add at Root Level**.

 For more complex security scenarios, you can create a hierarchy of roles.

Fill in the **Name**, **Display Name**, and **Description** fields in the right-hand side of the screen, as shown in the following screenshot:

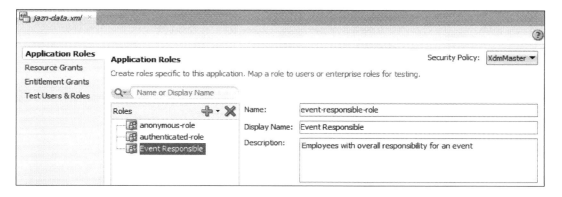

Repeat the preceding procedure to create `operations-staff-role` with **Display Name** set to `Operations Staff`.

Implementing the user interface security

In the user interface, you can apply security to either pages or task flows. Remember that the ADF Security wizard, by default, locks down everything, so you won't have access to any part of your application until you have explicitly granted access.

Securing task flows

To apply security to task flows, navigate to **Application | Secure | Resource Grants**. If you already have opened the `jazn-data.xml` file, you can also just select the **Resource Grants** tab in the left-hand side of the screen. Set **Resource Type** to **Task Flow** and make sure that you check the **Show task flows imported from ADF libraries** checkbox in order to see the task flows defined in the subsystem workspaces.

Then, choose the task flow and click on the plus sign next to **Granted To**. Choose **Add Application Role** in order to grant access to that task flow to a specific application role. While securing the user interface for a normal ADF application, the only element under **Actions** that you need to select is **view**. The other options are relevant only if you deploy your application as a portlet to Oracle WebCenter, where it can be customized and personalized in different ways.

For the example used in this chapter, assign `person-timeline-flow` to `event-responsible-role` and assign `task-overview-edit-flow` to both `event-responsible-role` and `operations-staff-role`, as shown in the following screenshot:

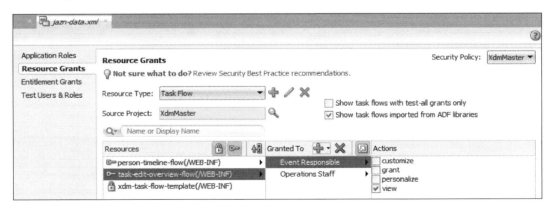

All of your task flows should be shown with a key icon, as shown in the screenshot—this indicates that access has been granted to at least one application role. If any of your task flows have the padlock icon, it means that nobody has been granted the right to execute them—in effect, they are locked and inaccessible.

Securing pages

Remember that your task flows are normally implemented with page fragments and are placed inside a dynamic region on a page. In order for your users to be able to view the application, you must also grant the **view** privilege on the page. It is often the case that every authenticated user is allowed to see the page—in this case, you grant the **view** privilege on the master page of your application to the built-in role, `authenticated-role`. If you want to allow even unauthenticated users to access your page, grant the **view** privilege to the built-in role, `anonymous-role`, also.

 Even if you grant access to the page, `anonymous-role`, anonymous users still won't have access to the task flows unless you also explicitly grant access to the task flow, `anonymous-role`. Access to pages and task flows are completely separate.

Using entitlements

If you have many resources, you can create **entitlements** to group the resources together and then grant the whole entitlement to a role in one operation.

Implementing data security

In addition to the user interface security, it is also possible to apply security rules at the data level—to the entity objects.

Applying data security is an additional security layer that you can use to protect, especially, important or sensitive data. Your page fragments should, of course, only display the information that each user is entitled to see, but if you add data security at the entity level, you have an additional layer of protection. In an enterprise application that might be changed by a maintenance programmer five years after the project was initially built, this helps ensure that someone doesn't accidentally make data available to users who shouldn't be able to see or change it.

Implementing entity object security is a two-step process. It is detailed as follows:

1. Define the operations you want to secure (read, update, and delete).
2. Grant these operations to specific application roles.

Defining protected operations

You can define the operations that you want to protect in the `CommonModel` project (or wherever you keep your entity objects). Data security is different from user interface security in which the data in an entity object is accessible by default, unless you decide otherwise. ADF data security checking only happens if you define security on any of the three operations (read, update, or delete).

Protecting an entity object

To protect a whole entity object (all attributes), you open it in JDeveloper, choose the **General** subtab, and scroll down to the **Security** section. Here, you define which operations you want to secure. The operations that you *don't* select here are *not* secured, that is, if you leave **read** unchecked, as shown in the following screenshot; all users can read the data presented by this entity object (if they have access to a task flow that uses it, of course).

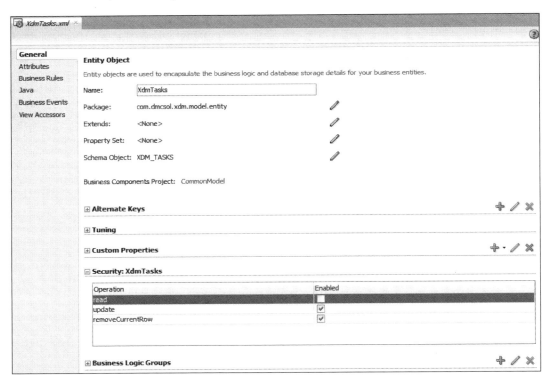

Protecting an attribute

In addition to the protection of a whole entity object, you can also protect the update operation for an individual attribute. To do this, navigate to the **Attributes** subtab and choose the attribute that you want to protect. Open the **Security** tab and check the **Enabled** checkbox next to the **update** operation.

Securing attributes secures the data but does not change the user interface. If you remove the update privilege from an entity object, a user won't be able to change the value, but the user interface element doesn't automatically get disabled. For a good user experience, you should set the **ReadOnly** attribute with an expression language so that it is displayed as read-only if the user can't change it. You can access user authorization in the expression language using #{securityContext...}; this is documented in *Chapter 41* of *Fusion Developer's Guide for Oracle Application Development Framework* (http://docs.oracle.com/middleware/1212/adf/ADFFD/ adding_security.htm).

Granting operations to roles

Now that you have defined which entity objects to protect, you can grant specific operations to specific application roles. This is done in the master application.

Go to the **Resource Grants** subtab in the jazn-data.xml dialog by navigating to **Application | Secure | Resource Grants**. In the **Resource Type** drop-down menu, select **ADF Entity Object** and check the **Show entity objects imported from ADF libraries** checkbox.

Your entity objects should now appear in the **Resources** column, and you can assign various actions to the application roles, as shown in the following screenshot:

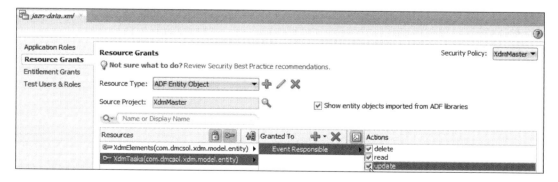

Even more data security

If you require even more sophisticated data security, you can use **Virtual Private Database (VPD)** or **Real Application Security (RAS)**. These are the features of the Enterprise Edition Oracle database — VPD in 11*g* and RAS in 12*c*. This technology allows you to associate policies with individual database tables and execute advanced PL/SQL to calculate additional restrictions on data access at runtime. You could use this, for example, to restrict a regional manager from seeing the sales figures only for his/her region.

In order to do this, you must perform some setup in the database and then override the `prepareSession()` method on the application module to send the actual logged-in user to the database before any data operations are executed.

Google `oracle adf vpd` for more information.

Users and groups

As a developer, you can define the application roles. However, you don't necessarily know about the users and groups in the organization actually running the application. In the example used in this book, DMC Solutions is building an application that they hope to sell to hundreds of different organizations.

Therefore, when the application is deployed, the application roles must be **mapped** to the groups of users defined in the organization.

Enterprise roles or groups?

Enterprise roles and user groups are two names for the same thing. Some identity management systems use the terminology that users are members of groups, and others use the terminology that users are assigned enterprise roles.

Mapping the application to the organization

Integrating your application server with your identity management system (Microsoft Active Directory, Oracle Internet Directory, or some other system) is the task of your application server administrator. This procedure is outside the scope of this book but is well-documented in the Oracle Fusion Middleware documentation — start with the *Oracle Fusion Middleware Security Overview* manual and follow the references provided by it.

When this task is done, the application server knows the enterprise roles (or groups) that are used in your organization. This allows the person deploying your ADF application in the application server to perform the mapping of application roles (defined by the application developer) to enterprise roles (defined by the organization).

This approach means that the application developer is free to define the application roles that make sense in the application, and the organization is free to define the groups that correspond to their organization.

Example users and enterprise roles

You do not normally integrate the built-in WebLogic server that comes with JDeveloper with your identity management system, but you will still need to test the security of your application. You normally do this using a simple file-based identity management system that you can set up using dialog boxes in JDeveloper. As the users that you set up here only exist in your own system, you are free to create and delete users as needed.

With the simple, local solution, you can perform the following tasks:

- Define test users
- Define test enterprise roles
- Assign members to your enterprise roles
- Assign application roles to enterprise roles

The first three steps establish an identity infrastructure, such as the one you might have in Microsoft Active Directory or Oracle Internet Directory in your production environment, and the last step mimics the task that the application deployer performs when putting your application in production.

To create your example users, you should navigate to **Application | Secure | Test Users** and then choose **Roles** to bring up the `jazn-data.xml` file. This file represents a simple user repository and can be used for testing your security. JDeveloper recognizes this file as part of the security configuration and presents you with a nice overview tab—but you can click on the **Source** tab to see the raw XML data if you want to. Click on the green plus sign to add a user and provide a name and password.

Password policy

The password must satisfy the security policy of the built-in WebLogic application server—in JDeveloper 12c, the requirement is that the password must be at least eight characters and contain at least one numeric or special character.

For the purposes of this chapter, create users SR (`Steven Robertson`) and JF (`Jennifer Fisher`), as shown in the following screenshot:

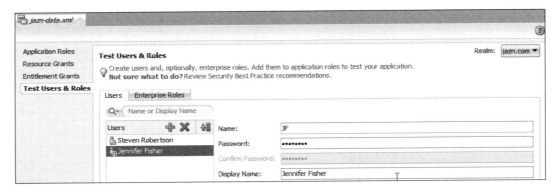

Note the little padlock on the user icon—it indicates that they don't have access to anything yet.

Then, change to the **Enterprise Roles** tab to define the groups in which your users will be the members. If you are building an application for in-house use where you already know the groups that the organization uses, you should define all or some of the real user groups. If you are working for an independent software vendor, such as DMC Solutions, and you don't know the organization where your application will be deployed, create some example user groups.

For the XDM application, create the enterprise roles, `OperationsManagerRole` and `TourGuideRole`, at the root level. In the **Members** subtab, add SR as a member of Operations Manager and JF as a member of tour guides, as shown in the following screenshot:

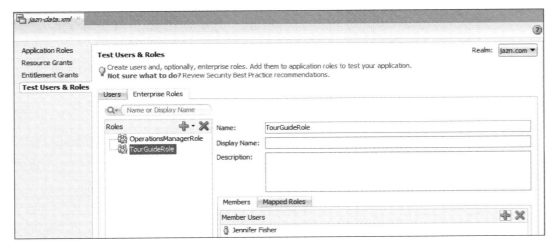

Again, note the padlock on the enterprise role icon, indicating that these enterprise roles do not have access to anything yet—they have not been assigned any application roles.

Assigning application roles

To assign the application roles you have defined to your enterprise roles/user groups, switch back to the **Application Roles** subtab where you defined the application roles. Here, you use the **Mappings** subtab to assign enterprise roles to each application role.

Select the `Event Responsible role` and click the green plus next to **Mapped Users and Roles**. Select **Add Enterprise Role** and check the checkbox for the enterprise role `OperationsManagerRole`

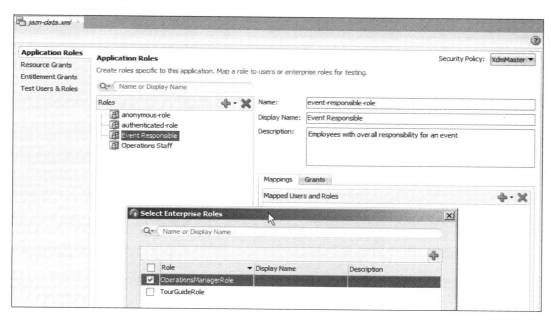

Similarly, map the enterprise role, `TourGuideRole`, to the application role, `Operations Staff`.

Anonymous and authenticated

Note that you have two application roles available in addition to those you defined yourself: `anonymous-role` and `authenticated-role`. If you want some pages or task flows to be accessible to users who are not logged in yet, you can grant access to `anonymous-role` for using these pages or task flows. If there are pages or task flows that you want every authenticated user to be able to see, irrespective of enterprise role or group membership, grant access to `authenticated-role` for using these pages and task flows. Pages that need to be accessible to everyone, whether they are logged in or not, need to be accessible to both of the roles.

Running the application

When you have saved your `jazn-data.xml` file, you can run the application as usual (by right-clicking on the `Xdm.jspx` page and choosing **Run**). You will be met with a very simple username/password page—this is the autogenerated `login.html` page that JDeveloper has built for you.

If you log in with the user `SR`, you will see the application working as before because the user `SR` has the Operations Manager role, which, again, has the Event Responsible role assigned to it. It gives access to the whole application.

If you log in with the user, `JF`, on the other hand, you will see a blank page if you select the **Timeline** menu item. This is because `JF` only has the Tour Guide role, which also, has the Operations Staff application role. It does not give access to the person timeline task flow.

Removing inaccessible items

For the best user experience, users should not be able to see the select menu items that won't show them anything. You can handle this in two ways, which are as follows:

- You can hide the menu item completely by setting the **Rendered** attribute to **false**. Use this if you don't want to confuse your users with menu items that are not relevant to them.

- You can show the disabled menu item (grayed out) by setting the **Disabled** attribute to **true**. Use this if you want to show your users that additional functionality exists but is not accessible to them.

You can use an expression language to set an attribute on the menu items that is not accessible to a user. As mentioned previously, you can have access to the current security context in an expression language using the `#{securityContext...}` functions.

To disable the **Timeline** menu item for users who do not have access to the timeline task flow, you can set **Disabled** to `!#{securityContext.taskflowViewable['/WEB-INF/person-timeline-flow.xml#person-timeline-flow']}`.

Refer to *Chapter 41, Enabling ADF Security in a Fusion Web Application*, in the Oracle manual, *Developing Fusion Web Applications with Oracle Application Development Framework*, for details on accessing the security context using an expression language.

Summary

In this chapter, you have applied ADF Security to your master application so that users would be prompted to log in when starting the application. We just used the default login page, but you can easily build your own login page and integrate this with the application. You defined the application roles and implemented security on pages, task flows, and entity objects, thus specifying what each application role can do. Finally, you used the built-in user and group repository to test your application.

You can tell your manager that the XDM application is secure and implements all of the required logic to ensure that only properly authenticated and authorized users can access functionality and data. He/she will be happy to hear that and will ask you to package the application for deployment to the test server. That's the subject of the following (and last) chapter.

11
Packaging and Delivery

When a tailor has taken all of the measurements of his or her customer, he or she cuts pieces of cloth according to the agreed style. However, 36 pieces of cloth do not make a jacket—just like 36 individual ADF Libraries do not make up an application.

What remains is to sew all of the parts together into one deliverable package for installation—first, on your test environment, and then on your production environment. This package should include your executable code, any database scripts, and the necessary documentation.

After each cycle of test and rework, you need to create a new deliverable package until it passes all of the tests. Then, the *same* package goes to the operations staff to be installed in the preproduction or production environment. In case your package does not install cleanly on this environment, you can go back to the drawing board, fix the code or the documentation, and create a new package.

This deployment happens from the master application that includes all of the common ADF Libraries, as well as all of the task flow libraries containing your business components, web pages, and task flows.

The contents of a good deployment package

When the development team is done and hands the application over to production, the package should include the following:

- The runnable application
- Any database code
- Installation and operation instructions

The runnable application

The enterprise ADF application that you and your team have built is a **Java Enterprise Edition (JEE)** application. Therefore, it is delivered in the standard JEE application form as a Java Enterprise Archive (.ear) file.

A .ear file is just a compressed file containing the application code and a bit of metadata. You can open the file with an unzip utility to see what's inside—normally, the .ear file contains a **Web Archive** (.war) file that you can again unzip to see what's inside.

Your EAR file will contain the application roles and other security features that you have configured in *Chapter 10, Securing Your ADF Application*.

Database code

If your application contains new or changed database objects, you will of course need to supply SQL scripts for your database administrator to run. If you are using advanced security, such as **Virtual Private Database** (**VPD**), there will also be database scripts to run in order to implement this. Since this is the same for all database applications, we will not discuss SQL scripts much in this chapter.

Installation and operation instructions

Finally, your installation package needs to include the necessary instructions for your database and application server administrators to install the application.

Your instructions must include exactly the version of WebLogic and ADF that you need—there is a WebLogic version matching each version of JDeveloper. You also need to point your application server administrator to the *Oracle Fusion Middleware Administrator's Guide for Oracle Application Development Framework* for instructions on how to prepare the WebLogic environment for ADF. If you are using customization, as described in *Chapter 9, Customizing Functionality*, there are additional steps to set up a database-based metadata repository (MDS).

In addition to the basic instructions (such as deploy this file and run this script), your installation instructions must include the data source name of any database connection used by the application so that the application server administrator can make sure that this connection name is available. You will also have to provide the name and intended use for each of the application roles that your application defines so that the application server administrator or security administrator can map these roles to the user groups or enterprise roles already defined in the organization.

Finally, you need to tell your system administrators where your system will write its logfiles so that they can help find the cause of any problems, as well as the jobs set up to archive and/or clear old logs.

Preparing for deployment

Preparing your application for deployment involves cleaning up the code and setting the application parameters for production use.

Cleaning up your code

Just as the tailor shouldn't leave pins in your finished jacket, you should not leave development artifacts in your installation package. Some things that might accidentally slip into the deployment package include the following:

- Test users and groups
- Print statements
- Commented-out code
- Debug settings in `web.xml`

Use JDeveloper's automatic reformatting functionality to reformat all of the XML and Java files. For readability and maintainability, all code should have a uniform format. If you are not happy with the default formatting, you can change it by navigating to **Tools | Preferences | Code Editor | Code Style**.

Test users and groups

You might remember from *Chapter 10, Securing Your ADF Application,* that we created test users and groups in order to test our security settings. A WebLogic server running in the development mode (like your standalone development server) will accept any users and groups deployed as part of the application, so you need to tell JDeveloper not to package these into your final application. To do this, navigate to **Application | Application Properties** to bring up the **Application Properties** dialog and then choose **Deployment**. The following screenshot shows the **Security Deployment Options** wizard:

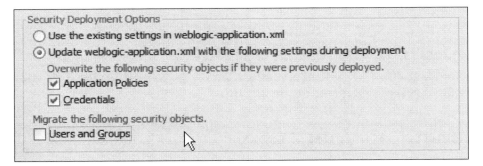

Under **Security Deployment Options**, deselect the **Users and Groups** checkbox. Then, click on **OK** to close the dialog.

> Your preproduction and production WebLogic servers should run in the production mode. You will get a deployment failure if you try to deploy an application containing users and groups onto a production server.

Depending on the choices you made in the ADF Security wizard, you might also have a `test-all` role with access to all of the screens and task flows in your application. If you allowed a `test-all` role, you should use the security dialogs, as described in *Chapter 10, Securing Your ADF Application,* to make sure that your final application does not contain any grants to the `test-all` role.

Other development artifacts

Of course, you have used the logging method that you all agreed upon in the project team and did not write any simple `System.out.println()` statements in your code. However, somebody else might have done so. To check for these kind of impurities in your project code, you can use JDeveloper's global file search capability. Navigate to **Search | Find in Files** to search through your active project or application (or any user-defined path in the filesystem), as shown in the following screenshot:

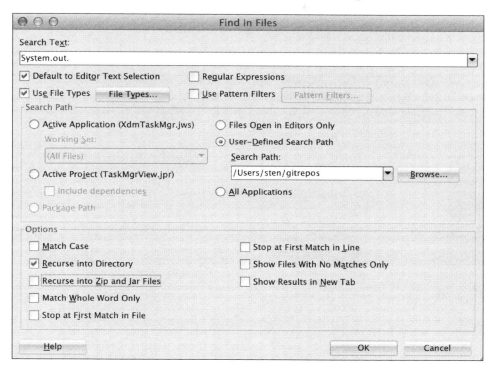

Your finished application should not contain any commented-out code. If there are code snippets that you want to keep for later use, place them on the development Wiki.

In *Chapter 8, Changing the Appearance*, we set `org.apache.myfaces.trinidad.DISABLE_CONTENT_COMPRESSION` in the `web.xml` file to `true` in order to see the full names of CSS styles. This setting should be set back to `false` before you deploy your application to production. If you changed other settings for development or debug purposes, you should also set these back to the default.

Performing code audit

JDeveloper can also perform code auditing—a static analysis of your code to see whether it meets the specific standards. Audit rules test whether some feature is present or not. For example, a rule might require a class name to start with an uppercase letter. JDeveloper will report a rule violation if this is not the case.

To run a code audit in JDeveloper, select a project and navigate to **Build | Audit**. In the **Audit** dialog box, choose the **ADF Best Practice Rules** profile. You can click on **Edit** to select the rules that are included in this profile. When you click on **Run**, JDeveloper analyzes your code and comes up with a report, as shown in the following screenshot:

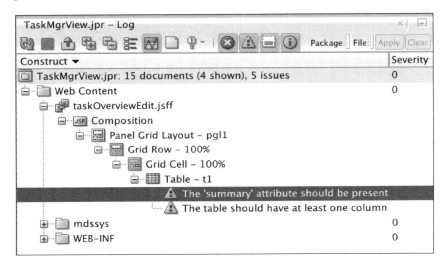

You want your code audit report to be clean. If you decide that some rules are not relevant for your project, you can click on **Edit** in the **Audit** dialog, change the rules that are validated, and save your new audit profile.

Ignoring rules

For Java code, JDeveloper 12*c* allows you to explicitly ignore each individual warning. This allows a programmer to take responsibility for deviating from the rules so that you can still get a clean audit report.

JDeveloper doesn't offer a similar feature for the XML code that makes up much of an ADF project. However, Oracle ACE Director, Wilfred van der Deijl and ADF Developer, Richard Olrichs have developed a JDeveloper 12*c* plugin that allows you to ignore individual warnings in the XML files. You can download this plugin under **Help | Check for Updates**. Check the **Open Source and Partners Extensions** checkbox and install the **Suppress Audit Warnings** plugin. Wilfred has also written a blog post explaining how it works at `http://www.redheap.com/2013/11/jdeveloper-extension-to-suppress.html`.

Checking more rules

The built-in rules check a number of basic things, but there are many more things that you might want to check in your code. Fortunately, the flexible auditing framework allows you to create your own audit rules completely with suggested fixes.

Wilfred and Richard Olrichs have done just that and built the **ADF EMG Audit Rules** plugin for JDeveloper 12. This plugin can be downloaded, as mentioned earlier, and it validates your code against a number of the rules in the official Oracle ADF code guidelines. Richard has written a blog post about it which is available at `http://www.olrichs.nl/2013/12/adf-emg-audit-rules-10-released.html`

Setting application parameters for production use

In addition to making sure that you don't have development and debugging stuff in your application, you want to make sure that your application has the right stuff—the configuration settings that are necessary for a good performance.

Application module tuning

The most important settings for the performance of your ADF application are the settings for the application modules. To access these settings, open the application module and choose the **Configurations** tab, as shown in the following screenshot:

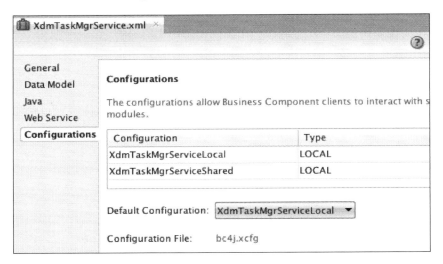

Select the configuration line that ends with ...Local and click on the pencil icon to bring up the **Edit configuration** dialog. In this dialog, you can access the important tuning parameters on the **Pooling and Scalability** tab.

> The configuration that ends with ...Shared is only used if you decide to share an application module across the whole application. This can be a good idea if you have read-only application modules that deliver data for value lists. See *Chapter 14* of *Developing Fusion Web Applications with Oracle Application Development Framework* (http://docs.oracle.com/middleware/1212/adf/ADFFD/bclookups.htm) for more information on shared application modules.

The most important parameter on the **Pooling and Scalability** tab is the **Referenced Pool Size** parameter. The ADF framework will keep this number of application module instances in memory (the default number is 10), ready to serve your users. As long as you have fewer concurrent users than this value, each user will get the same application module each time the browser communicates with the application server. Once you have more users than this number, the users will have to share the application modules. To allow this sharing, ADF has to store all of the internal states of the application module in the database in order to free it up for another user. This is called **passivation** and is an expensive operation, so as long as your application is running on one server, you want to avoid it as much as possible.

To minimize passivation, set **Referenced Pool Size** as close to the maximum number of concurrent users you expect as possible. Of course, if you set this value very high and run out of memory on your application server, your application server will start swapping the memory to disk, which is even more expensive. You need to work with your application server administrator to find the "sweet spot", where application modules are not passivated too often, and your application server machine does not run out of memory.

There are many ADF tuning settings, and they can be set for each application module individually to match how that application module is expected to be used. The online help describes each setting, and *Chapter 8* of *Tuning Performance Guide* (`http://docs.oracle.com/middleware/1212/core/ASPER/adf.htm`) gives tuning guidelines. You'll have to look at the section on *Advanced Tuning Considerations* for information on tuning the ADF Business Components.

Controlling database locking

When several people are using a database application at the same time, they might attempt to change the same record in the database at the same time. This situation can be resolved in the following two ways:

- With pessimistic locking
- With optimistic locking

Pessimistic locking assumes that this conflict is likely to occur (hence, *pessimistic*) and locks the record as soon as the first user tries to change it. This has the advantage that the second user will not be allowed to change the value at all. On the other hand, this has the disadvantage that if the first user goes away without changing the record, the lock remains, and the second user is barred from changing the record. The server can't tell if the users' browser crashed or if they have left for a three-week vacation, so it has to perform a cleanup of the locked records on some schedule. In an ADF web application, this happens when your web session times out.

Optimistic locking assumes that this conflict is not likely to occur (hence, *optimistic*). Bob is allowed to change his copy of the record, and Alice is allowed to change her copy. This has the advantage that the application server doesn't have to perform a regular unlocking of stuck records, and nobody has to wait for these locks to be released. The disadvantage to this approach is that if Alice commits her change to the database first, Bob will be turned away—in effect, he will be told that his change cannot be stored in the database because another user has already changed the value.

Oracle recommends the default Optimistic setting for web applications such as the one we have built in this book (web applications make up 95 percent or more of all of the ADF applications). You can change the global default value in the adf-config.xml file that you will find under **Application Resources | Descriptors | ADF META-INF**. On the **Business Components** subtab of the **Overview** tab, you can set the default locking mode for the whole application, as shown in the following screenshot:

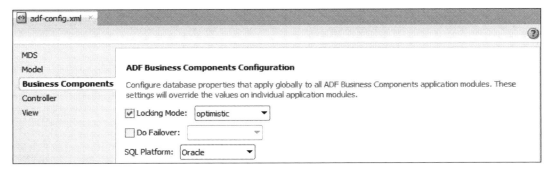

Tuning your ADF application

A whole book could be written on ADF tuning—but this book is not the one. There is a lot of good ADF tuning advice in the chapter on *Oracle Application Development Framework Performance Tuning* in *Tuning Performance Guide* (http://docs.oracle.com/middleware/1212/core/ASPER/adf.htm). This chapter has a section on tuning the user interface (the ADF Faces part), as well as a section on tuning the ADF Business Components.

Tune the Business Components first

Mysteriously, the section on ADF Faces in this guide is called "basic tuning", and the section on ADF Business Components is called "advanced tuning". Tuning ADF Business Components has much more impact than tuning the user interface, so start with the *Advanced Tuning* section.

Additionally, a lot of material on ADF tuning is available on the Oracle technology network and elsewhere on the Internet. For more information, google oracle adf tuning.

Setting up the application server

While developing the application, you were probably just clicking on the **Run** button to run your application. As you have noticed, this means that your application runs in the built-in WebLogic server on your local machine. This instance of WebLogic is integrated with JDeveloper, so it contains all of the necessary libraries and settings for running ADF applications.

In addition to these built-in WebLogic instances, your development server administrator must set up at least a test/integration server where you can collect all of the components of the application for integration testing. Your environment might also include preproduction or other WebLogic server instances before the final production environment.

Number of servers

The minimum requirements of a production environment are as follows:

- The WebLogic server integrated with JDeveloper for development on each developer's workstation
- A standalone server for integration and testing
- The production environment

In an enterprise setting, you should use the following:

- The WebLogic server integrated with JDeveloper for development on each developer's workstation
- A standalone development server for integrating the code
- A standalone test server that your test team will work on
- A preproduction server that your operations' people can use to test the final deployment and where stress/performance tests can be run
- The production server
- Depending on how much training you plan to give your users, you might also need an education system

Since there are licensing costs involved, your IT manager is also likely to have an opinion on how many environments you will need.

Deciding who is in charge

You will need one standalone server that the development team has full root/administrator access to. During your project, there will be times when you need to make some code available for a demo or a discussion of possible solutions without having to involve people and procedures outside of the team.

In an enterprise setting, the operations group manages all of the other servers, thus following the systems management procedures and guidelines of your organization.

Installing WebLogic 12*c* standalone for ADF

In WebLogic 12*c*, you have the choice of a simple installation (just a ZIP file to unpack), or a complete WebLogic installation. Unfortunately, the simple installation doesn't run ADF, and the complete installation requires an infrastructure database.

However, it is possible to run a single instance of WebLogic 12*c* as an integration or test server without a database. This approach is documented by Duncan Mills, Oracle Senior Director of Product Management, on his blog at `https://blogs.oracle.com/groundside/entry/setting_up_a_standalone_weblogic`. Duncan explains why the database is normally necessary and rightly points out that this is not a supported configuration in any way. However, for a simple test or integration server, it is sufficient.

Creating a data source on the server

Once you have your server and domain set up for ADF, you need to create a data source on the server.

The easiest way to do this is through the WebLogic console that you access through a web browser with the URL of your WebLogic installation, including the port, followed by `/console` (for example, `http://test.dmcsol.com:7001/console`). The WebLogic console appears as shown in the following screenshot (it takes a bit of time for the application to load the first time you use the console):

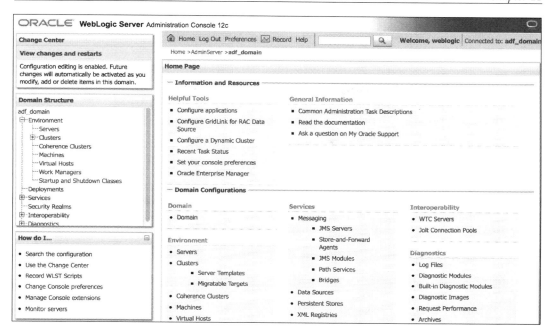

Click on **Services** and then on **Data Sources** to bring up the **Summary of JDBC Data Sources** page. Navigate to **New | Generic Data Source** to define a new data source, as shown in the following screenshot:

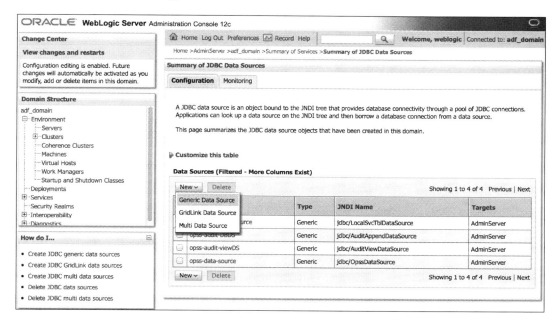

Give your data source a name matching the one you used in your application module (for example, XdmDS) and a JNDI name also matching your application module (for example, jdbc/XdmDS). Set **Database Type** to **Oracle** and click on **Next**. Select the **Oracle's Driver (Thin) for instance connections** driver and click on **Next**.

Remember to select the right driver

For ADF applications, you should select **Oracle's Driver (Thin)**. Unfortunately, the default driver that is selected when you enter this screen is a **Thin XA** driver. This is not supported for ADF applications. See http://www.oracle.com/technetwork/developer-tools/ jdev/documentation/1212-cert-1964670.html.

On the next screen, leave the default **Transaction Options** value and click on **Next**. Provide connection information (database, server, port, username, and password) and click on **Next**. In the final step of the wizard, be sure to click on the **Test Configuration** button. You should see a **Connection test succeeded** message, as shown in the following screenshot:

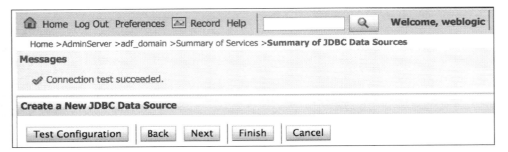

If there is something wrong with your connection information, you get an error message instead.

Click on **Finish** to close the wizard. You'll see your new data source on the **Summary** page, as shown in the following screenshot:

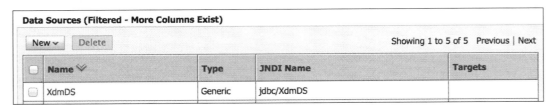

Note that your connection doesn't automatically acquire a target—the **Targets** column is blank. You need to click on your connection, choose the **Targets** tab, and check the checkbox next to your server name, as shown in the following screenshot:

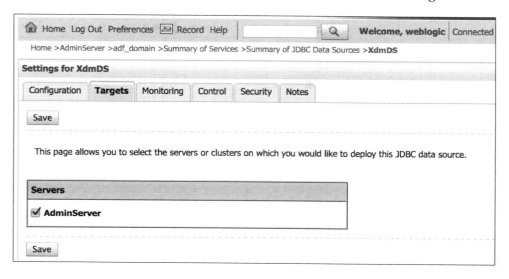

On the simple development server that you are managing in the development team, you will only need AdminServer. On the other WebLogic servers managed by the operations people, there is going to be one AdminServer managing multiple **managed servers** inside the same WebLogic instance.

When you have saved your configuration, you should see your JDBC connection being associated with your server, as shown in the following screenshot:

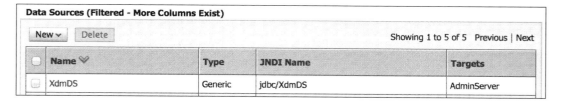

Deploying the application

With all of the development scaffolding removed from your application and the standalone application server prepared, it is time to deploy the application. Initially, you will do this directly from JDeveloper to the standalone development server, but the end goal is to deploy your application to an EAR file that you can hand over to an application server administrator to install.

 If you are building a new database or have made any changes to an existing one, you also need to deliver matching database scripts.

Direct deployment

For the first test of your deployment procedure, you should deploy your application directly from JDeveloper to the application server. This approach gives you more feedback and makes it easier to fix any deployment errors. This is also the approach that you normally use to deploy to the standalone development server that the development team owns.

Creating an application server connection

To deploy your application directly from JDeveloper, you first need to create an application server connection to your test/integration server. Navigate to **File | New | From Gallery** and then to **General | Connections | Application Server Connection** to start the **Create Application Server Connection** wizard. Once the wizard starts, perform the following steps:

1. In step 1, give your connection a name, set **Connection Type** to **WebLogic 12.x**, and click on **Next**.

2. In step 2, provide a username and password for an administrator account on the server (the default username is `weblogic`, and you set the password when you installed the server).

3. In step 3, fill in the hostname of your server and the name of the WebLogic domain where you want to deploy your application. You created this domain when you installed the server. The **Configuration** wizard is as shown in the following screenshot:

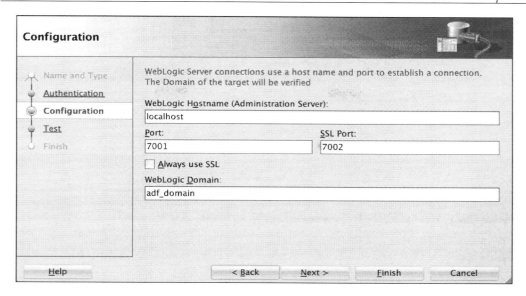

4. In step 4, test if your connection works. All of the 11 tests should pass, as shown in the following screenshot:

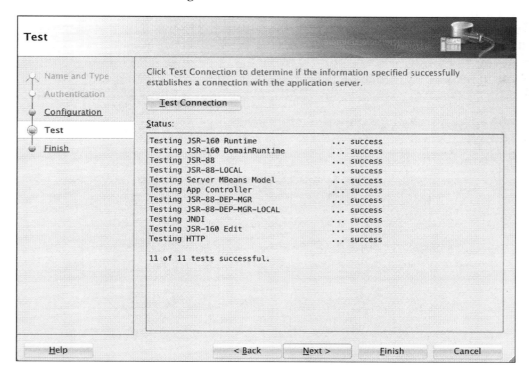

5. When you click on **Finish**, your connection should be shown in the **Application Servers** window, as shown in the following screenshot:

Deploying your application directly

First, open the **Project Properties** dialog for your XdmMaster project and choose the **Deployment** node. Click on **New** to add a new project deployment profile, choose the **WAR File** profile type, and name your profile XdmMaster. All of the default settings for this deployment should be correct, so you can just click on **OK** to create the profile and again close the dialogs.

Then, open the **Application Properties** dialog and navigate to **Deployment | WebLogic** in the tree. Make sure that the **Auto Generate and Synchronize WebLogic JDBC Descriptors During Deployment** checkbox is not checked. Then, click on the **Deployment** node and delete any default application deployment profile that you might find. Click on **New** to create a new deployment profile, set **Profile Type** to **EAR File**, and name your deployment profile (typically, the same as your master workspace name—for the XDM application, this would be **XdmMaster**).

In the **Edit EAR Deployment Profile Properties** dialog, choose the **Application Assembly** node and make sure that XdmMaster is selected, as shown in the following screenshot:

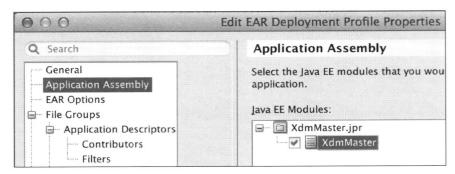

Click on **OK** a couple of times to close all of the dialogs.

Now, you can navigate to **Application | Deploy** and choose the name of your application deployment profile (XdmMaster). You will get a dialog box where you can choose **Deployment Action**—choose **Deploy to Application Server** and click on **Next**. In the next step, choose the application server connection that you just created and click on **Finish** (you don't need to change any settings in the remaining steps of the deployment wizard).

This process first builds a Web Archive (WAR file) and then packages it into an Enterprise Archive (EAR file). It then calls the application server using the connection information that you have defined and installs your application on the application server.

You should see a new **Deployment** tab, which appears at the bottom of the screen, containing a series of the following deployment messages:

```
[09:28:28 AM] ----  Deployment started.  ----
[09:28:28 AM] Target platform is  (Weblogic 12.x).
[09:28:28 AM] Retrieving existing application information
[09:28:28 AM] Running dependency analysis...
[09:28:28 AM] Building...
[09:28:29 AM] Deploying 2 profiles...
[09:28:29 AM] Wrote Web Application Module to C:\JDev …
[09:28:29 AM] Wrote Enterprise Application Module to … [09:28:29 AM]
Redeploying Application...
[09:28:39 AM] [Deployer:149194]Operation 'deploy' on …
[09:28:39 AM] Application Redeployed Successfully.
[09:28:39 AM] The following URL context root(s) were …
[09:28:39 AM] http://192.168.138.44:7001/NgdmMasterApp
[09:28:39 AM] Elapsed time for deployment:  10 seconds
[09:28:39 AM] ----  Deployment finished.  ----
```

If you don't get any error message, you should now be able to start your application from your test server with a URL as the one you see when running it locally. If you deploy the XDM application to a standalone development server called matano in the default managed server running on port 7001, the URL to start the application would be http://matano:7001/Xdm/faces/Xdm.jspx.

Remember that Xdm is the **context root** of your application set under **Project Properties | Java EE Application**. Xdm.jspx is the name of the JSPX page that you created in the master application as the starting point for your application.

Deploying the file through the console

Direct deployment is fine for testing your deployment procedure and deploying to the development server, but the package that you need to deliver to the operations people in order to install it is an EAR file.

Creating the EAR file

To do this, navigate again to **Application** | **Deploy** and then to the name of your application deployment profile. In the **Deployment Action** dialog, choose **Deploy to EAR**, click on **Next**, and then click on **Finish**.

In the **Deployment** tab at the bottom of the screen, you'll see a shorter series of deployment messages, as follows:

```
[11:38:37 AM] ----  Deployment started.   ----
[11:38:37 AM] Target platform is  (Weblogic 12.x).
[11:38:37 AM] Running dependency analysis...
[11:38:37 AM] Building...
[11:38:40 AM] Deploying 2 profiles...
[11:38:41 AM] Wrote Web Application Module to C:\JDev …
[11:38:41 AM] Wrote Enterprise Application Module to …
[11:38:41 AM] Elapsed time for deployment:  4 seconds
[11:38:41 AM] ----  Deployment finished.   ----
```

In the `Wrote Enterprise Application Module…` line, you can see where JDeveloper wrote the `.ear` file—this will normally be a `deploy` directory under your application directory. If your master application workspace is stored in `C:\JDeveloper\mywork\XdmMaster`, you can find the `XdmMaster.ear` file in `C:\JDeveloper\mywork\XdmMaster\deploy`.

As mentioned earlier, an `.ear` file is a normal compressed file. You can double-click on the link in the log window to open it inside JDeveloper, as shown in the following screenshot:

XdmMaster.ear ⨯			
Path	Date	Size	Compressed
META-INF/Xdm-jdbc.xml	12/8/13 1:45 PM	1,003	1,003
META-INF/application.xml	12/8/13 1:45 PM	464	464
META-INF/cwallet.sso	12/8/13 12:29 PM	3.20 KB	3.20 KB
META-INF/weblogic-application.xml	12/8/13 12:28 PM	1.62 KB	1.62 KB
XdmMaster.war	12/8/13 1:45 PM	3.91 MB	3.91 MB
adf/META-INF/adf-config.xml	12/8/13 12:28 PM	1.19 KB	1.19 KB
adf/META-INF/connections.xml	12/8/13 12:29 PM	966	966
adf/META-INF/wsm-assembly.xml	12/8/13 12:28 PM	127	127
lib/adf-loc.jar	12/8/13 1:45 PM	273	273

Most of the actual application content is inside the `.war` file—you can double-click on this to see the content of the WAR file with all your classes, pages, and so on.

 You can also open the EAR and WAR files with your choice of uncompression application.

Deploying the EAR file

To deploy the EAR file you just created to your standalone development server, bring up the WebLogic console in your web browser again (the URL is your test/integration server name and port, followed by `/console`). The deployment procedure uploads your EAR file from your local filesystem to the server filesystem and then installs the application.

 Production deployment

Oracle Enterprise Manager (OEM) also has the deployment functionality. For deployment to a preproduction or production test/integration server, use OEM. This is also the only tool that allows you to map the existing users and groups to application roles.

Click on **Deployments** in the **Domain Structure** box. You'll see quite a few deployments already; these are all of the infrastructures that you don't need to worry about. You'll also see the application that you deployed directly from JDeveloper—in order to test deployment through the EAR file, you'll need to select this and click on **Delete**. Then, click on **Install** to start installing your application from the EAR file.

In the first step of **Install Application Assistant**, you need to point to your EAR file. Remember that you just built your EAR file on your local machine, and you are now running the console application on your test/integration server. This means that you have to click on the **upload your file(s)** link to copy your EAR file from your development machine to the server. This link is somewhat hidden inside the text paragraph that starts with **Note: Only valid file…**.

 Separate filesystems

Your EAR file is generated on your local machine, but the content of the **Path** field in the WebLogic console refers to the locations of the file on the test/integration server. Unless you generated your EAR file to a network drive accessible to the test/integration server, you have to upload your EAR file.

In the next step of the wizard, click on the **Browse** button to select your local EAR file.

You should get a message that your EAR file was successfully uploaded. This means that the file is now present in the filesystem on the application server.

It should also be listed at the bottom of the screen for you to select, as shown in the following screenshot:

If you have uploaded several files for different applications, the console web page might list multiple files. Select the one you just uploaded and click on **Next** to start the actual deployment. Choose the option to install this deployment as an application and click on **Next**. Then, give your application a name and click on **Next**. In the final step of the installation assistant, choose the **No, I will review the configuration later** option and click on **Finish**.

You will probably see the **Change Center** box in the upper-left corner of your WebLogic window, as shown in the following screenshot:

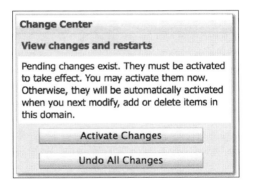

Click on **Activate Changes** to activate your new deployment.

Similar to deploying directly, your application should now be available on the test/integration server with the same URL.

Scripting the build process

During the project, you will be building and deploying many times, so it makes sense to create scripts that handle this whole process. A good tool for handling this scripting is Apache Ant (`http://ant.apache.org`).

> **Working with Maven and ADF**
>
> Oracle is improving the Maven support in JDeveloper in each version, and Maven is supported as a dependency-management and build tool in JDeveloper 12*c*. With built-in dependency tracking, Maven is very promising as a build tool for enterprise ADF applications using various ADF Libraries. However, in the version of JDeveloper that was currently used at the time of writing this book, using Maven as a build tool requires some tweaking.

Creating a build task

When working with Ant, you create a **build file** (traditionally called `build.xml`) to specify how to build a project. This XML file consists of a number of **targets** that define the different goals that you might want your build process to achieve, for example, `clean`, `init`, `compile`, `test`, or `deploy`. Within each target are a number of steps called **tasks**. Ant comes with a large number of prebuilt tasks, and many tools that integrate with Ant supply their own tasks. If you are not already familiar with Ant, there are several books and many online resources available — for example, the online manual available at `http://ant.apache.org/manual/index.html`.

JDeveloper offers to help you create the Ant build files for your project.

Creating a build task for the master project

To create a build file, right-click on your master view project (for example, `MasterView`) and choose **Project Properties**. Under **Features**, click on the green plus sign and move **Ant** to the right-hand **Selected** box. Then, click on **OK** to return to your project.

> You can select **Use Ant** in step 6 of the **Create ADF Fusion Web Application** wizard when you create the application workspace. This also adds the Ant libraries, but only creates an empty build file (because it is built before the project and application had any content).

To build or rebuild your Ant files, navigate to **File | New | Buildfile from Project** to bring up the **Create Buildfile from Project** dialog, as shown in the following screenshot:

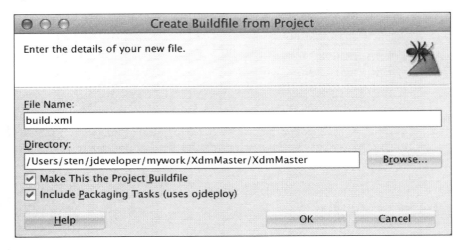

It is important that you check the **Include Packaging Tasks (uses ojdeploy)** checkbox – this tells JDeveloper to also generate targets and tasks for packaging and deploying your application.

> **JDeveloper deployment without the user interface**
>
> The ojdeploy referred to by the dialog box is a command-line Java program that can do anything JDeveloper can do with regards to deployment. This program is included with JDeveloper so that you can automate your build process, as described in this section. It uses some JDeveloper libraries, so you need JDeveloper or a special JDeveloper library installed on the machine where you run it. Refer to the documentation for a thorough explanation of the many options with ojdeploy.

When you click on **OK** (accept to overwrite if you already had Ant files), you'll see that two new files were created for you in the Application Navigator: the build. xml file defining how to build the project, and the build.properties file containing some constants such as directory names. You will need to modify the properties file to match your local environment. The little insect icon on the build.xml file, as shown in the following screenshot, shows that JDeveloper has recognized the file as an Ant build file.

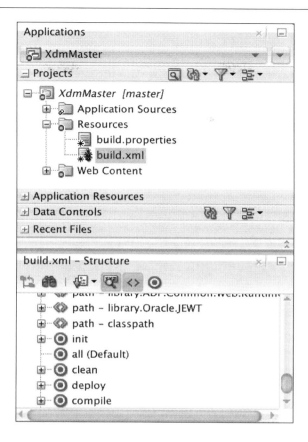

The **Structure** window in the bottom-left corner of the JDeveloper window will also show targets and tasks in your build file.

You can right-click on an Ant build file and run individual targets from within JDeveloper.

Creating build tasks for ADF Libraries

Inside each of the projects in your common workspace, you can also create Ant tasks that build the library. The default build files that JDeveloper creates include tasks for running all of the deployment profiles in your project; this means that you automatically get a target that builds each ADF Library.

Similarly, create an Ant build file in each of your subsystems to build the ADF Libraries from these.

Creating a build task for the master application

In the master application, you also want a task that actually builds the whole application. To create this, navigate to **File | New | From Gallery,** and then to **General | Ant | Buildfile from Application**. Again, remember to check the **Include Packaging Tasks** checkbox and overwrite any existing file. The application-level Ant files will show up under **Application Resources | Build Files** in the **Applications** window.

You can include the Ant build files from the common workspace and the subsystems using an `<ant>` task in the master build file to call the other build files. You will find a complete example of a master build file in *Chapter 8, Build and Deploy*, of the book *Developing Web Applications with Oracle ADF Essentials*, *Packt Publishing*.

The default build files that JDeveloper creates include tasks for running all of the deployment profiles in your project or application. This means that if you choose to run the `deploy` target in the application-level Ant file and your application has a deployment profile for an EAR file, Ant will build that EAR file.

Moving your task to the test/integration server

When you have tested your Ant script, you need to move it to your own standalone development server in order to enable the automatic build on this server, and you'll have to install the Ant software on the server. Additionally, you'll need the `ojdeploy` runtime code. To get `ojdeploy` onto the server, simply install JDeveloper.

Once you have Ant and the `ojdeploy` libraries on your standalone development server, copy the `build.xml` and `build.properties` files to the server. After copying these files, you need to open the `build.properties` file and change it to match your server environment. This file is a simple collection of keys and values—you need to change all of the path values to match your test/integration server environment.

Adding a checkout

Now, we're able to run the build process on the test/integration server, but we don't have any code to build on the server yet. We don't want our build process to be based on what some developer happens to have on his of her development workstation—we want to build our process from the checked-in code in our source code repository.

Ant does not come with a built-in version control integration, but for Subversion, you can use the SvnAnt task available at `http://subclipse.tigris.org/svnant.html`. This task depends on having access to a Subversion command-line client; if your Subversion installation didn't include this, there are several options available (for example, the CollabNet client at `http://www.collab.net` or the Slik SVN client at `http://www.sliksvn.com`).

With this software installed on your test/integration server, you can add an additional target to your `build.xml` file for checking out the source code using a `<svn>` task. Your code might look something like the following lines of code:

```
<svn username="${username}" password="${password}">
  <checkout url="http://matano:8088/svn/repos/xdm/trunk"
    revision="HEAD" destPath="build" />
</svn>
```

If you add your `checkout` task to the `depends=` property of your deploy target, Ant will automatically check out the latest code before running `ojdeploy` to package and deploying your application to the WebLogic server.

There is no similar Ant task if you are using Git, but you can, of course, use the `<exec>` tasks to execute the `git` command-line tools. You can also google `git ant task` for various partial solutions.

Adding the database

If your enterprise ADF application includes any changes to the database (new or modified objects), you can use Ant's `<sql>` tasks to run these scripts as part of your build process.

More scripting

Once you have your basic build script, you can add many other things. They are as follows:

- You can tag each nightly build in Subversion using the `<copy>` operation to copy the revision you check out to your Subversion `/tags` directory
- You can run your JUnit unit tests as part of the build with `<antunit>`
- You can run your Selenium user interface tests as part of the build with `<selenese>`

Automation

Your build script ensures that a developer only has to issue one command to build the whole application and also ensures that nothing is left out or forgotten.

However, scripting is only the first step toward true automation. As all of your tasks can now be started by another program, you can begin by using continuous integration tools, such as Hudson (`http://hudson-ci.org`), to automatically run the nightly builds or even start a new build every time a developer checks the code in.

Summary

The XDM application has been cleaned up, and the parameters have been checked for deployment. You have set up your standalone development server and checked that you can package, deploy, and run the XDM application. Together with database scripts and installation instructions, you are now ready to deliver a deployment package to the operations team to install on the test environment. You have also seen how you can use Apache Ant to script this process.

When your test team has completed testing and you have corrected any issues the test has uncovered, you use the same procedure to create a new final deployment package that your operations team will install on the production server.

Your ADF enterprise application is ready for business.

Internationalization

In the book, *The Hitchhiker's Guide to the Galaxy*, Douglas Adams describes a world where people can place a "Babel fish" in their ears to instantly understand any language. While the real-life "Babel fish" at sites such as `http://translate.google.com,` do a fair job of automatic translations, an enterprise application intended for people speaking different languages still has to be translated at least in part by humans.

Even if you are only planning to run your application in one language, read this appendix to see how easy it is to internationalize your application. If you do the internationalization while developing the application, it's easy—if you have to do it later, it's hard.

Localization lingo

Internationalization means building your application so that it can be adapted to different languages and countries. People who work in this area often shorten a very long word to just `i18n` (eighteen characters in the middle of the word are removed).

Localization means actually preparing your application for a specific language and country. This will not only involve translating the user interface text, but also changing the date formats and making other changes for the specific country. This is sometimes abbreviated as `L10n`.

Automatic internationalization

In order to make it easier to internationalize Java applications, the Java language offers a mechanism for centralizing all of the strings that a user might see. This is called a **resource bundle** and can be implemented in several ways as described later in the chapter. The application will use a key (for example, START_DATE_LABEL), and there will be a resource bundle for each supported language, thus mapping that key to the user interface string in that language.

JDeveloper is built for enterprise applications so that it automatically uses the resource bundles to prepare your application for localization. Let's take the XDM Common Model, shown in the following screenshot, as an example:

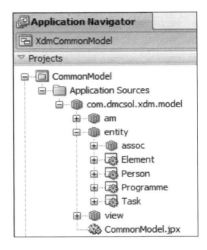

Now, watch what happens when we go into the Task entity object and define **Control Hints** for an attribute, as shown in the following screenshot:

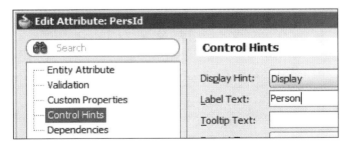

As `PersId` is something that might be shown to the application end user, for example, as a prompt for a drop-down list, JDeveloper doesn't just hardwire the literal string into the application. Instead, JDeveloper automatically creates a resource bundle for you. You can see this new file in the **Application Navigator** window, as shown in the following screenshot:

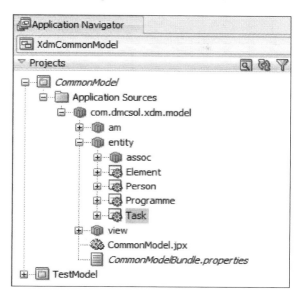

Notice the new `CommonModelBundle.properties` file. If you open this file, you'll see something similar to the following screenshot:

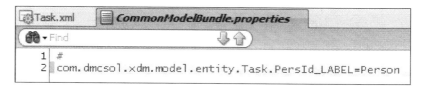

JDeveloper has automatically executed the following tasks:

- Extracted the value that you defined as the label control hint for the attribute
- Created a resource bundle file
- Placed the text that you entered into the resource bundle and assigned a key to it
- Inserted a reference to the resource key in the entity object

If you click on the **Source** tab for the entity object, you can see that the `ResId` attribute for the label points to the `com.dmcsol.xdm.model.entity.Task.PersId_LABEL` key, as shown in the following screenshot. This is the key that JDeveloper automatically created in the resource bundle.

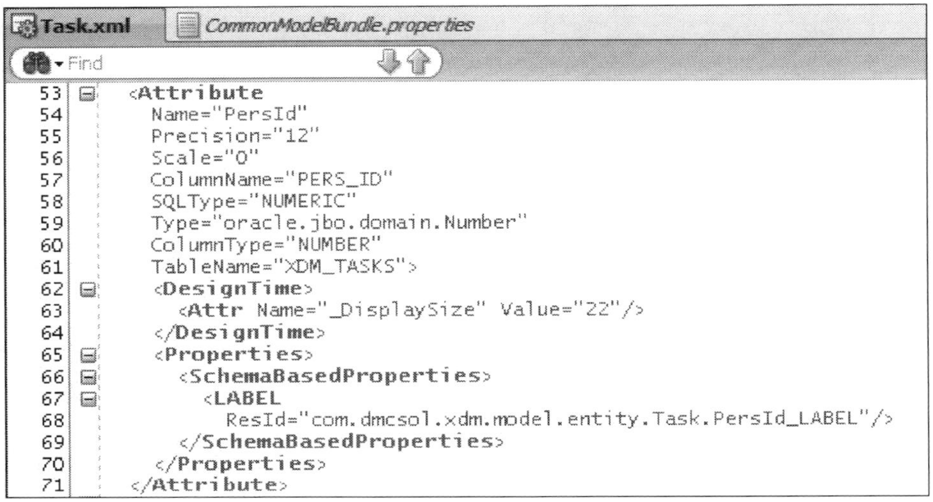

```
53    <Attribute
54       Name="PersId"
55       Precision="12"
56       Scale="0"
57       ColumnName="PERS_ID"
58       SQLType="NUMERIC"
59       Type="oracle.jbo.domain.Number"
60       ColumnType="NUMBER"
61       TableName="XDM_TASKS">
62       <DesignTime>
63          <Attr Name="_DisplaySize" Value="22"/>
64       </DesignTime>
65       <Properties>
66          <SchemaBasedProperties>
67             <LABEL
68                ResId="com.dmcsol.xdm.model.entity.Task.PersId_LABEL"/>
69          </SchemaBasedProperties>
70       </Properties>
71    </Attribute>
```

How localizable strings are stored

There are three ways to store localizable strings in an ADF application. They are as follows:

- In a simple `.properties` file
- In an XLIFF file (an XML file format)
- In a Java `ListResourceBundle` class

The preceding example uses a simple `.properties` file, which is the easiest to work with.

If you will be using a professional translation service to translate the user-visible text strings, they are likely to ask you for an XLIFF file. **XLIFF** stands for **XML Localization Interface File Format**, and professional translation software will be able to read and write XLIFF files. Oracle Metadata Services also uses XLIFF files to store customized strings, as we saw in *Chapter 9, Customizing Functionality*.

The last option is to define all of your strings in a Java class that extends `java.util.ListResourceBundle`. This class must implement a method to return all of the localizable strings in an `Object[][]` array as follows:

```
package com.dmcsol.xdm.model;
import java.util.ListResourceBundle;
public class ModelBundle extends ListResourceBundle {
  private static final Object[][] contents =
  {
    { "com.dmcsol.xdm.model.entity.Task.PersId_LABEL",
      "Person" },
    { "com.dmcsol.xdm.model.entity.Task.StartDate_LABEL",
      "Start time" }
    { "com.dmcsol.xdm.model.entity.Task.StartWhere_LABEL",
      "Start location" }
  }

  public Object[][] getContents() {
    return contents;
  }
}
```

The class has to define an array with an element for each of your localizable strings. This element is again an array containing exactly two values: the key and the localized value. As the `ListResourceBundle` class is much more difficult to read and write, you typically don't use this if you are using only static strings. If you try to deliver a file like this to your localization team, you can be sure that the commas and curly brackets won't all be correct in the file that you get back. However, it does make sense to use a `ListResourceBundle` class if you plan to keep all of your localizable strings in a database. In this case, your resource bundle class can access the database to retrieve the values.

You can choose the way in which you want to store your localizable strings for each project by setting **Project Properties**. In this dialog, choose the **Resource Bundle** node in the left-hand side and the desired **Resource Bundle Type** in the right-hand side, as shown in the following screenshot. For the XDM application, we choose the XLIFF format because we expect the application to become an international success, and we expect to send out the application UI strings to a translation agency when that happens. The **Resource Bundle** settings dialog looks as shown in the following screenshot:

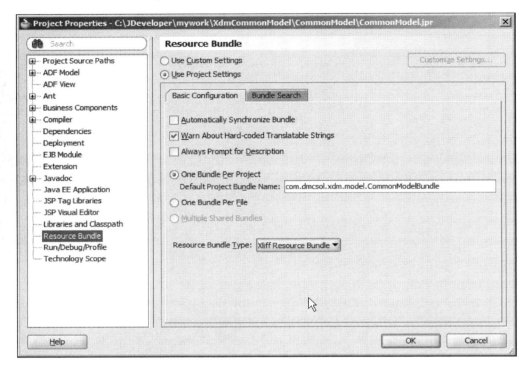

A binding choice

Once you have selected the resource bundle type, your project will use that type. If you go back into the **Properties** dialog and change the resource bundle type after you have started using another type, you will need to delete the resource bundle that was started by JDeveloper for you in order to start over with the new type.

It's a good idea to check the **Warn About Hard-coded Translatable Strings** checkbox. This tells JDeveloper to present you with a warning if you hard code a string into a translatable field, such as the **Label** field. This will be shown with an orange border around the properties that should come from a resource bundle, as shown in the following screenshot:

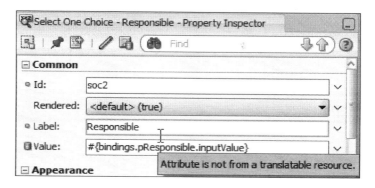

The warning will also be shown in the source view for a page or Business Component.

Defining localizable strings

Every string the user sees can be localized—labels for fields, mouseover texts, validation messages, and so on.

In some cases (such as the preceding `entity` attribute), JDeveloper can automatically register a new string and create an associated key in a resource bundle. However, you will normally work in the **Select Text Resource** dialog to define your strings because this dialog provides the option to select an already defined string for a new purpose. You can invoke this dialog from many places, which are detailed as follows:

- To set a Business Component attribute (for example, `Label`), you click on the search icon in the right-hand side of the field in the **Control Hints** dialog

- To set a text for a user interface element from **Property Palette**, you can click on the little triangle in the right-hand side of the field and choose **Select Text Resource** from the pop-up menu

- To set a text for a user interface element from the visual page designer, right-click on the element, choose **Select Text Resource for**, and then choose the element you want to define (for example, **Label**), as shown in the following screenshot:

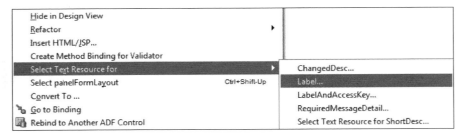

All of these bring up the **Select Text Resource** dialog, where you can define new strings or choose among the existing ones. The dialog looks as shown in the following screenshot:

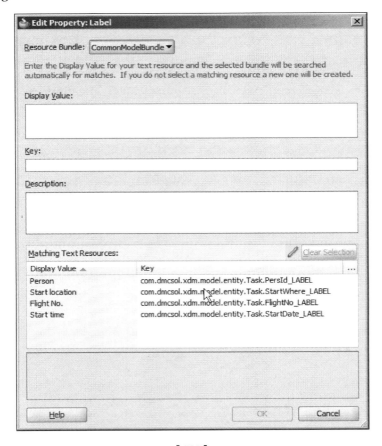

As you start typing in the **Display Value** field, JDeveloper automatically fills in the **Key** field with a suggested key. At the same time, the **Matching Text Resources** box is automatically reduced to the elements matching the display text that you are entering. If an already defined text resource contains the text you want, you can select it in this box and click on **Select**. Otherwise, type the display value, accept or change the suggested key, and click on **Save and Select** to store your new key/value pair in the resource bundle.

The **Description** field is optional unless you have checked the **Always Prompt for Description** checkbox under **Resource Bundle** in the **Project Properties** dialog.

Give us a clue

It is very hard for a translator to translate an individual word without any indication of the context where it is used. If you don't provide proper descriptions, you'll either be spending a lot of time answering questions from your translator or a lot of time in correcting the language errors once you show your enterprise application to the native speakers of your target language.

Performing the translation

Now that you have your strings separated from the components and user interface, it's time to translate them. You have a resource bundle (the `.properties` file, XLIFF file, or Java class) with your default text, but you haven't really told the ADF framework about the language. To add this information, you can add a suffix to the file using a two-character ISO 639 language code. If, for example, your default language is English, you should add _en to the filename (for example, `ModelBundle_en.properties`).

If you wish to specify the version of the language of a specific country, you can add an additional suffix using a two-character ISO 3166 country code. For example, French as spoken in France would be `ModelBundle_fr_FR`, while French as spoken in Canada would be `ModelBundle_fr_CA`.

To start your translation process, you can create copies of your default file or class with different suffixes for all of your target languages. You can then send out your property or XLIFF file to be translated.

Don't send a Java `ListResourceBundle` class to be translated unless your translator happens to be a Java programmer in his or her spare time.

When you get your translation back, you need to place all of your translated resource files in the filesystem next to the original default resource files in your project, as shown in the following screenshot:

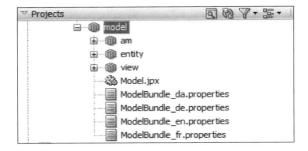

Additionally, you will have to define the languages that your application will offer in the `faces-config.xml` file. You will find this file in your `View` project under `Web Content / WEB-INF`. On the **Application** subtab, scroll down to the **Locale Config** section, set **Default Locale**, and add all of the languages that your application supports, as shown in the following screenshot:

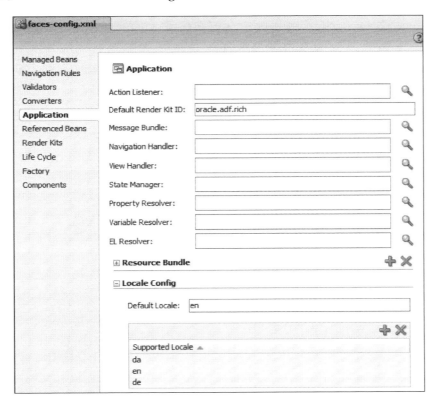

Running your localized application

With the translated files back and integrated into the application, it's time to test the localized versions.

Testing the localized Business Components

When you right-click on an application module to run it through the Business Component Browser, it will run by default in the language selected in your operating system. If you are running Microsoft Windows, the Business Component Browser will show the label-control hint in the language that you have selected in the Windows Control Panel (under **Region and Language**).

You can override this by setting the default language of your application module. This is done by right-clicking on the application module, choosing **Configurations**, and then **Edit**. On the **Properties** tab, scroll down to the `jbo.default.language` property and set a value to force the Business Component tester to show your application module in that language, as shown in the following screenshot:

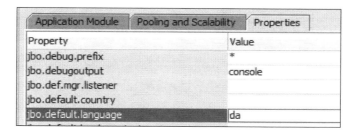

Testing the localized user interface

When you are running the application, you will be running web pages in a browser. It is part of the HTTP protocol that the browser will send an ordered list of the languages in which it would like to see content, so that the web server can serve up this content if it is available.

You can set the language preferences in the browser as shown in the following screenshot:

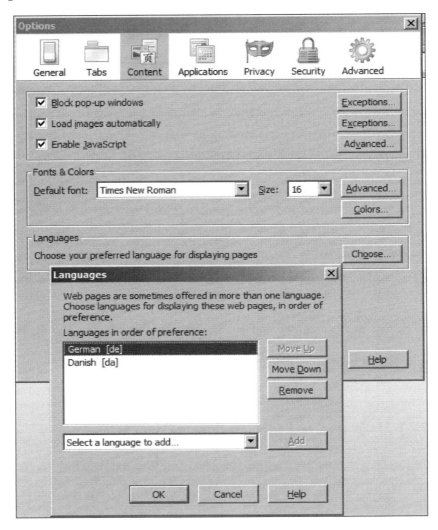

Note that the browser language settings determine a priority, so the preceding setting means to first ask for a German version of the page and then a Danish one. If your ADF application does not support any of the requested languages, it will revert to the default language defined in the `faces-config.xml` file.

To test your application in different languages, it is enough to change the order of the languages in your web browser and refresh the page — the page will be redrawn in the first language that your application supports.

Localizing formats

When you change the language in your browser, you will see that the date and number formats change automatically, as well. When, for example, running the application in Danish, Christmas Eve is displayed as **24.12.2011**, while, when running it in English, the same date is shown as **12/24/2011**. Note that both the day/month order and the separator character have changed. If you have chosen a date format that includes the names of the month, these will be localized as well.

ADF will also automatically change the decimal character between a period and a comma, matching the locale to which your browser is set.

Don't use the Currency format

You have the option to select **Currency** as **Format Type**. Don't use this format (or use it with extreme care) — ADF doesn't know exchange rates. This means that if you format something with a currency symbol and change your browser settings, the same amount might suddenly be displayed as Pesos instead of U.S. Dollars. Use a normal number field and place the currency symbol in a label or prompt next to it.

More internationalization

The error messages that you define for the business rules in your entity objects should also point to a string in a resource bundle instead of containing hard-wired error or warning messages.

If you have data in several languages in your tables and want to present, for example, a list of values in a user language, you need a managed bean and a bind variable in your view object. The managed bean has access to the browser session variables and can retrieve the UI language and store it in a variable. The view object can then use a bind variable assigned with a value using the built-in `adf.context` object to refer to the bean value. Therefore, if you have a `LocaleHelperBean` class with a `Session` scope and a `userLanguage` parameter, you would assign your bind variable to the `adf.context.sessionScope.LocaleHelperBean.userLanguage` expression.

You will notice that the standard texts that ADF supplies (for example, **Sort Ascending**, when pointing to a table column header) will also be localized. ADF comes in all of the languages to which Oracle normally localizes their end user software — several dozen at the last count. As we discussed in *Chapter 8, Changing the Appearance*, these strings are a part of the skin; if you are not happy with Oracle's standard texts in a language, you can create a skin that overrides them with your own texts.

It is also possible to change the language programmatically. However, it's a bit of an advanced topic and falls outside the scope of this book as it involves creating and registering a phase listener to ensure that the chosen language is always set before the page is rendered.

Summary

You have seen how to use resource bundles to ensure that your application can easily be localized into different languages, and how the application magically changes the language to match the user's environment.

You are now ready to build ADF enterprise applications for the world!

Index

L

Label property 58
LabelStyle property 284
layout containers
  arranging, Structure window used 61
Layout property 67
lead programmer 100
listeners, recorded sessions
  Aggregate Graph 275
  Graph Results 275
  View Results in Table 275
  View Results Tree 275
localization 379
localized application
  business components, testing 389
  testing 389
  user interface, testing 389, 390

M

Make Active button 159
Managed Beans 203, 236
managed servers 365
master application
  aspects 231
  dynamic region, creating 234-236
  libraries 232, 233
  master page, creating 233
  master workspace, setting up 232
  task flow switching 237
master application workspaces 120
master page
  creating 233
  layout, creating 234
  menu, adding 234
master workspace
  about 119, 334
  setting up 232
Maven
  working with 373
MaxEndDate attribute 229
maximum productivity
  focusing on 152, 153
  time, focus mode 153
  time, recharge mode 153
  time, work mode 152
Members subtab 346

N

Messages window 150
MinStartDate attribute 229
model layer 12
model-view-controller (MVC) pattern
  about 12
  controller layer 12
  model layer 12
  view layer 12
modular architecture
  about 116, 117
  Application Common Workspace 117
  database workspace 119
  master workspace 119
  subsystem workspaces 119

N

naming conventions
  about 121
  ADF elements 124
  database objects 123
  file locations 125, 126
  general 121
  Java packages 121
  test code 126
nesting 17
new files
  versioning 219
new workspace
  setting up 221
non-functional requirements
  about 74
  aspects 73
  NFR002 73
No Proxy for field 273

O

Object-oriented programming 95
OFA 307, 308
OK button 218
online chat, collaboration tools 113
OPSS 333
optimistic locking 359
Oracle
  alternatives 277
Oracle Application Testing Suite
  contents 277

Thank you for buying
Oracle ADF Enterprise Application
Development – Made Simple
Second Edition

About Packt Publishing

Packt, pronounced 'packed', published its first book "Mastering phpMyAdmin for Effective MySQL Management" in April 2004 and subsequently continued to specialize in publishing highly focused books on specific technologies and solutions.

Our books and publications share the experiences of your fellow IT professionals in adapting and customizing today's systems, applications, and frameworks. Our solution based books give you the knowledge and power to customize the software and technologies you're using to get the job done. Packt books are more specific and less general than the IT books you have seen in the past. Our unique business model allows us to bring you more focused information, giving you more of what you need to know, and less of what you don't.

Packt is a modern, yet unique publishing company, which focuses on producing quality, cutting-edge books for communities of developers, administrators, and newbies alike. For more information, please visit our website: www.packtpub.com.

About Packt Enterprise

In 2010, Packt launched two new brands, Packt Enterprise and Packt Open Source, in order to continue its focus on specialization. This book is part of the Packt Enterprise brand, home to books published on enterprise software – software created by major vendors, including (but not limited to) IBM, Microsoft and Oracle, often for use in other corporations. Its titles will offer information relevant to a range of users of this software, including administrators, developers, architects, and end users.

Writing for Packt

We welcome all inquiries from people who are interested in authoring. Book proposals should be sent to author@packtpub.com. If your book idea is still at an early stage and you would like to discuss it first before writing a formal book proposal, contact us; one of our commissioning editors will get in touch with you.

We're not just looking for published authors; if you have strong technical skills but no writing experience, our experienced editors can help you develop a writing career, or simply get some additional reward for your expertise.

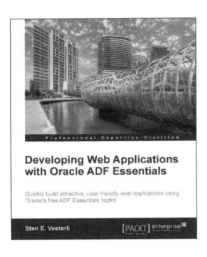

Developing Web Applications with Oracle ADF Essentials

ISBN: 978-1-78217-068-6   Paperback: 270 pages

Quickly build attractive, user-friendly web applications using Oracle's free ADF Essentials toolkit

1. Quickly build compete applications with business services, page flows, and data-bound pages without programming

2. Use Java to implement any business rule or application logic

3. Choose the right architecture for high productivity and maintainability

Oracle ADF 11*g*R2 Development Beginner's Guide

ISBN: 978-1-84968-900-7   Paperback: 330 pages

Experience the easiest way to learn, understand, and implement rich Internet applications using Oracle ADF 11*g* R2

1. Implement a web-based application using the powerful ADF development framework from Oracle

2. Experience the fun of building a simple web application with practical examples and step-by-step instructions

3. Understand the power of Oracle ADF 11*g*R2 and develop any complex application with confidence

Please check **www.PacktPub.com** for information on our titles

Oracle E-Business Suite R12 Integration
and OA Framework Development and
Extension Cookbook

A practical step-by-step guide to develop end-to-end extensions
to Oracle E-Business Suite Release 12, with detailed illustrations
and explanations

Andy Penver

Oracle E-Business Suite R12 Integration and OA Framework Development and Extension Cookbook

ISBN: 978-1-84968-712-6   Paperback: 398 pages

A practical step-by-step guide to develop end-to-end extensions to Oracle E-Business Suite Release 12, with detailed illustrations and explanations

1. Gain key skills learning to extend Oracle E-Business Suite Release 12

2. Learn how to personalize Oracle Application Framework (OAF) pages and understand the structure of an OA Framework page

Oracle SOA Suite 11g
Developer's Cookbook

Over 65 high-level recipes for extending your Oracle SOA
applications and enhancing your skills with expert tips and
tricks for developers

RUBICON RED

Antony Reynolds   Matt Wright

Oracle SOA Suite 11g Developer's Cookbook

ISBN: 978-1-84968-388-3   Paperback: 346 pages

Over 65 high-level recipes for extending your Oracle SOA applications and enhancing your skills with expert tips and tricks for developers

1. Extend and enhance the tricks in your Oracle SOA Suite developer arsenal with expert tips and best practices

2. Get to grips with Java integration, OSB message patterns, SOA Clusters, and much more in this book and e-book

3. A practical Cookbook packed with recipes for achieving the most important SOA Suite tasks for developers

Please check **www.PacktPub.com** for information on our titles

75785659R00237

Made in the USA
Columbia, SC
23 August 2017